READING DISABILITIES
IN
COLLEGE & HIGH SCHOOL

READING DISABILITIES IN COLLEGE & HIGH SCHOOL:
DIAGNOSIS & MANAGEMENT

P. G. Aaron
Catherine A. Baker

 Parkton, Maryland

YORK
PRESS

12/96

This book was manufactured in the United States of America.
Typography by Brushwood Graphics, Inc., Baltimore, Maryland.
Printing and Binding by Maple Press, York, Pennsylvania.
Cover design by Joseph Dieter, Jr.

Library of Congress Catalog Card Number 90-72124
ISBN 0-912752-23-8

Contents

Preface

This book is written for learning skills specialists, reading specialists, administrators, counselors, and all other personnel who are concerned with the organization and administration of learning skills and reading disability programs that are intended to enhance the academic achievements of students in high schools and colleges. It may also be helpful to those students who are struggling with their high school or college studies.

Many students in high schools lack reading skills and not all students who are admitted into colleges are equipped with adequate learning skills to cope with the academic demands. These students constitute a sizeable proportion of the student population and are considered to be "at risk." A large number of these at-risk students exhibit discipline problems in high schools; many of the at-risk students who enter colleges eventually drop out. Because the academic skills of many of these at-risk students can be improved, these problems, to some degree, can be averted.

There are two categories of at-risk students: the *underprepared* and the *reading disabled*. Students who, for some reason or other, do not put forth the effort needed to learn to read, are underprepared; students who, despite their effort and adequate intellectual ability, fail to learn to read, are reading disabled. The information and techniques presented in this book can be effectively used to deal with the problems of both kinds of at-risk students. The latter category of poor learners, namely students with reading disabilities, is often referred to as *learning disabled*. In this book we have preferred the use of the term *reading disabilities* because reading disabilities can be defined more or less unambiguously and diagnosed with a reasonable degree of accuracy. More importantly, appropriate corrective measures can be undertaken and, if implemented conscientiously, students with reading disabilities can be expected to improve their reading skill.

In contrast, learning disabilities are defined so broadly that they include deficits in perceptual, social-personal, and a plethora of non-verbal skills. This lack of rigor in defining learning disabilities has made diagnosis and treatment of learning disabilities imprecise and unreliable.

The fact that some college students have reading disabilities is not a new finding but has been recognized for a long time. For instance, Smith (1965) reports that between the years 1924 and 1935, a total of 654 studies on reading were conducted and reading disability was one of the most frequently investigated topics; among those studies that investigated reading disability, more were reported on college reading than either on elementary or high school reading. Smith further notes that of the 35 doctoral dissertations published on reading disabilities during this period, studies concerned with reading at the college level outnumbered those conducted on other levels of education. Interest in reading disability among mature students abated somewhat during the war years but there was a resurgence of interest in the teaching of reading skills at high schools and colleges in the late 40s and early 50s. This is reflected in the title of the Forty-Seventh Yearbook of the National Society for the Study of Education (1948): *Reading in the High School and College.* The Yearbook recognized two different kinds of reading programs in high schools and colleges: a developmental program that was geared to foster high levels of competence of reading in normal readers, and a remedial program designed to rectify the deficiencies of poor readers. The present book is written with these two types of programs in mind.

In the '50s and '60s many colleges initiated reading programs for their students partly because of the awareness created by publications such as the 47th Yearbook and partly because of the realization that *large numbers* of college freshmen could not read well enough to pursue their studies successfully. According to a survey conducted by Causey and Eller (1959), of the 418 colleges investigated, almost three-fourths had reading programs for their students and these programs served 57,052 students. These programs, however, were not systematically organized and executed but were often viewed by administrators as irksome encumbrances. According to Smith (1965)

> Because of lack of experience in developing reading programs at the secondary level, lack of training in reading for high school teachers, and in many cases, lack of guidance from a reading specialist, the programs are sometimes growing in lop-sided and irregular ways (p. 370).

There is no compelling reason to believe that the situation has changed a great deal since 1965. It is the hope of the authors that the present book will provide a theoretical and a pragmatic basis for the systematic organization and execution of reading programs that will increase the learning skills of students.

At present, we do not have reliable figures about the number of high school and college students who have reading disabilities. Estimates, however, suggest that at least 10% of all high school students have reading disabilities. The corresponding figure for college students, even though much lower, is still substantial. According to Sandoval (1988), even in a highly selective university such as the University of California, as many as 0.5% of the student body may have symptoms of reading disability. One can, therefore, expect about 100 students to have reading disability in a university of about 20,000 students. In universities where the admission criteria are less stringent, this figure can be significantly higher. This most certainly is true of community colleges that practice an open admission policy. Anderson (1982) reports that the number of students enrolled in developmental and remedial studies programs range from 10% to 50% of the total community college student population. The number of students who can benefit from a well organized learning skills program, therefore, is quite substantial.

The contents of this book can be divided into two broad categories: theoretical and practical. The first two chapters deal with the theory of the reading process and the nature of reading disabilities. The next three chapters are built on this theoretical foundation; they describe procedures that can be used in the diagnosis of the different kinds of reading disabilities and principles that can be useful in managing these disabilities. Chapter 6 presents the basic principles that will be useful in advising and counseling students with reading disabilities. The final chapter describes the organizational and administrative pattern of a model program.

The pragmatic aspects of the program described in this book are derived, for the most part, from our experiences with students with reading disabilities. We wish to express our indebtedness to these students. We are grateful to Dr. Michele Boyer of the Department of Counseling Psychology, Indiana State University, who reviewed the section on counseling and made many important suggestions. Finally we wish to thank Ms. Elinor Hartwig, senior editor and President of *York Press*, for her valuable editorial comments and, of course, her patience.

P. G. Aaron
Catherine Baker

REFERENCES

Anderson, T. W. 1982. Functions for school psychologists in community colleges. *Psychology in the Schools* 19:221–25.
Causey, O. S., and Eller, W. 1959. Starting and improving college reading programs. *Eighth Yearbook of the National Reading Conference.* Fort Worth, TX: Christian University Press.
Sandoval, J. 1988. The school-psychologist in higher education. *School Psychology Review,* 17(3):391–96.
Smith, N. B. 1965. *American Reading Instruction.* Newark, DE: International Reading Association.
Forty-seventh yearbook of the National Society for the Study of Education. 1948.

Chapter 1

The Psychology of Reading

INTRODUCTION

The learning problems of more than eighty percent of the children re-ferred to school psychology clinics originate from poor reading skills. This statement is equally applicable to students in high schools and col-leges; learning difficulties of a majority of older students also can be traced to poor reading skills. For this reason, the terms *reading disability* and *learning disability* are used interchangeably in this book even though the former is the preferred term. This book focuses on improv-ing reading and writing skills of students in secondary and postsec-ondary institutions; other skills such as listening, note taking, and test taking also are addressed. In this chapter, we provide an overview of the psychological processes that underlie reading. The nature of read-ing disabilities and recommendations for corrective actions to be un-dertaken in order to improve reading and writing skills presented in this book are based on the psychology of reading process described below. An acquaintance with this information is, therefore, essential to appreciate the rationale of the diagnostic and corrective procedures presented later in the book.

Components of Reading

The diagnostic and treatment approaches presented in this book are based on the premise that even though reading is a complex skill, it is made up of certain identifiable components. A component can be de-fined as an elementary information process that operates upon internal representations of objects and symbols (Sternberg 1985). A process that is elementary enough to be labelled as a component depends upon the independence of the process from other processes, as well as the de-sired level of theorizing chosen by the researcher. While some re-searchers identify the components of reading at a very basic level (c.f., Leong 1988), others resort to a more fine-grained analysis (c.f., Fred-eriksen 1982). Because of this, the number of components that con-stitute the reading process reported by researchers varies. For our pur-pose, reading is approached at a basic level and is considered to be made up of two major components: (1) the ability to pronounce the written word, either overtly or covertly, and (2) the ability to comprehend the word and the text. Findings of experimental, neuropsychological, and developmental studies support the two-componential view of reading.

In one experiment, Jackson and McClelland (1979) studied undergraduates and found that comprehension ability and reaction time in a letter-matching task accounted for nearly all of the variance seen in reading ability. Investigations by Hunt, Lunneborg, and Lewis (1975) and by Palmer et al. (1985) also report that comprehension and speed of decoding print are the two most important components of reading.

Neuropsychological patients who have lost their ability to read, and are labelled either as "deep dyslexics" or as "surface dyslexics," also demonstrate the independence of phonological decoding and comprehension of written language (Marshall and Newcombe 1973; Patterson, Marshall, and Coltheart 1985). The most salient symptoms of "deep dyslexia" are an almost total inability to read aloud pronounceable nonwords, difficulty in reading grammar words correctly (e.g., *for* → and, *the* → yes, *in* → those), and a tendency to commit paralexic errors (e.g., *father* → "dad"; *child* → "boy"). In contrast, the predominant symptoms of "surface dyslexia" include a mechanical pronunciation of words without a proper understanding of them (e.g., *listen* → "Liston," the boxer; *sale* → "Sally," a girl's name). These two disorders indicate that some patients can comprehend words far better than they can pronounce them, whereas other patients can pronounce words far better than they can understand them.

Developmental studies also lend support to the notion that comprehension and the ability to pronounce the written word are the most important predictors of reading achievement. Furthermore, reports that children with dyslexia can comprehend much better than they can read aloud (Frith and Snowling 1983) and descriptions of hyperlexic children who can decode print with extraordinary skill but cannot comprehend what they have read (Aaron 1989a; Healy 1982) indicate that decoding and comprehension are dissociable components of reading and that one or the other skill may be developmentally arrested.

Our choice of two components is motivated by empirical as well as pragmatic considerations. The empirical consideration is that the two-component view is in agreement with neuropsychological and experimental findings; the practical consideration is that the proposed model of reading based on this two-component view leads to relatively easy diagnostic procedures that can be carried out quickly and easily without the need for complicated instruments and a multitude of tests.

The first component, the ability to pronounce the written word, is also referred to as *decoding skill, phonological encoding skill,* and *grapheme-phoneme conversion skill.* It is an operation that is specific to the written form of the language. The second component, comprehension, is used in this book as a generic term to encompass both reading and listening comprehension. The decision not to distinguish between these two forms of comprehension is based on empirical evidence presented in Chapter 3. Treating reading and listening comprehension as a single higher order mental process also has practical implications for the diagnosis of reading disabilities.

Normal reading requires that the integrity of these two components be preserved. Inefficient operation of either one of these components can, therefore, disrupt the reading process and result in reading disability. Furthermore, because these two components are independent of each other, deficiencies in different components can lead to different kinds of reading deficits. It follows then, with reference to the two-component view of the reading process, the following three kinds of reading disabilities can be expected to occur: (1) poor decoding with adequate comprehension, (2) poor comprehension with adequate decoding, and (3) poor decoding and poor comprehension. In this book, reading disability of the first kind is referred to as *specific reading disability* or *developmental dyslexia*, the second kind as *nonspecific reading disability*, and the third kind as *low ability reading*. The componential view of the reading process naturally leads to the conclusion that not all poor readers are alike and, depending on the nature of their deficit, poor readers are likely to respond differently to different corrective procedures. Experimental and clinical evidences that support these premises as well as the procedures necessary for making the differential diagnosis of the reading disorders along with different treatment methods are described later. Identifying the nature of the reading disability of a poor learner and targeting appropriate corrective procedures for the learning problem are major objectives of the reading disabilities program.

In addition to these two component skills, reading involves sensory, perceptual, and motor processes. Because the ability to encode the written word into its phonological equivalent and the ability to comprehend language, whether written or spoken, are the two basic components of the reading process, much attention is given to these two skills in our discussion of the psychology of reading.

Since all these processes function in unison, reading is considered an interactive process. For our discussion, however, the reading process will be described as though it were carried out in a series of discrete stages. Such an approach makes the elucidation of the reading process relatively easy. The reading process will be examined from the perspective of four substages: *sensory encoding, word recognition, sentence comprehension,* and *passage comprehension*. Because each one of these stages is a potential source of reading difficulty, processes associated with these stages are examined.

The ability to monitor one's own performance and appraise it accurately is an important correlate of reading performance. This ability is referred to as metacognition, which is discussed in the concluding part of this chapter.

THE ENCODING STAGE

Eye Movements

It has been known from the beginning of the present century that when we read, our eyes do not move smoothly and continuously over the printed line, but make a series of moves interspersed with stops. The moves are referred to as *saccades* and the stops as *fixations*. Each saccade lasts approximately 15 to 35 milliseconds (msecs) depending on how far the eyes travel and the average fixation duration is about 250 msecs even though factors such as familiarity and ambiguity of the fixated word can influence the fixation duration so that it can range anywhere from 150 to 500 msecs (Rayner and Pollastek 1989). The average fixation duration of 250 msecs fits neatly in with the observation that proficient readers can read about 250 words per minute. This means that approximately four words can be processed per second. Generally speaking, a single word is fixated and processed during a single fixation even though two adjacent words could be processed if the second word is short and is predictable from context (Just and Carpenter 1987). Examples of these include function words such as *and*, *the*, and *on* which, at times, are skipped altogether. During the saccades, the neural system inhibits visual input and information is taken in only during the fixations. But for this neural phenomenon, the printed line and, indeed, the entire visual world, would appear to us as a big blur.

The Iconic Store

During the initial stage of reading, specifically during fixations, the photic stimulus is transduced into neural impulses, and the mapping of the visual stimulus onto the sensory system is accomplished. Experimental studies suggest that the visual stimulus that is transformed into sensory input is retained in a temporary store called an *icon*. The iconic store is thought to have a very short duration but a relatively "large" capacity. Studies by Sperling (1960) indicate that the iconic duration is 100 msecs or less and the iconic capacity is about 12 items. The capacity of the icon is considered "large" because it exceeds that of the short-term memory (STM) which ranges from 7 to 9 items. Interestingly, the extremely short duration of the icon falls well within the average period of the eye fixation and the iconic capacity of about 12 items is sufficient to process most of the written words in the English language. This is not to say that every letter in a written word is analyzed one by one and processed, but it appears that letters in the word are the basic units of analysis and that all the letters in a word are processed simultaneously, in parallel.

Even though the psychological reality of the iconic store is questioned by some, it is apparent from eye movement studies that whatever the nature of the store is, the initial visual input has to be cleared from the temporary store in less than a quarter of a second to make room for the subsequent input. If this does not happen, the first visual input can linger on and interfere with the subsequent input. In order to avoid such a logjam, a reader may have to slow down the movement of his or her eyes to allow time for the icon to be cleared, which would retard the rate of reading. For this reason, the iconic process of poor readers has been investigated to see if this could be the origin of reading disabilities. Even though studies that examined this question are equivocal in their findings, there is no convincing evidence to show that poor iconic functioning, or any problem associated with visual perception, plays a causal role in reading disabilities. As a matter of fact, a number of studies show that a dyslexic reader's visual memory for nonverbal material is as good as or even better than that of normal readers (Aaron, Bommarito, and Baker 1984; Fisher and Frankfurter 1977). Furthermore, as will be seen later, reading disabilities in general are manifest in the form of syndromes comprising many symptoms, including poor spelling. Thus, the reading problem is not limited to the input aspect of information processing but also involves output processes, such as spelling, which cannot be explained by deficiencies of the visual input system. Once the mapping of the visual stimulus into sensory input is accomplished, the word is ready to be recognized.

THE WORD RECOGNITION STAGE

Studies that have tracked the movement of the eyes during reading with the aid of computers suggest that, generally speaking, the word that is fixated is recognized before the eyes move and fixate on the next word. A written word is recognized when the sensory input corresponding to the word makes contact with the representation of the word stored in the long-term memory (LTM). The written word is most likely represented in terms of its features such as pronunciation, spelling pattern, and meaning. These are referred to as the *phonological, orthographic,* and *semantic* properties of the word, respectively. Thus, recognition of a word includes retrieving not only its pronunciation but also accessing its semantic properties. It is also likely that its grammatical status is determined at the same time. The orthographic features of the word are also retrieved when writing. The notion that all these properties of a written word in a sentence are realized just as the reader encounters it, rather than relying on a "wait-and-see" strategy (until the phrase or the sentence in which the word appears is read), is referred to as the *immediacy hypothesis* (Just and Carpenter 1987). Even though the immediacy hypothesis is true as a general statement, there appear to be some exceptions, such as when the reader encounters ambiguous statements and anaphoric references (Rayner and Pollatsek 1989). For example, realization of the full import of the word *what* in the sentence "What Johnny wants to do is to read all day and all night" cannot be accomplished immediately upon its first encounter but will have to wait until the entire sentence is processed. In spite of these exceptions, it appears that the properties of a majority of words are realized before the eyes move and make the next fixation. Just and Carpenter (1987) also note that when readers encounter an uncommon word, they tend to spend longer fixation time than when they come across a familiar word. For example, readers have been observed to fixate longer at the word *sable* than on the word *table*. This observation is taken as evidence that the eyes do not move until the word is recognized. If the eyes had moved before word recognition had occurred, they move back and refixate on the unprocessed word. Such a regressive movement indicates that a reader is keeping track of his or her comprehension and, if comprehension fails, is able to take adequate measures to correct the situation. Regressive movements, therefore, cannot be considered a cause of reading disability but could be the result of the reader's corrective actions. It is also reported (Just and Carpenter 1987) that when a reader encounters an ambiguous word with more than one meaning (e.g., *rose* = flower, or past tense of rise) all the meanings of the word are temporarily but simultaneously activated and a final selection is made on the basis of semantic and syntactic contexts.

But how is the word recognized on the basis of its phonological, orthographic, and semantic properties? Considering the fact that a skilled college student may know as many as 150,000 words (Aitchison 1987), the ability of the average reader to recognize and pronounce a written word within a fraction of a second is an astounding feat. It is obvious that in order to accomplish such a quick retrieval, information regarding the phonological, semantic, and orthographic features of words have to be organized and arranged in the brain in some systematic fashion.

Psychologists and psycholinguists often use metaphors such as "dictionary" and "library" to describe such an organization of information. In fact, this putative organization of word knowledge is called the *mental lexicon*. That the mental lexicon is not organized on an alphabetic basis can be easily demonstrated by asking someone to recall the names of the months of the year first in the chronological sequence starting with January and then in the alphabetical order, starting with April and ending with September. The fact that the second task takes much longer than the first should come as a surprise to no one. But how can the difference in the recall time be explained? One reasonable explanation is that names of the months are stored in our memory in chronological order rather than in alphabetical order. This explanation is based on the assumption that reaction time (RT) reflects the nature of the organization of the mental lexicon, and if two words are recalled in quick succession, they should be close to each other in the lexicon. In fact, experimental psychologists who study the mental lexicon use reaction time as a major dependent variable to make inferences regarding several aspects of the mental lexicon. With some practice, it is possible to learn to recite rather quickly the names of the months in the alphabetic order. This shows that we can create lexical files in our long-term memory on the basis of new formats, if we want to. It also shows that the format in which information is filed in the lexicon has much influence on its recall. In other words, if the pattern of input is unsystematic and disorganized, recall will be poor. Poorly organized input can, therefore, be one source of learning problems. Because the mental lexicon is part of the long-term memory, the nature of the organization of the mental lexicon has much influence on our ability to remember and recall not only individual words but also sentences, passages, and concepts. An understanding of the mental lexicon can, therefore, provide us with useful information regarding the nature of reading disabilities.

In order to understand more about the nature of the mental lexicon, we raise three questions: (1) How many lexicons are there? (2) How is information organized in these lexicons? (3) How is a connection made between a word on the paper and its representation in the mental lexicon?

These are not trivial questions; they contain potential answers to the puzzle of reading disabilities. Before we try to answer these questions, we should point out that psychologists cannot provide straightforward answers to these questions. Rather, the questions are answered in terms of *models*. Psychological models are metaphors that do not describe things as they are, but tend to explain them in terms of phenomena that are familiar to us. That is why analogies such as "library," "dictionary," and "network" are often used to describe the mental lexicon. In a way, a model is a confession of our inability to understand a phenomenon in its original form.

Answers to the three questions raised about the lexicon are presented in terms of models. Information on the basis of which these models are constructed comes from two sources: observation and experimentation. Some of these observations are based on common facts such as our ability to pronounce words that we have never seen before, from unusual instances such as slips of tongue, and from clinical symptoms such as the selective inability of some neurological patients to pronounce grammar words and word suffixes. Experimental data are primarily collected by using *lexical decision tasks, semantic decision tasks,* and *priming tasks.* In the lexical decision task, the subject is presented with a string of letters (e.g., *bromp*) and is asked to decide whether it is a word or a nonword. In the semantic decision task, the subject is presented with a word (e.g., *chicken*) and is asked to decide whether or not it is an animal. In the priming task, the target word is preceded by another word that may or may not be related to the target word and the reaction time for pronouncing the target word is measured. In all of these experiments, RT is the dependent variable, the assumption being that the larger the difference in RT between two words, the farther away from each other they are represented in the mental lexicon. For instance, in the lexical decision task, if the RT for words such as *robin* and *finch* are closer to each other than the RT for *robin* and *chicken*, it is inferred that *robin* and *finch* are closer to each other in the lexicon than are *robin* and *chicken*. In the priming task, if the RT for *nurse* is shorter when preceded by *doctor* than when preceded by *milk*, it is assumed that the words *nurse* and *doctor* are represented closer to each other in the lexicon than *nurse* and *milk*.

We will now attempt to answer the three questions we raised regarding the mental lexicon.

How Many Lexicons Are There?

As Aitchison (1987) puts it, humans must know at least three things about a word: rules to pronounce unfamiliar words and to construct syntactically correct sentences, pronunciation of familiar words, and the meaning of words. Information regarding these properties are presumed to be stored in the *phonological rules lexicon*, the *word pronunciations lexicon*, and the *semantic lexicon*.

The Phonological Rules Lexicon   The phonological rules lexicon is envisaged as a holding place that contains all the rules that are needed to pronounce and spell words correctly. Several sources of evidence suggest that the phonological lexicon is independent of the word pronunciation and semantic lexicons. In a previous section we saw that two outstanding symptoms of "deep dyslexia" are an inability to read aloud nonwords and an impaired ability to read aloud grammar words even though these subjects could demonstrate better comprehension of words. It is assumed that because nonwords cannot be found in any mental lexicon, reading them correctly requires the utilization of spelling-pronunciation rules. Similarly, because grammar words do not refer to things, actions, or properties, they cannot be pronounced by accessing the semantic lexicon and identifying their meaning first. Thus, it appears that "deep dyslexia" is caused by a defect in the phonological rules lexicon. It was also noted that in the converse condition known as "surface dyslexia," the neurological patient tends to pronounce words by applying pronunciation rules in a more or less mechanical fashion but fails to understand the word correctly. Taken together, "deep dyslexia" and "surface dyslexia" suggest that the phonological and semantic lexicon are independent of each other. The developmental reading disorder known as *hyperlexia* also suggests that the semantic lexicon and phonological rules lexicon are separable. Children with hyperlexia can pronounce words and nonwords quite well but have severe deficits in comprehension (Aaron 1989a). Their ability to read nonwords indicates that pronunciation is possibly accomplished by applying spelling–pronunciation rules. Several such rules that are useful in pronouncing written words have been identified by researchers (c.f., Calfee, Venezky, and Chapman 1969; Wijk 1966).

A defect in the spoken language caused by neurological impairment is referred to as *aphasia*. Several kinds of aphasias are described in the neuropsychological literature, and Broca aphasia is one of them. Patients with Broca aphasia tend to omit small grammar words and word suffixes when they speak. Their ability to understand spoken language, however, remains relatively intact and their comprehension of content words is almost normal. These patients also show a similar defect in their reading performance (Benson 1977). Because function words (such as prepositions and conjunctions) do not have meaning, reading of these words probably has to be mediated by either the phonological or word pronunciation lexicon. The same statement can be made with regard to suffixes. Being bound morphemes, they also do not have semantic content and may have to be processed by the phonological mechanism. Experimental and clinical studies show that when we are read, complex words are decomposed into root morphemes and suffixes and then processed separately. For example, the root word *play* in the morpheme *played* may be stored in the semantic lexicon, whereas its inflexional suffixes such as "ed" or "ing" may be stored in a different lexicon. Kean (1977) has argued that deficits of grammar seen in Broca aphasia can be traced to deficits in phonology since grammatical morphemes, lacking in meaning, depend on phonology for processing. This view receives further support from the observation that patients who have difficulty in reading grammatical morphemes also have difficulty in reading nonwords and in spelling words correctly (Patterson 1982; Langmore and Canter 1983). These observations lead to the conclusion that we can postulate a lexicon that contains rules for pronouncing words which is independent of the semantic lexicon. This proposition is further supported by the observation that children and adolescents with developmental dyslexia tend to omit suffixes when they read and write and that they experience a great deal of difficulty in spelling and reading unfamiliar words, nonwords, and function words correctly even though they can comprehend spoken language far better (Aaron 1989a).

On a rational basis alone it can be argued that because we can correctly pronounce nonwords such as *slint*, we should have in our possession some means of pronouncing such words which, of course, are not in our semantic lexicon. Experimental studies also provide support for postulating a lexicon that contains phonological rules, which is independent of the semantic lexicon. In lexical decision tasks, normal subjects say "yes" faster to common nouns such as *cat* and *house* than "no" to nonwords such as *neet* and *cleer*. This may be because two different lexicons are tapped in such tasks; the "yes" decision may be made after searching only the semantic lexicon, whereas the relatively slow "no" decision may be due to a conflict between a "no" decision from the semantic lexicon and a "yes" decision from the phonological lexicon. As noted earlier, there is experimental evidence to show that when suffixed words are read, the suffix is stripped and processed separately from the root morpheme (see Hankamer 1989 for a description of this process). This is likely to be so in the case of agglutinative languages such as Turkish, Finnish, Hungarian, Tamil, and Kannada. In agglutinative languages, grammatical features such as tense, person, negation, interrogation, etc., are indicated by inflectional suffixes and are attached to bases and to one another in a definite order (Çapan 1989). This process of adding suffix to suffix results not only in huge words but also in a large number of words. According to Hankamer (1989), in the Turkish language the agglutinative morphology is estimated to have the potential of creating nearly 200 billion morphemes. It is not conceivable that all these elements could be stored as independent entries in the semantic lexicon. A reasonable set-up would be to list a limited number of root morphemes in the semantic lexicon and to list the limited number of suffixes and store them separately along with the rules required to generate compound words. Because defects in the proper use of suffixes and a deficit in nonword reading skill tend to co-occur, rules of pronunciation and rules of the use of syntax may be represented in the same lexicon. We can, therefore, expect slow reading, poor spelling, and incorrect use of syntax to occur together in the same person.

The Word Pronunciation Lexicon   Unlike the phonological rules lexicon, in which rules for pronouncing words are represented, the word pronunciation lexicon is thought to contain word-specific pronunciations. Thus, while the rules lexicon helps in assembling the pronunciation of words, the pronunciation lexicon enables the reader to address and retrieve appropriate pronunciations of words wholistically, as single units. While the operational basis of the rules lexicon can be viewed as algorithmic, that of the pronunciation lexicon can be viewed as associative. The fact that we can pronounce "exception words" which do not obey spelling–pronunciation rules (e.g., have, sew, pint) is sometimes cited as a reason for postulating a lexicon in which whole word pronunciations are listed. Exception words, which are also referred to as "irregular words," do not conform to the conventional spelling–pronunciation rules (e.g., *have* does not conform to the rule by which words such as *cave, pave,* and *rave* are pronounced) and, therefore, cannot be pronounced by applying spelling–pronunciation rules.

Neuropsychological literature provides evidence for the independence of the rules lexicon from the pronunciation lexicon. That is, the existence of patients who could pronounce written real words rather well but are very poor in pronouncing nonwords is documented (c.f., Funnell 1983; Lytton and Brust 1989). These patients apparently use an associative process for pronouncing real words but are unable to apply pronunciation rules to words they have not encountered before. Furthermore, whether a word is classified as "regular" or "exception" has no influence on the reading performance of these patients. This means they pronounce the word by retrieving the pronunciation as a whole without assembling it. Recently, we studied a developmental analog of this form of reading disability (Aaron, Frantz, and Manges 1990). The subject was a 19-year-old girl with borderline IQ who could read written words at about the fourth grade level but could not read even a single item from a list of 36 nonwords. She also read "regular" and "exception" words equally well. Children described in developmental reading literature as "word callers" are similar to this subject.

The strategy used in retrieving whole word pronunciation by accessing the word-pronunciation lexicon is primarily an associative process and, as such, requires repeated exposure to the written word. A limitation of this process is that the number of word-pronunciation associations that can be formed and stored in memory is limited. The girl described above had a sight vocabulary only of an average fourth grader. Languages such as Chinese use a nonalphabetic form of script and depend primarily on the associative process for learning to pronounce the written morpheme. Readers of such scripts are said to have a sight vocabulary limited to three or four thousand morphemes.

The Semantic Lexicon   The semantic lexicon can be thought of as a store that contains all the meanings we associate with the words we know. There is evidence to show that a good portion of the information we have about the world is organized on a conceptual basis. For instance, the priming effect of conceptually related words on one another is larger than conceptually unrelated words. The verbal learning task called the *free recall task* provides further support for the belief that the semantic lexicon is conceptually organized. In this task the subject is presented with a random list of words and is asked to recall them in any order he wishes. The words may represent different categories such as clothing items, fruits, animals, etc. It is generally observed than even without specific instruction, subjects tend to recall items in categories rather than in a random fashion. For instance, subjects are likely to recall the names of animals and fruits in groups even though the list was not presented to the subjects on such a conceptual basis. This suggests that learners tend to organize and store what they learn in conceptual categories.

In addition to experimental evidence, clinical data also support the notion of an independent semantic lexicon. For instance, neurological patients described as "deep dyslexics" are unable to pronounce non-words (e.g., *slint*) but demonstrate much better ability to comprehend the meaning of written words. This indicates that these patients comprehend the general meaning of written words but are unable to pronounce them correctly. Deep dyslexia, therefore, can be considered as support for the belief that the semantic lexicon where word meanings are represented is distinct from the lexicon or lexicons that mediate pronunciation.

To this list of three lexicons, we would like to add one more lexicon, the *orthographic lexicon*. Because the status of this lexicon is ambiguous, it is not listed here as a separate lexicon. Orthography is the visual representation of a language and can be defined as the written patterns of a language and their mapping onto phonology and meaning. In alphabetic scripts, the spelling pattern of the written language serves as a means of accessing the pronunciation of a word and its meaning. In reading, apprehending the meaning of the word is more important than pronouncing it. Alphabetic orthographies, therefore, give precedence to semantics over phonology. This often is the case in the English language. Thus, even though word pairs such as *sign—signature, know—knowledge,* and *part—separate* are pronounced differently, their spelling patterns are preserved. Conversely, homophones have the same pronunciation but different meaning and are spelled differently (e.g., *no—know, meet—meat, reed—read*). Thus, the allegiance of orthography is to meaning and not always to pronunciation.

Do we have any evidence for the existence of an independent orthographic lexicon? It is said that some children lag behind in the development of word recognition skill even though they have adequate phonological skills. If phonological skill is all that is necessary for word recognition, these children should be good at this task. The poor word recognition skill of children with good phonological skill is, therefore, thought to indicate that word recognition requires some other skill in addition to phonological skills. It is speculated that this additional skill is orthographic memory that probably is visual–perceptual in nature. Children with adequate phonological ability but poor word recognition skill are thought to have poor orthographic memory. It is, therefore, proposed that decoding skill is a necessary but not sufficient condition for the acquisition of reading skill and that the ability to form, store, and access orthographic representations accounts for some of the variance seen in word recognition skill that is not accounted for by phonological factors (Stanovich and West 1989). If this turns out to be true, then poor orthographic representation can result in yet another form of reading disability.

One piece of evidence cited in support of the orthographic lexicon is that sometimes children correctly write a few words they cannot pronounce. In addition, mature readers are able to spell exception words correctly, a task that cannot be accomplished by relying on spelling–sound rules. The same statement can be made with reference to homophones. Obviously some form of visual representation of the word is used to write these words correctly. Besides these rational arguments, some experimental studies also indicate that there might exist an independent orthographic lexicon. For instance, Seidenberg and Tanenhaus (1979), found that in an aurally presented rhyme detection task, words that were orthographically similar (e.g., pie—tie) were identified as rhymes faster than rhymes that were orthographically dissimilar (e.g., rye—tie). The difference in RT is thought to be due to the arousal of orthographic representations (dissimilar in the case of *rye—tie*) that create a conflict. Stored visual orthographic representation of words, therefore, appears to play a role in the identification of words.

Even though some evidence in support of the existence of an independent orthographic lexicon can be cited, the precise nature of such a lexicon is not clear. Ehri and Wilce (1980) suggest that the orthographic representation may not be stored as rote-memorized visual images but as sequences bearing systematic relationships to acoustic and/or articulatory segments detected in the word's phonological identity. The capacity of the orthographic representation, which presumably is visual, also appears to be limited to two or three items. Orthographic representations that exceed this limit may have to be sustained by phonological support to be retained in working memory. It should come as no surprise if the orthographic lexicon eventually turns out to be a component of the word pronunciation lexicon and the ability to spell correctly is more dependent on phonology than on visual memory. A study of 180 children from third through eighth grade corroborated this statement as we obtained a correlation coefficient of .72 between spelling and nonword reading (Aaron and Simurdak 1989).

But how important is the role played by orthographic memory? Stanovich and West (1989) studied college students and concluded that *some* of the variance seen in word processing skill could be attributed to differences in orthographic processing skill but that reading experience is closely related to the orthographic variance. A study by Olson et al. (1989) also found that phonological processing skill associated with word recognition had a sizeable heritability, whereas the variance associated with orthographic processing was largely nonheritable. Thus, reading experience appears to be an important variable associated with orthographic processing skill. Failure to learn to read because of inadequate learning experience generally is not considered as a form of reading disability.

How is Information Organized in the Lexicon?

A knowledge of the format in which lexicons are organized can be useful because it can help us choose between alternate explanations put forward to account for slow retrieval of information by poor readers. It is often reported that poor readers are slow in retrieving information and that they perform poorly in RT tasks. Two possible explanations have been advanced to account for this. One is that the neurological mechanism of a poor reader takes longer to process written language than spoken language; the second explanation is that the lexicon of poor readers is organized in an unsystematic fashion that does not permit efficient retrieval of information or that the relevant information is not stored in the lexicon.

Two basic formats of lexical organizations have been proposed. Other proposed formats are either hybrids or modifications of these two basic models. Furthermore, these models are efforts to describe the semantic lexicon; there is no reason to extend the same form of organization to the other lexicons. While the semantic lexicon is organized on a conceptual basis, it is quite possible that the phonological rules lexicon is organized on the basis of phonemic properties of the word and the orthographic lexicon on the basis of letter patterns.

Evidence on which the models of the semantic lexicon are built are almost solely based on data obtained from RT studies. Two organizational formats of the semantic lexicon have been proposed. These are the *network model* and the *set model*.

The Network Model   This model proposes that lexical entries are arranged on a conceptual basis in the form of a hierarchy of network.

As one moves up the hierarchy, the concepts become more and more generalized. For example, the superordinate of *canary* is *bird* and the superordinate of *bird* is *animal*. Thus, *canary* is at the bottom of the network, *bird* above it, and *animal* farther up. Concepts relevant to *canary* alone will be linked to that word, whereas concepts relevant to birds in general will be linked to the word *bird*. For example, "yellow" would be attached to *canary* whereas "wings" will be attached to *birds*. When information has to be retrieved, a subject enters the lowest level of the network and proceeds farther up until information necessary to answer the question is obtained. For instance, in this example, it takes longer to answer the question "Is a canary an animal?" than to answer the question "Is a canary a bird?". It is, therefore, inferred that *canary* is closer to *bird* than to *animal*. Even though a temporal–conceptual relationship has been demonstrated for several concepts, too many exceptions have been reported so that the network model does not appear to provide the best fit for the mental lexicon (Bower and Hilgard 1981). For example, it takes longer to verify the statement "cantaloupe is a melon" than to verify the statement "cantaloupe is a fruit" even though in the network model *cantaloupe* and *melon* should be closer to each other than *cantaloupe* and *fruit*.

The Set Model   In this model, semantic information is thought to be arranged in discrete sets. Each set may be envisaged as a deck of playing cards that includes all instances of a particular semantic unit as well as all its attributes. For instance, the semantic unit *dog* may contain the names of all breeds of dogs as well as their defining characteristics such as "dogs are animals," "dogs bark," "dogs are pets," etc. Furthermore, the attributes within the set as well as the set themselves may be stacked on top of each other with the most frequently encountered units occupying the top-most level. It is also assumed that an information search is serial in nature and proceeds from top to bottom. This form of organization can explain the experimental observation that in lexical decision tasks the RT for high frequency words is shorter than for low frequency words.

A modified version of this model hypothesizes that highly familiar words may be represented twice, once in the main set and again in a subset. The subset contains highly familiar words and is somewhat like an abridged pocket dictionary that contains common words and is used for quick reference. When readers encounter a word, they may first search the quick reference subset, and if the search fails to turn up the word, they would proceed to search the large set.

An implication of the set model, in its originally proposed format, is that all the units of information in a set are checked against the input information, one at a time, until the correct match is obtained. The incredible speed with which we can recognize a word is not compatible with this model unless it is modified to adopt a search procedure in which all items stored in a set are matched with the input item simultaneously. This, of course, is parallel search. However, for parallel search, a hierarchical organization of semantic units based on word frequency and familiarity is not necessary.

This brief review shows that both models of lexicon have their relative weaknesses. Perhaps the lexical organization is far more complex than we had imagined. A more important problem, however, is how the written word is recognized.

How is a Connection Made
Between the Written Word and the Lexicon?

How is a connection made between a word on the paper and its representations in the mental lexicons? This question can be reformulated to read, "How is a word recognized when the reader encounters it?" or "How is information associated with a word retrieved from the lexicon?"

Several hypothetical models have been proposed to explain the word recognition process, and they can be placed in two broad categories: *lexical activation* and *lexical search*.

Lexical Activation and Lexical Search   The activation model assumes that the search is carried out simultaneously, in parallel, and that the word representation that is in tune with the sensory input stands out and is recognized. The lexical search model, on the other hand, assumes that a systematic serial search of the lexicon is carried out until the word representation that matches the sensory input is identified. A modified version of the activation model, however, proposes that the parallel search can be limited to a selected group of viable candidates. A modified version of the lexical search model proposes that the search need not be carried out on an item-by-item basis, but subgroups of candidates in the lexicon can be searched on a set-by-set basis. The reader would realize that after these modifications, the difference between these two basic models becomes rather blurred. In the present context, an explanation of the word recognition process is presented from the perspective of the activation model.

According to one version of the activation model, words are represented in the lexicon in terms of their semantic, phonologic, and orthographic features. Moreover, when the visually coded information arrives at the lexicon, it presumably activates all these representations, viz., semantic, phonologic, and orthographic, at once. This activation is carried out in a parallel fashion and is presumed to activate several

viable candidates that resemble the input. For example, the word
"house" may activate in the semantic lexicon the representation *house*
in addition to activating related representations such as *home, hut,* or
family. In the phonologic lexicon the target word may activate phonemes such as /h/, /ho/ (rhymes with *go*), /ho/ (rhymes with "ho" in
hop), /hou/ (rhymes with *how*). In addition, it may also activate orthographic patterns such as "ho," "ou," or "se," and word pronunciations
such as *house,* and *hose,* and *horse* in the orthographic and word-
pronunciation lexicons. When the summed-up contributions of these
representations exceed a certain threshold, the code that represents the
word stands out, and the word represented by that code is recognized.
It is possible to describe the simultaneous comparison process with the
help of an analogy borrowed from Just and Carpenter (1987). Suppose
from among an array of tuning forks of differing pitch, one has to
choose the one that matches a standard fork. The task can be accomplished by hitting the standard tuning fork so that it vibrates and then
holding it against the array of forks. The one fork with a pitch corresponding to that of the standard will vibrate in harmony even though
all the tuning forks were exposed to the standard fork simultaneously.
In this analogy, the standard tuning fork is similar to the printed word,
and the array of forks is similar to the representations of words stored
in the lexicon. The search is simultaneous and parallel.

A model described by Morton and Patterson (1980) is representative of this family of activation models. The model advanced by these
investigators also allows for the word frequency and recency effects by
proposing that these factors lower the threshold needed for recognition. Consequently, familiar words and words that have been recently
encountered are identified more readily than unfamiliar words. In accord with the description given in the previous paragraph, this model
proposes that a group of words that resemble the target word visually
and phonologically also will be activated. For example, when the word
throng is presented, it could also activate similar looking words such as
through, thorough, and *though,* and similar sounding words such as *gong*
and *wrong*. But most of the lexical evidence would converge on the
word *throng*, which will then be identified. It is, nevertheless, possible,
as often happens in the case of poor readers, that the wrong word may
be identified and uttered.

One of the issues in word recognition that continues to be contro-
versial is the role played by the phonological feature of the written
word. Not only the importance of pronunciation of the word and the
point in time when it may occur are questioned, but doubts about the
very need for pronunciation in reading are also raised. Some researchers contend that conversion of the written word into its phonological counterpart is not necessary for word recognition. They be-

lieve that the meaning of the written word can be captured without resorting to pronunciation, whether overt or covert. Several other investigators, however, believe that a phonological conversion of the written word is essential for reading, but they are not in agreement as to the stage when phonological representation of the word comes into play, before word recognition or after it. When phonological realization of the written word precedes word recognition, such a conversion is termed as *prelexical*; when the meaning of the word is first realized and then it is pronounced, the phonological conversion is *postlexical*. Apart from those who advocate the prelexical or postlexical conversion of print into phonology, there is also an opportunistic group that believes that the input races toward the phonological and semantic lexicons and the lexicon that is accessed first is used in word recognition. It is, however, assumed that, generally speaking, visual representation reaches the semantic lexicon sooner than the phonological representation and, therefore, phonology plays a lesser role, particularly in skilled reading.

We believe that even though prelexical and postlexical conversions of print into phonology are possible and that a race may take place between processes, all the representative lexical features of the written word are used simultaneously in word recognition process. That is, a word's semantic, phonological, and orthographic representations in the lexicons are used simultaneously for its recognition. Furthermore, weakness in utilizing any one of these representations can bias the recognition process and lead to errors. We call this the *concurrent model* of word recognition.

The Concurrent Model of Word Recognition   This model draws heavily from models proposed to explain speech recognition, particularly the *cohort model* proposed by Marslen-Wilson (1989). The cohort model tries to account for the experimental observation that spoken words generally are recognized in context in less than 200 msec from word onset, a point at which the available sensory information is incomplete to allow correct identification of the word. That is, a listener can recognize a word in a sentence even before the word is completely uttered. This means, during this early stage, that additional information such as the semantic and syntactic properties as well as contextual cues converge and activate viable candidates in the lexicon. This initial group of representations constitute the word-initial cohort. As more of the word is heard, there is a successive pruning of the number of candidates that do not fit the accruing input stimulus. This process of winnowing continues until there remains only one candidate that still matches the sensory input. This is recognized as the word. The *concurrent model* of written word processing differs from the cohort model in two ways: (1) unlike the spoken word, the written word requires a mechanism to convert the stimulus into its phonological equivalent; (2) the concurrent model assumes that the word is recognized all at once without undergoing a successive reduction in the number of activated candidates. The concurrent model proposes that a number of viable semantic, phonological, and orthographic candidates may be activated, but selection of the single representative is made all at once without going through a successive elimination process. The word recognition problem is solved much like a problem of simultaneous equations. Consider the following example which contains two equations. Finding the correct solution to this problem requires the use of both equations simultaneously.

$$
\begin{array}{rcl}
x + y &=& 3 \\
2x + y &=& 4 \\
\hline
x &=& 1
\end{array}
$$

In this example neither equation alone could provide the correct solution. Assuming we are dealing with positive integers, equation (1) alone would give four values for x (0, 1, 2, and 3), and four values to y (0, 1, 2, and 3). Similarly, equation (2) alone would give three values for x (0, 1, and 2) and three values for y (0, 2, and 4). When the two equations are solved simultaneously, however, only one value for x and only one value for y is possible and the correct solution is obtained. It is proposed that during word recognitions, representations from the semantic lexicon, phonological rules lexicon, word pronunciation lexicon, and possibly orthographic lexicon are treated like separate equations in an algebraic problem and are used simultaneously, in a one-step operation.

The model is illustrated with an example (figure 1.1). In the sentence, "The house has a pool," the word *house* activates semantic representations such as *house, home, hut, live,* and *place*; in the phonologic lexicon it activates rules for pronouncing the graphemes and syllables such as /h/, /ho/, /ou/, or /use/. At the same time, in the word-pronunciation lexicon, it activates pronunciations associated the words *house, home,* or *horse* and in the orthographic lexicon, it activates letter patterns such as "ho," "hou," and "ho . . e."

In Figure 1.1 the matrix is entered simultaneously from all of these lexical dimensions and the intersect is recognized as the word. The solid arrows result in correct recognition; the broken arrows represent the recognition process of a poor reader who has specific weakness in the phonological rules lexicon. Under this circumstance, the rules lexicon has no significant input and the semantic lexicon assumes an overriding power. The word is incorrectly recognized as *home* because it agrees with the limited orthographic input "ho" and fits the sentence context.

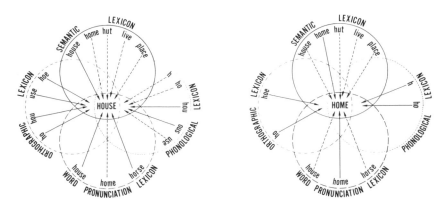

(A) Correct pronunciation of the word 'house'.

(B) Incorrect pronunciation of the word 'house' because of faulty phonological lexicon.

Figure 1.1.   A schematic diagram of the concurrent model of word recognition.

The concurrent model is "form-based" and not "time-based." That is, errors of word recognition are attributed not to an inability to retrieve information quickly but to the possibility that one or more of the lexicons is deficient in its content or organization. This conclusion is based on the observation that many dyslexic children do not improve their word recognition performance even when allowed an unlimited amount of time. One implication of the concurrent model is that the conversion of the written word into its phonological representation is very helpful for the correct recognition of the word. Weakness of this skill leads to approximations of the correct solution because under such a circumstance, word identification is accomplished by the semantic and orthographic lexicons alone. The paralexic errors committed by patients with "deep dyslexia" probably represent such approximations. In the concurrent model, the issue of whether or not the phonological conversion is pre- or postlexical also becomes irrelevant because lexical access is based on the simultaneous involvement of all the lexicons.

Even though in this book we do not provide experimental evidence in support of the concurrent model, reading errors committed by neuropsychological patients and poor readers do lend empirical support. Patients described as "deep dyslexics" and children who have developmental dyslexia probably have an impaired or poorly developed phonological rules lexicon and patients described as "surface dyslexics" and children who are hyperlexic probably have an impaired or underdeveloped semantic lexicon.

Correct recognition of the word ensures that the comprehension process is progressing along the right lines. Reading, however, is more than the ability to recognize individual words; it involves comprehension of the entire sentence and the text.

SENTENCE COMPREHENSION

Once the word is recognized, it is thought to be kept in the short-term memory (STM) store for a brief period until a unit of meaning accrues due to the accumulation of words into a group. Subsequently, the meaning unit is processed further into the long-term memory (LTM). When all the units of meaning in a sentence reach LTM, the entire sentence is comprehended.

The construction of meaning units is based on the accumulation of words and this takes time. For this reason, individual word representations have to be kept in a temporary store until a memory unit is completed. Short-term memory is believed to play an important role in storing word representations temporarily and thus facilitating the building of meaning units. Any deficiency of the STM, therefore, can be a potential source of reading difficulty.

Short-Term Memory and Working Memory

A tendency to dichotomize memory into short-term and long-term memories has a long history dating back to the end of the last century. At times, it is debated whether such a division represents psychological reality or is an outcome of our subjective experience. Nevertheless, classifying memory into two components has been experimentally productive and is defensible on operational grounds.

Even though STM can be acoustic or visual in nature, the word representations realized from the lexicon are thought to be stored in some phonological form in the acoustic STM. The STM, much like the iconic store, is considered to have a relatively short duration and limited capacity. Unlike the iconic store, however, the STM has some strategies that help it overcome these limitations. The temporal limitation could be overcome through a process of covert rehearsal; the capacity limitation through grouping or chunking input information. For instance, the term *deoxyribonucleic acid* contains letters that exceed the capacity of the STM which is limited to 7 or 9 items. The term, however, could be grouped into the following 5 chunks: *de oxy ribo nucleic acid*, which reduces the cognitive load placed on STM considerably and enables the rehearsal and retention of the information until it is transferred to LTM. Rehearsal and chunking can be accomplished more readily by converting the written word into its phonological representation than into its visual representation. This representation obviously is realized in the phonological rules lexicon or in the word pronunciation lexicon. The precise nature of the phonological representation, however, is not clear even though ability to pronounce the written word overtly is closely associated with ability to form the phonological representation of the word. Observations of dyslexic children struggling to read indicate that an inability to pronounce the written word without expending much effort is a serious impediment to becoming a skilled reader.

A number of studies show that the written word is stored in phonological form. In a letter memorization task, more intrusion errors (and consequently, poor performance) were found for similar-sounding letters such as *b, v, p, c, t,* than for letters with dissimilar sounds such as *n, s, x, l, o* (Baddeley 1966a). A similar finding for words is also reported by Baddeley (1966b). In this study, it was found that, in immediate recall tasks, more confusion errors occurred for phonologically similar words (e.g., *mad, man, can*) than for dissimilar words (e.g., *cow, day, pen*). If, however, the words were recalled after a delay of 20 minutes, more intrusion errors occurred among words with similar meaning (e.g., *huge, wide, big*) than among words that differed in meaning (e.g., *late, thin, wet*). This indicates that STM is phonology-based but LTM is meaning-based. It follows that an inability to convert the written word into its phonological equivalent will severely restrict STM operation. This, in fact, appears to be a proximal cause of specific reading disability.

When the STM is discussed from the perspective of its functions and the strategies it uses to perform these functions, it is referred to as *working memory.* The concept of working memory can be considered as a descriptive label for STM. It was introduced by Baddeley and Hitch (1974) and represents a system for the temporary holding and manipulation of information. It is conceived of as having a central executive system along with satellite systems in which information is stored in the form of articulatory and visual representations. Of these satellite systems, the articulatory system, which corresponds to the phonological STM described in the previous section, has been studied quite extensively.

One of the outcomes of this reformulation of the concept of STM is to focus more attention on the function than on the structure of STM and to emphasize its performance more than its capacity. This shift in emphasis is in line with the recent trend to explain differences in performance on memory tasks in terms of the speed with which STM carries out mental processes rather than in terms of its capacity. This statement is examined closely in the following paragraph because poor STM is often proposed as a correlate of specific reading disability.

Interpreting the results of tests of memory in terms of the speed with which operations are executed in STM, rather than its capacity, is based on the following evidence. Some studies show that the memory span of individuals can be determined by the number of items they can subvocalize in 1.8 to 2.2 seconds (Standing et al. 1980; Nicholson 1981). English-Welsh bilingual subjects have a larger STM for digits in English than in Welsh and it was found that Welsh digits take longer to articulate than English digits (Ellis and Hennelly 1980). The number of digits that can be processed by STM within a given time, therefore, will be smaller in Welsh than in English.

Furthermore, Hulme et al. (1984) found a linear relationship between speaking rate and STM for subjects ranging in age from four years to adulthood. These studies show that speed of processing rather than capacity may be the factor that limits the efficiency of STM in poor readers. Slow processing of information in poor readers, however, does not seem to be the result of slow neurological processes, but is brought about by a poorly organized phonological lexicon that impedes quick retrieval of information.

Psychologists and linguists have studied extensively these and other factors that promote or impede comprehension and have developed a more or less coherent view about sentence comprehension. They believe that the basic unit in sentence comprehension is not single words but a group of words that form a natural unit of meaning. These units are referred to as *propositions* (Kintsch 1977) or *idea units* (Chafe 1985).

Propositions and Idea Units

A proposition is a sequence of words that represents a meaningful unit. Even though propositions often correspond to clauses, the former represent semantic units whereas the latter are defined in terms of syntax and grammar. The term *idea unit* is often used in the context of speech perception, and the term *proposition* in the context of reading comprehension, but we see no reason for strictly adhering to this classification. In this book, these two terms, viz., propositions and idea units, are used interchangeably. According to Chafe (1985), an idea unit is spoken with a single coherent prosodic contour ending in a clause-final intonation and is followed and preceded by pauses. In written language, punctuation marks and conjunctions often, but not always, take the place of pauses. The idea unit is hypothesized to be a unit that can hold only the information a speaker can handle in a single focus of attention. In the spoken language, an average idea unit contains about seven words, a number that corresponds to STM capacity. From a psychological point of view, a proposition or an idea unit can, therefore, be defined as a unit of meaning made up of a sequence of words that can be held in STM at any given moment. The permanent nature of the written language permits propositions to be made up of a few more words. The additional words, however, are generally used for embellishing the written language and, therefore, may not add substantially to the memory load.

It is proposed (c.f., Kleiman 1975) that phonological representations of words that have been recognized in the lexicon are held in the STM until they are reconstituted into propositions and then processed further onto long-term memory. This momentary holding in STM provides an opportunity for the subject's knowledge of the world to be utilized in the comprehension process and by facilitating the construction of propositions. If, for some reason, a word needed for the construction of an idea unit is lost or not available, the reader uses his or her world knowledge to install an appropriate substitute for the missing word. Also, when such omissions are deliberately introduced in the text by the writer, a reader infers the missing items and makes appropriate restitutions.

At this point, when the semantic interpretation is processed on to the LTM, memory for the exact words in STM decays. This view is in agreement with the general observation that immediate recall of information, presumably from the STM, invariably is verbatim, whereas delayed recall, presumably from the LTM, often is not verbatim but is reformulated on the basis of meaning. For these reasons, sentence comprehension is considered an active, constructive process that requires information above and beyond that which is on the printed page. This is in accord with the view that reading disability is partly due to the "passive attitude" adopted by a learner toward the text instead of utilizing an active approach (c.f., Torgesen and Licht 1983).

Mere recognition of words in a sentence does not ensure comprehension of that sentence nor could propositions be constructed by assembling words in a serial fashion. A sentence is more than a collection of words, and comprehending the sentence correctly requires that it be placed in the appropriate syntactic format. Frequently, sentences are written with the assumption that a reader already has certain knowledge about the subject matter under discussion and leaves some information unsaid, expecting the reader to fill the gap by making appropriate inferences. For example, consider the simple sentence: "We went to McDonald's and had a good time." In order to understand the full import of the sentence, the reader should know what McDonald's is and make the inference that the writer had a meal at McDonald's. Knowing that McDonald's is a fast food place is part of the reader's world knowledge. This knowledge background that the reader brings to bear on the reading task is referred to as *schema*.

Schema

Many researchers believe that the schema (plural = schemata) a reader possesses has much influence on reading comprehension. Consider the following passage:

> Chicago hosts the LA Rams to determine the NFC's Super Bowl representative. There will be no sideshows in this one as it doesn't need any. Walter Payton running one way and Eric Dickerson the other is plenty, and add to that the Refrigerator and friends snacking on Ram Quarterback Dieter Brock (Hunt 1986).

A correct understanding of the above statement requires a sound background knowledge of the current American football scene. In fact, some British psychologists who listened to this statement thought it was about a county fair or picnic. Inadequate background knowledge or schema is one of the major sources of difficulties in comprehension experienced by students in high schools and colleges.

Being in possession of the schema, by itself, does not guarantee the correct comprehension of a sentence. First, the appropriate schema has to be selected, and then it has to be activated. The importance of selecting the appropriate schema for proper comprehension is demonstrated by a series of studies done by Pichert and Anderson (1977). As part of their research, they required subjects to read about what two boys did at one boy's home while skipping school. The readers' schemata were manipulated by assigning different perspectives; one third of the subjects were instructed to read the story from the perspective of a potential home buyer, one-third from the perspective of a burglar, and one-third were given no special perspective. It should come as no surprise that the assigned perspective had a powerful influence on learning and recall. The home-buyer perspective group recalled more items regarding the quality of the home whereas the burglar-perspective group recalled more information relevant to illegal entry and escape. This suggests that a student and his or her lecturer may use different schemata when dealing with the same topic and a student may read a passage in a textbook without being aware of what the author thinks is important. Under such circumstances, a student cannot be said to have comprehended the sentence in the strict sense. Activation of the proper schema is, therefore, necessary for efficient learning and recall.

Schemata are part of our LTM, whereas propositions are formed in the STM. If schemata play a role in the building of propositions, it is obvious that LTM influences some of the activities of the STM. This is described as *top-down* or *concept-driven* process. Processing information in the opposite direction, from the icon to the lexical level, is considered as *bottom-up* or *data-driven*. Because of the simultaneous involvement of both top-down and bottom-up processes, reading is described as an interactive process. As we move from sentence comprehension to text comprehension, it becomes increasingly necessary to consider reading as an interactive process.

TEXT COMPREHENSION

Just as a sentence is more than a collection of words, so is a text more than a mere collection of sentences. The text usually contains a coherent theme and is, therefore, a more natural unit than is a random group of words or sentences. Generally speaking, sentences within the text are arranged in such a way as to present information in a cohesive manner and not to tax the cognitive resources of the reader excessively. Principles that govern the structuring of text on the basis of coherence and logical arrangement of sentences constitute what is known as *story-grammar*.

Story-Grammar

The concept of story-grammar simply means that a text is not a haphazard collection of sentences and that both the writer and the reader have to be sensitive to the principles of organization of the text. Texts and passages that students come across in high schools and colleges can be classified into three categories: narratives, descriptions, and expositions. By and large, a majority of texts are expository in nature because they contain explanations of objects, people, and phenomena that are intended to communicate knowledge to the reader and, thus, expose him or her to new ideas and facts. The nature of story-grammar has received some research attention in recent years, but most of the investigations have been limited to children's stories. These stories show that, in general, they contain a theme, a plot, and a resolution. The theme of the story is made obvious by the writer in the early parts of the story or higher in the story-grammar hierarchy. Even children in elementary school appear to be aware of this. For instance, in one study, Cirilo and Foss (1980) inserted the following sentence at two different levels in two different stories: "He could no longer talk at all." One story was about a king who was cursed by a witch so that he could not speak. The other story was about a soldier who was rewarded by the king for a good deed and was rendered speechless by the magnitude of the reward. The critical sentence in the first story is thematic in nature and naturally appeared high up in the story, whereas the same sentence, being about a relatively unimportant consequence, appeared toward the end of the second story. It was found that children spent more time reading the sentence in the first story as compared to the second story. It was reasoned that readers spend more time on thematic sentences because they are aware of their importance and pay careful attention to them by spending more time processing them. A reader who is insensitive to such story grammar features may allocate equal time to all the sentences in the text.

Most high school and college texts do not contain stories but, as noted earlier, are expository in nature. Nevertheless, the story-grammar principles apply to them as well. For instance, the theme of the story is equivalent to the *main idea* in expository text. The main idea is usually introduced in the beginning of the text, and ideas that support the main idea are provided farther down in the text. Awareness of this structure facilitates reading comprehension. Equally important is the fact that sensitivity to story-grammar can help students also to write well-organized essays.

Identification of the main idea of the text also helps a reader activate the appropriate schema early in reading and thereby build expectations and a contextual base. The following passage (Sanford and Garrod 1981) illustrates that as we read each sentence we build up expectations based on the schema that is aroused. When the sentence does not fit the context, that particular schema is abandoned and a new one is installed.

> John was on his way to school. He was terribly worried about the mathematics lesson. He thought he might not be able to control the class again today. He thought it was unfair of the instructor to make him supervise the class for a second time. After all, it was not a normal part of a janitor's duties (p. 132).

The opening sentence in the passage activates the schema of a "school boy," which is replaced in the third sentence by the schema of the "teacher," which, in turn, is replaced by the schema of a "teaching assistant." This schema, too, is shelved in the last sentence. Most expository texts do not lead the reader down the garden path like this passage does but make the main idea quite explicit, usually at the beginning of the passage. In the above passage, the writers have misled the reader deliberately in order to make a point. Many poor readers fail to anticipate the reader's expectation and unintentionally write confusing essays.

Failure to activate the appropriate schema is one of the sources of comprehension failure. According to Baker and Brown (1984), comprehension failure can occur for three reasons: (1) the appropriate schemata are not available to the reader because the reader does not have enough knowledge about the topic to make appropriate inferences; (2) the appropriate schemata are available, but the author has not conveyed his or her ideas clearly enough so that the appropriate schema can be activated; and (3) the reader is able to interpret the text correctly, but not the way the author intended; that is, the reader understands the text, but misunderstands the author.

The large amount of information contained in expository texts places a great deal of demand on a reader's memory. These memory demands can be minimized by being sensitive to the grammatical features of the story as well as by integrating thematically related propositions and by discarding irrelevant items so that a compact and coherent theme emerges. These constitutional processes are sometimes expressed in the form of rules such as deletion, generalization, and construction. Paying particular attention to these rules can speed up the reading process and facilitate learning.

METACOGNITION

At the beginning of the chapter we noted that readers make regressive eye movements when they feel they have come across a word that does not fit the context or when a sentence does not make sense. This form of corrective action indicates that a reader is monitoring his or her comprehension as he or she reads and is aware of comprehension failure. This awareness is known as *metacognition*, and keeping track of comprehension as one reads along is referred to as *on-line monitoring*. Metacognition can be defined as cognition about cognition or "knowing what one knows and knowing what one does not know." According to Garner (1987), because cognition involves perceiving, understanding, and remembering, metacognition involves thinking about one's own perceiving, understanding, and remembering. Reading teachers are familiar with children who plunge into text heedlessly, read aloud paying little or no attention to prosody and punctuation, and hardly ever self-correct their oral reading errors. These children are not aware that they are not comprehending the text; they lack metacognitive skills.

Metacognition is thought to have two components, on-line monitoring of comprehension and taking the necessary corrective action if the reader encounters difficulty. Baker and Brown (1984) have classified metacognitive skills under two headings: reading for meaning (comprehension monitoring) and reading for remembering (studying). A number of studies show that as children grow older, their metacognitive skills also keep up with their development and that poor readers are not as good as skilled readers in using metacognitive strategies (see Baker and Brown 1984 for a review of these studies).

Comprehension monitoring: The on-line monitoring component of metacognition embraces all aspects of cognitive functioning including sentence comprehension as well as sensitivity to story-grammar in text comprehension. In the previous section we mentioned three sources of comprehension failure described by Baker and Brown. In addition to knowing that comprehension is not proceeding smoothly, the reader has to be aware of the source of comprehension failure. The last two sources of comprehension failure, viz., where the author is at fault and where the author's point of view is different from the one adopted by the reader, are quite elusive to metacognition because many students have an implicit faith in authors and a naive respect for the printed material. In more advanced classes a change in this attitude can be initiated by encouraging critical thinking.

Reading for remembering, metacognitive aspects of reading for re-membering (study skills), involves three components: *self knowledge, task knowledge,* and *text knowledge.*

Self Knowledge

Self knowledge includes an objective appraisal of one's own schematic background, reading speed, and memory skill. For instance, if stu-dents know that they are slow readers, they can take appropriate steps to remedy the situation by allocating more study time. Similarly, cor-rective measures can be taken to improve memory performance and background knowledge about the topic being studied. An awareness about one's own cognitive style (described in the next section) is an-other aspect of self knowledge. For example, a self knowledge that "I read globally and tend to leave out details" can help the reader to be more careful when reading a physics or chemistry textbook.

Task Knowledge

This includes assessment of one's own ability to identify what is re-quired; does the text call for detailed study, or does it require only skimming and scanning? Does it require paraphrasing of the major theme, or does it require memorization of details such as formulas? Poor readers in grades as high as six are known to equate reading with being able to sound out the words correctly and not necessarily with comprehension (Canney and Winograd 1979). Children studied by these authors also claimed that they could read any passage regardless of its difficulty level. Another study (Myers and Paris 1978) showed that while sixth graders understood that the purpose of skimming was to pick out the informative words, second graders said they could skim by reading easy words. These studies show that task knowledge cannot be taken for granted and that poor readers may need deliberate train-ing in this aspect of metacognition.

Text Knowledge

The metacognitive aspect of text knowledge requires that a reader be able to evaluate his or her own knowledge about text organization, story-grammar, main ideas, and supporting ideas. This aspect of metacognition also develops as children grow older. Some older children, however, are found to be deficient in this respect. Furthermore, some children who are able to identify main ideas in simple stories have more difficulty in rating the importance of themes in more complex passages. Thus, complexity of the text is an important variable that can be expected to pose difficulty in identifying the main idea and in separating it from supporting ideas even at the college level. When this metacognitive skill is not well developed, it can lead to the student's allocating equal time to all statements in the text, regardless of the degree of their importance. Another skill that is of great value is to be able to recognize redundant items and to separate ideas related to the main theme from those whose purpose is mainly cosmetic. This is an important skill, particularly in high school and college where a great deal of material is to be read within a limited amount of time. A realistic appraisal of one's own ability to perform this task is another aspect of the metacognitive skill.

Even though the section on metacognition has focused on the reading process, most of what is said is equally applicable to learning through listening. Identifying the main idea in a lecture and separating it from the redundant and being able to focus on the essence are important skills. Knowing one's own level of skill in performing these functions is a metacognitive skill.

Simple, informal means of assessing metacognitive skills and means of creating awareness about metacognitive skills in students are discussed in Chapters 3 and 4.

Cognitive Styles

The term *cognitive style* is defined as "consistent individual differences in the ways of organizing and processing information and experience . . . ; these styles represent consistencies in the manner or form of cognition as distinct from the content of cognition or the level of skill displayed in the cognitive performance" (Messic 1976, p. 5). Cognitive style is concerned with the process rather than the product, style rather than content. Being stable and enduring, cognitive styles are considered resistant to training. Even though there is some question as to whether all cognitive styles reported in the literature can satisfy this definition (Tiedemann 1989), certainly individuals differ in the way they process information. Studies show that field-dependent individuals are more influenced by textual context than field-independent children and that impulsive children are likely to make more reading errors than reflective children (Kagan et al. 1964). Another cognitive style described by Aaron and Whitefield (1990) and known as *dysfluency*, is characterized by extreme slowness in the processing of symbolic information such as the written text. Individuals who can be characterized as dysfluent have no reading disability as such, but are slow in reading. As a result, they do not perform well on timed tests. Because they are not aware of the nature of their own reading difficulty, they misinterpret their poor performance in terms of poor comprehension and questionable intellectual skill. Careful assessment of their reading performance and proper counseling can help these students become aware of their own cognitive styles.

Chapter 2

Varieties of Reading Disabilities and Their Nature

INTRODUCTION

In this chapter, three different kinds of reading disabilities are presented and the symptoms associated with each one of these are described. The three kinds of reading disabilities are: specific reading disability (SRD; also referred to as developmental dyslexia), nonspecific reading disability (NSRD), and low ability reading (LAR).

The fact that reading is a complex skill that is made up of several subskills leads to the possibility that suboptimal functioning of any one of these subprocesses can be a potential proximal cause of reading disability. Malfunctioning of different subprocesses may lead to different forms of reading disabilities. More importantly, such malfunctioning also leads to the expectation that corrective instruction that takes into account the origin of reading disability and targets instruction at the nature of the reading disability can be more effective than an undifferentiated remedial procedure that treats all forms of reading disabilities alike. Sometimes a distinction is drawn between *process factors* and *content factors*. Process factors refer to how data are processed. In contrast, content factors refer to the kinds of data that are processed (Pearson 1984). Operations such as decoding, inference making, and metacognition are process factors, whereas the vocabulary and schemata of the reader are content factors. Comprehensive assessment of the reading skill of an individual involves the evaluation of both process and content factors.

In this chapter, we will describe the different varieties of reading disabilities and their nature. We will follow the format presented in Chapter 1 and examine the three major stages of the reading process to see if these reading disabilities (SRD, NSRD, or LAR) can be traced to any of the stages.

VARIETIES OF READING DISABILITIES

The Encoding Stage

Eye Movements Visual factors may be potential contributors to reading disability. One such factor that has been studied extensively is faulty eye movements. It is known that poor readers make many more regressive eye movements during reading than do normal readers. Sometimes this is interpreted to mean that one source of reading difficulty is faulty eye movements, particularly regressive movements. It is now generally accepted, however, that regressive eye movements are not a source of reading disability that normally is encountered in the classroom. There are several reasons for arriving at such a conclusion. During the reading process, it is the brain that guides the eye and not the other way around. For this reason, regressive movements cannot be considered as causes of reading problems but are themselves the result of some cognitive difficulty experienced by readers. Furthermore, regressive eye movements are indicative of the fact that readers are monitoring their reading performance and that when they become aware of some difficulty in decoding or in comprehension, they take a "second look" at the word. This causes regressive eye movements. This explanation of regressive eye movements is further buttressed by several experimental studies that report that when nonverbal stimuli such as an array of lights is used, dyslexic readers do not show regressive movements. According to Just and Carpenter (1987), some early training programs misguidedly attempted to improve the comprehension of poor readers by training them to make short fixations and to reduce the number of regressive movements. Because these programs ignored the cognitive processes responsible for poor reading and focused on superficial phenomena associated with reading, they were unsuccessful.

It has been reported that the reading performance of some dyslexic readers improved significantly if they wore specially tinted prescription glasses while reading. Even though it is claimed that such glasses can "cure" dyslexia, in fact, what they appear to alleviate are symptoms of scotopic sensitivity. Scotopic sensitivity is a problem associated with photo receptors in the visual system which increase the sensitivity of the eye to light and can cause reddened or watery eyes, make the print appear blurry and fuzzy, and result in erratic eye movements. If glasses can improve reading performance, it is obvious that some optical processes associated with the physiology of vision contribute to this form of reading difficulty. As Richardson (1989) puts it, dyslexia is a language disorder whereas scotopic sensitivity is a vision disorder. Because reading disabilities are considered psychological phenomena associated with cognitive processes, reading defects that arise from visual-optical processes cannot be considered reading disabilities.

Finally, it has to be noted that reading disabilities are syndromes made up of many symptoms. These symptoms include faulty spelling and errors in the use of syntax, defects that are associated with the output processes and cannot, therefore, be accounted for by defective visual input processes.

The Iconic Store   As noted earlier, during the encoding operations, the iconic store has to be cleared of the initial input very rapidly, probably in less than 250 msecs, in order to make room for the subsequent input. A tardy icon, if such a thing exists, could therefore, lead to reading difficulties. Researchers have used two methods to see if reading disability can be caused by slow iconic processes.

The first method involves presenting the visual stimulus and following it with a mask at varying intervals to determine the shortest interstimulus interval in which the subject fails to report the first stimulus. A mask is usually a jumble of letters that virtually wipes the icon clean of the visual stimulus that precedes it. If the interstimulus interval is larger for poor readers than it is for normal readers, it can be concluded that the poor readers' icon is not cleared as quickly as that of normal readers. The second method is to present two different stimuli (such as a short horizontal line and a short vertical line) in rapid succession and gradually increase the interval between the presentation of the two stimuli until the subject reports that he or she sees two distinct stimuli rather than a single figure (in this instance, a cross). If normal readers require a shorter interstimulus interval to perceive the unified figure than do disabled readers, it may be concluded that poor readers and normal readers differ in the duration of iconic persistence.

Even though a few studies of iconic duration have reported differences between normal and poor readers, many studies that have employed these techniques have failed to find a significant difference between normal and poor readers. Other investigators who have discussed this issue have also concluded that there is insufficient evidence to show that a deficit at the iconic stage contributes to developmental dyslexia (see, for example, Ellis and Miles 1978; Vellutino 1979; Mitchell 1982). Apart from the fact that many studies have failed to detect any abnormality in the iconic processes of reading-disabled children, there are other reasons for excluding iconic processes as potential causes of reading disabilities. For instance, dyslexic readers have difficulty not only in reading sentences where continual clearance of successive words in the iconic memory is obligatory, but they also have difficulty in reading isolated words where rapid clearance of the icon is not required. Furthermore, in addition to being slow, as the icon store defect hypothesis would predict, disabled readers commit spelling and syntactic errors when they write. These symptoms associated with the output aspect of language processing cannot be explained by a hypothesis that is limited only to the input facet of reading. (For a brief review of some of the relevant experimental studies in this area, see Aaron 1989).

The Word Recognition Stage

It was noted in Chapter 1 that a word is recognized when the sensory input makes contact with its corresponding phonological *and* semantic representations stored in the lexicons. Word recognition, as it is used in this book, therefore, includes the recovery of the phonological representation of a word as well as its meaning. The phonological representation of a word may be in an articulatory form (i.e., its pronunciation) or in some abstract form of which we know little. Thus, phonological representations of words can play a role in both oral and silent reading.

The Role of Phonology in Reading   Whether the meaning of a word can be understood or not without recovering its phonological representation is a major question in reading research. It is possible that the meaning of isolated printed words can be accessed without the help of their phonology, much as the message in some road signs is understood. Such direct accessing of meaning depends on an associative learning process and requires repeated exposures to the written word. For this reason, comprehending the written word without making use of its phonology may not be possible when the reader encounters unfamiliar and uncommon words. Furthermore, in order to comprehend the meaning of a sentence, the string of words in the sentence is to be kept in the working memory until the meaning of the entire sentence is constructed. Many studies indicate that words are retained in working memory as phonological representations rather than as visual representations (c.f., Baddeley 1966a; Conrad 1964).

The phonology of a written word can be recovered either by assembling its pronunciation or by directly accessing its pronunciation from the word–pronunciation lexicon. Assembling the pronunciation of a word requires the use of spelling–sound rules located in the phonological rules lexicon, a process commonly referred to as decoding. The ability to decode the written word is a much needed skill in the early primary grades when children begin to learn to read. The ability to decode words serves as a tool that can help the child to read words he or she has not encountered before without resorting to outside help and thus enables the pupil to be a self-tutor. Children who are deficient in this skill rely on outside help for word recognition and when such help is not readily available, tend to make wild guesses. Because under such a condition reading becomes a strenuous and often uninteresting exercise, these children may give up reading altogether. Consequently, the extent of their sight vocabulary also tends to remain small which, in turn, limits their ability to access whole word pronunciation of the written word through the associative process. These children, therefore, grow up to be poor readers, and their decoding deficit can persist through college age and well into adulthood. Phonology, therefore, plays a vital role in reading. Even though decoding skill may appear to be relatively more important for beginning readers than for skilled readers, the ability to pronounce the written word cannot be relinquished at any age without greatly sacrificing the ability to read unfamiliar and uncommon words.

The ability to decode a word by utilizing spelling–pronunciation rules is a skill that is independent of general intelligence. As a matter of fact, the correlation coefficient between IQ and decoding skill as measured by a test of nonword reading turns out to be insignificant among college students (Aaron 1985). This agrees with the general observation that individuals with specific reading disability can have average or superior intelligence. For this reason, decoding ability is sometimes described as a modular skill.

A modular ability is characterized as being domain-specific, fast, informationally encapsulated, and not subject to the influence of higher level cognitive functions (Fodor 1983). Consequently, a reader with specific reading disability could be deficient in decoding skill but still have adequate comprehension. If the reading comprehension of these individuals appears to be subaverage, it could be because poor decoding operates as a factor that limits comprehension. The apparent comprehension deficit seen in these readers is, therefore, not a primary weakness but is secondary to poor decoding skill. If the comprehension ability of such individuals is assessed with the aid of a test of listening comprehension, which obviously does not require decoding, comprehension usually falls within normal range. This, indeed, has been reported for children (Riedlinger and Shewan 1984) and for college students (Aaron 1989a).

Phonological Processing and Reading Disability   One finding that has emerged unambiguously from studies during the past several years is that decoding skill, even though it alone is not a sufficient condition for successful reading performance, is nevertheless a necessity (for more details, see Shankweiler and Liberman 1989). Studies that have probed the decoding skill further suggest that the decoding deficit of poor readers could be traced to their poor phoneme awareness skill.

Phoneme awareness can be described as a knowledge of letter–sound correspondence that enables the reader to articulate the written word effortlessly and automatically. Phoneme awareness should be differentiated from two related skills: phoneme discrimination and phonetic skill. Phoneme awareness is an ability to analyze and isolate the different sound units in a word (e.g., *cat* = /k/ae/t/; *book* = /b/u/k/) whereas phoneme discrimination involves the ability to tell whether two phonemes such as /k/ and /r/ (in *cat* and *rat*) are the same or not. Phonetic skill refers to the ability to name the letters of the alphabet.

Recognizing that the word *cat* has three phonemes (/k/ae/t/) involves phoneme awareness; naming the three letters in the word *cat* (c,a,t) is phonetic skill. Of these three skills, phoneme awareness seems to be the most difficult to acquire and, when not mastered, is known to disrupt reading. This conclusion is supported by a number of studies that show that children who do poorly on phoneme awareness tasks also are severely reading disabled (Fox and Routh 1980; Stanovich, Cunningham, and Cramer 1984). Lundberg, Olofsson, and Wall (1980) tested a group of Swedish kindergarten children and found that the ability to segment words into phonemes was the single most powerful predictor of future reading achievement. Similar results were obtained for children who speak French (Alegria, Pignot, and Morais 1982) and for children who speak Italian (Cossu et al. 1988). More importantly, available evidence indicates that phoneme awareness skill can be taught, at least to children. It is reported that preschool children who received phoneme awareness training were less likely to fail in learning to read when they reached elementary grades than those who did not receive such training (Bradley and Bryant 1983; also see Lundberg, Frost, and Petersen 1988).

There is evidence to conclude that dyslexic adults also exhibit deficits in phonological awareness similar to the ones seen in dyslexic children (Byrne and Ledez 1983; Liberman et al. 1985). Katz and Tarver (1989) found that a group of dyslexic college students who had received a considerable amount of remediation and were succeeding in college were, nevertheless, poorer than their nondyslexic peers on two measures of phoneme awareness tasks. These investigators interpreted their results as suggesting that although the dyslexic subjects had improved their reading skills, (probably by having acquired a good sight vocabulary), there remained a fundamental deficit in their ability to process phonological information quickly and accurately. These and many other studies show that phonological processing skill, as assessed by measures such as phonological awareness tests and nonword reading tasks, is an important correlate of reading skill.

In addition to impeding the decoding process, a poorly developed phonological processing skill appears to have several secondary effects. For instance, poor phonological skill has been found to be associated with poor short-term memory (STM), difficulty in retrieving the name of a word quickly, poor spelling, and a suboptimal ability to repeat accurately orally presented nonwords and multisyllabic words. Although some of these symptoms have been considered at one time or another as causal agents of specific reading disability, there is reason to believe that poor phonological skill is the common denominator of all these symptoms. For instance, a limited STM, as measured by digit span tests, is often associated with reading disability (see Aaron 1989b for a discussion of this topic). This has been interpreted to mean that poor readers have limited STM capacity and that this is a cause of reading disability. This, however, does not appear to be the most accurate explanation of the link between reading disability and a limited STM. As noted in Chapter 1, many studies show that the number of items the STM can hold is determined by the speed with which information is processed and not by STM capacity. The poor performance of disabled readers in digit span tests may not be due to their limited memory capacity but may be due to the slow retrieval of phonological information. The factor responsible for the slow accessing of the lexicon by poor readers, however, does not appear to have a physiological or neurological basis because dyslexic children do not differ from normal readers in their speed of retrieving names of objects or pictures (Katz, Shankweiler, and Liberman 1981; Liberman et al. 1982; Perfetti, Finger, and Hogaboam 1978). Furthermore, the reading and spelling performance of subjects with SRD do not improve even if ample time is made available to them. Thus, the retrieval problem appears to be material-specific. For these reasons, it can be surmised that poor readers are slow in accessing verbal information because their phonological lexicon is either poorly organized or the entries in the lexicon are incomplete.

A similar explanation can be advanced to account for the poor performance of dyslexic children in tasks that require them to repeat orally-presented multisyllabic words and nonwords. Recognition of the spoken word involves two processes: identifying the phonemes of the input stimulus and relating them to the stored phonologic and semantic correlates of the word. Because nonwords do not have semantic components, they can be repeated only by identifying their phonemes and then by holding them temporarily in the STM. The phonological lexicon plays an important role in these operations. Repeating multisyllabic words may also depend a great deal upon these phonological mechanisms. To be sure, the listening comprehension of an individual with poor phonological skill can be affected when the spoken sentence is unusually long or if it contains structural ambiguities, an excess of embedded clauses, and unfamiliar multisyllabic words. Sentences with such complex structures are usually employed by psychologists for testing purposes and do not occur in ordinary conversation; even formal academic lectures, as compared to the written language, generally contain limited vocabulary and idea units (Chafe and Danielewicz 1987). For these reasons, a phonological processing defect can be more obvious in reading than in listening. As noted earlier, a decoding problem can remain as an isolated deficit without affecting general intelligence and comprehension of the day-to-day spoken language.

Reading disability that is caused by poor phonological skill and is limited to the written language and which does not encompass the comprehension of ordinarily spoken language is referred to in this book as specific reading disability (SRD). Another term that is used to describe this condition is developmental dyslexia. The nature of SRD is described later in this chapter.

The Role of Word-Knowledge in Reading   The basic unit of meaning and grammar is a *morpheme*. Even though morphemes are similar to words, the two terms are not synonyms. For instance, the word *playing* has two morphemes, the root morpheme *play* and the suffix *ing*, which is a bound morpheme. Furthermore, linguists identify two kinds of suffixes, inflected and derivative. An inflected morpheme signals information about number, tense, etc., (e.g., *s* and *ed* in *plays* and *played*) and the derivative morpheme signals the grammatical status of the morpheme (e.g., *er* in *player* indicates that it is a noun). Root morphemes themselves can be placed in two broad categories: an open class of words and a closed class of words. Content words represented by nouns, verbs, and adjectives belong to the open class, whereas function words such as conjunctions and prepositions that perform grammatical functions are placed in the closed class. It is believed that root morphemes are stored in the semantic lexicon, whereas function words and suffixes, lacking meaning, are mediated by the phonological lexicon or the word-pronunciation lexicon. Children and adults with SRD make an unusually large number of errors when they read and write function words and suffixes as compared to content words.

There is wide variation in the number of root morphemes or the size of the vocabulary individuals have. An average college student is estimated to have a vocabulary that ranges from 40,000 to 50,000 words, though there are wide differences among studies in this regard (Just and Carpenter 1987). Some studies estimate the figure to be as high as 150,000. Seashore and Eckerson (1940) reported that the vocabulary size of the top 10% of college students was about twice the size of those at the bottom 10%. Furthermore, a distinction has to be made between receptive vocabulary and expressive vocabulary, the former being much larger than the latter. This means individuals can understand many more words than they actually use when they speak and write.

The size of an individual's vocabulary is a powerful determinant of his or her reading skill (Anderson and Freebody 1981). According to Fry (1986), in the English language, there is a correlation of about .70 between vocabulary test score and reading comprehension score. Scores obtained in vocabulary tests also correlate highly with the overall IQ scores obtained from intelligence tests. It is not surprising, therefore, that a reader's vocabulary is one of the best predictors of text comprehension. Consequently, the source of this individual difference in

vocabulary has attracted the attention of researchers. Two major explanations have been advanced to account for individual differences in
vocabulary: (1) general intelligence, broadly defined as the ability to
learn, and (2) reading experience. It has to be noted that these two explanations are not mutually exclusive. The view that vocabulary and
comprehension are determined by general intelligence is sometimes
referred to as the "aptitude hypothesis" (see Maria 1990 for a discussion of this issue). The implication of this hypothesis is that the level of
vocabulary depends on the cognitive ability of an individual and that
acquisition of vocabulary can be promoted only by improving the individual's cognitive ability and not by direct teaching of vocabulary. The
second explanation attributes individual differences in vocabulary to
differences in reading experience. This implies that vocabulary size
can be increased beyond a minimal level only through reading and not
through listening, because spoken language is not a source of rich vocabulary. Several observations support this proposition. As children
move through grades 1 through 12, the size of their vocabulary increases more or less at a constant rate. According to one study (Smith
1941), children, on average, acquire the meanings of about 2,700 words
a year.

Because vocabulary in the spoken language seldom exceeds that
of the 7th grade level, reading is the most likely means of acquiring
many new words. According to Nagy and Anderson (1984), beginning
in about 3rd grade, the major determinant of vocabulary growth is the
amount of free reading a student does. Their study reveals a "stagger-
ing" difference in the amount of "outside" reading done by children.
According to their estimate, the least motivated children in middle
grades might read 100,000 words a year while the average children at
this level might read 1,000,000 words. Avid readers at the middle
grades might be exposed to as many as 10,000,000 words. Because new
vocabulary is best acquired in meaningful context and because reading
provides repeated exposure to the same words, beyond a certain age
vocabulary acquisition is facilitated primarily through reading. Individual differences in reading experience, therefore, can explain the individual differences in vocabulary size.

An important consequence of this relationship between reading
experience and vocabulary acquisition is that those who read less have
poor vocabularies and those who have poor vocabularies remain un-
skilled readers, forever falling farther and farther behind their skilled
peers. This reciprocal relationship between reading and vocabulary is
termed the "Matthew effect," an idea taken from the Gospel according
to St. Matthew:

> For unto every one that hath shall be given, and he shall have abundance;
> but from him that hath not, shall be taken away even that which he hath
> (Matt. 29:25).

(See Stanovich 1986 for a discussion of this topic.) The reality of the "Matthew effect" has been documented by several investigators (Aaron and Simurdak, in press; Van den Bos 1989). In the Aaron study, we examined the reading performance of 97 reading disabled children from grades 3 and 4 and their IQ was also determined. Three years later, we administered the same tests. We found that 65% of the children declined in their verbal IQ between the two testings with nearly 35% losing as many as 10 points. During the first testing, their word recognition skill, as determined by the Wide Range Achievement Test, was two years below grade level; three years later, it was 3.5 grades behind. Needless to say, a large number of high school and college students who are deficient in reading skills are victims of the "Matthew effect."

Thus, word knowledge is a fundamental ingredient of reading comprehension. The student with a limited vocabulary cannot comprehend much. Improving comprehension, therefore, requires vocabulary building, and this can be accomplished only through reading.

Identifying the source of the reading problem, whether it is due to low motivation coupled with limited reading experience or a genuine reading disability or a product of the two, is an important function of the diagnostic process. Careful analysis of the learning history of a poor reader in primary and early high school years is helpful in reaching such differential diagnostic decisions.

Semantic Processing and Reading Disability   Semantic processing of a word is made possible when the written word makes contact with its corresponding entry in the semantic lexicon. This enables a reader to realize all aspects of meaning associated with the word. As noted in Chapter 1, all the meanings a word represents may be made available during eye fixation, and then the one meaning that is appropriate for the context is selected. This is a reasonable description of the semantic processing of content words. Function words do not have entries in the semantic lexicon and, therefore, may be accessed from a different lexicon, probably the phonological or word–pronunciation lexicon. This conclusion is based on the observation that individuals with specific reading disability, in addition to having word decoding difficulty, also tend to omit or substitute function words when they read and write (Aaron and Phillips 1986; Blank 1985). This statement is also true of suffixes.

It is obvious that if semantic entries corresponding to the written words are not available in the semantic lexicon, comprehension of these words will be difficult. In other words, readers with limited vocabularies are also poor comprehenders. Even though the meaning of some unfamiliar words can be inferred from context, a majority of textbooks, particularly college textbooks, are not expressly written to facilitate comprehension from context. Consequently, the reader with a limited vocabulary runs into comprehension problems. Poor readers also may not know all the possible meanings a word represents, if the word happens to have more than one meaning. Perfetti (1985) cites studies that suggest that the vocabulary of high-ability readers is characterized by both breadth and depth. That is, good readers know not only more words, but they also know more about words.

Even if a reader's semantic lexicon contains all the appropriate entries, there is the possibility that a reader may not be able to recover the appropriate meaning of the word or that he or she may not be able to make a quick selection of the appropriate meaning. Perfetti (1985) speculates that in high-ability readers, the inappropriate meanings of the word are more quickly deactivated than in low-ability readers. This makes low-ability readers also slow readers.

Orthography and Reading Disability   In Chapter 1 orthography was defined as the written spelling pattern of words in alphabetic languages as it relates to meaning and pronunciation of these words. The orthographies of some languages have a consistent, almost one-to-one correspondence with their spoken linguistic units. Because letters in the words written in these orthographies contain almost all the information needed to pronounce the words correctly, these orthographies are described as shallow or transparent. Some orthographies, however, have a much less straight-forward relationship with phonology. Pronunciation of words written in these orthographic systems cannot be readily accomplished by sounding out the constituent letters of these words but instead requires the use of complex spelling-to-sound rules and word meaning. These orthographies are, therefore, described as "opaque" or "deep." The English orthography is considered to be "deep," whereas Italian and Spanish are considered as relatively "shallow." Some educators believe that the opaque nature of English orthography is a major source of reading difficulties experienced by beginning readers. Spelling reforms and attempts to augment English orthography, such as the Initial Teaching Alphabet, therefore, represent efforts to make learning to read easy.

Investigations of school children who speak Italian, Spanish, and Greek, however, show that some children experience difficulties in learning to read fluently in these languages. Some of the errors committed by these children when they read aloud indicate that the errors are associated with the decoding process. Errors include difficulties in pronouncing unfamiliar words, parsing of multisyllabic words, and omission of word suffixes—all symptoms associated with developmental dyslexia. (See Aaron and Joshi 1989 for a number of these studies.) Thus, the nature of English orthography cannot be considered to be the sole source of reading problems in children even though it may exacerbate the decoding deficiencies that are already present in these children.

Because orthographic memory is thought to be helpful in spelling words correctly, defective spelling is sometimes attributed to poor orthographic skill. This explanation is advanced especially to account for unexpected spelling difficulty experienced by the so-called "good readers but poor spellers" (Frith 1980). It appears, however, that these "good readers" do have subtle reading difficulties. Careful testing of three college students who claimed to be "good readers but poor spellers" revealed that these subjects could not pronounce nonwords very well and were also slow readers (Joshi and Aaron 1990). These observations suggest that orthographic memory is closely linked to phonological skill and may not be an independent component of reading. If orthography plays a role in reading disability, its contribution may be a minor one. In contrast, spelling ability appears to be closely related to phonological skills. This view receives support from the observations that poor decoders invariably are poor spellers and that spelling and nonword reading are highly correlated.

The Sentence Comprehension Stage

It should come as no surprise if students with limited vocabulary have difficulty in comprehending sentences and texts. Words and their meanings, after all, are the building blocks of propositions and idea units. But are there individuals who, in spite of having adequate decoding skill and vocabulary, experience difficulty in comprehending sentences and texts? Theoretically, such a condition is possible because a reader, in spite of knowing word meanings, can still fail to make the necessary inferences or fail to interpret a passage correctly because he or she does not have the appropriate schemata. This simply means that without adequate background knowledge of the subject matter, correct interpretation of the sentence and text is not possible. Evidence for the existence of individuals who have adequate decoding skills and vocabulary but still have comprehension deficits, however, is sparse. This may be because schemata and the ability to make inferences may themselves be products of reading experience rather than skills acquired in isolation. As noted earlier, reading experience helps vocabulary acquisition that, in turn, promotes skills required for sentence and text comprehension.

Are there poor readers who are deficient in one component and not the other; are there subjects who can decode rather well but still fail to comprehend the word or the sentence and, conversely, are there subjects who can not decode well but can still comprehend? A few subjects, indeed, display these patterns of reading disability. An extreme example of the first condition is represented by children described as having hyperlexia. In the regular classroom, children who display a mild version of this difficulty are referred to as "word callers." We have also seen cases of college students who can read aloud fluently but who demonstrate a level of comprehension far below that expected from their oral reading. In this book these subjects are described as having nonspecific reading disability (NSRD). Conversely, individuals who are deficient in decoding skill but have much better comprehension skill are described as having specific reading disability (SRD). Individuals who are deficient in both decoding and comprehension skills are considered as having low ability reading skill (LAR). A majority of children labelled as learning disabled display a combination of poor decoding and poor comprehension skill and, therefore, are low ability readers. A large number of students in post secondary institutions who have reading problems are also low ability readers.

THE NATURE OF READING DISABILITIES

In this book the term *reading disabilities* is reserved for reading problems that are attributable to some factor that is intrinsic to the reader. Examples of intrinsic factors include deficient phonological processing skill, comprehension deficit, and peculiar cognitive styles. Reading deficits that are caused by extrinsic factors such as poor motivation, limited reading experience, and an impoverished environment are referred to as *reading difficulties*. Recognizing the nature of the reading deficit, whether it is a form of reading disability or reading difficulty caused by environmental factors, has implications for corrective instruction and management of the reading problem.

When the individual's difficulty is limited to written language and does not involve ordinary spoken language, the individual is considered to have *specific reading disability;* when the deficit extends to include language comprehension, regardless of the modality of input, and when decoding remains relatively unaffected, the condition is referred to as *nonspecific reading disability.* The term *low ability reading* is applied to that group of subjects who have global cognitive deficits, poor reading performance being one of its manifestations. This condition is similar to the one referred to as "general reading backwardness" by Yule and Rutter (1976), in which the intelligence and the reading achievement of the subject are in line with each other.

Tests, tasks, and related procedures that are used in the differential diagnosis of these forms of reading disabilities are presented in Chapter 3.

Specific Reading Disability (SRD)

When the reading deficit is limited to the written form of language and does not extend to include the production and comprehension of ordinary spoken language, it is referred to as *specific reading disability*. Individuals with SRD also tend to have average or higher IQ scores and their listening comprehension is in line with their IQ rather than with their reading comprehension. The term *dyslexia* is also often used to refer to this condition. In this book the term *specific reading disability* is frequently used because it is more descriptive of the reading disorder than the term *dyslexia*. In addition, in the minds of many, the term *dyslexia* has come to have neurological as well as other unsubstantiated connotations.

From the beginning of the present century, ever since the term *dyslexia* was introduced into the educational literature, its status, and even its very existence, has been questioned. The reason for this skepticism is not that anyone would deny that some apparently bright children find it difficult to learn to read, but that the term is associated with brain dysfunction and neurological impairment. These concepts came to be linked with dyslexia because of its early association with medicine, particularly with neurology. During the latter part of the 19th century, reports of isolated instances of sudden but circumscribed loss of reading ability as a result of neurological impairment in literate adults began to appear in medical journals. The most complete accounts of such loss of reading ability, along with post-mortem findings, were provided in 1891 and 1892 by Déjeriné, a French neurologist. Déjeriné concluded that the reading disability was caused by damage to the corpus callosum and visual cortex of the dominant cerebral hemisphere. In 1895, James Hinshelwood, an ophthalmologist from Glasgow, published a similar report in the English language and called the loss of reading ability *word blindness*. A year later, Pringle Morgan, another British physician, happened to examine an intelligent healthy boy who was referred to him by his teacher who suspected that some visual problem hindered the boy from learning to read. Morgan, who was familiar with Hinshelwood's paper, was quick to observe the similarities between the traumatic reading disability seen in adult patients and the developmental disability seen in the boy. Attempting to explain the disorder in neurological terms, with which he was familiar, Morgan called this condition *congenital word blindness* and attributed the problem to faulty development of the angular gyrus. A few years later, Hinshelwood published a monograph describing several children with reading disability and frequently referred to it as *congenital dyslexia*, a term he had borrowed from neurological literature. In the United States, during the mid-twenties, extensive observations from a neurological perspective were made on reading disabilities in children by Samuel Orton, also a physician. Even though Orton used the term *congenital word blindness* in his early writings, later on he coined his own term, *strephosymbolia,* to emphasize what he thought to be an important symptom, namely a deficit in the sequential processing of written language. Contrary to general belief, he did not consider reversals in reading and writing to be the most salient feature of developmental reading disability. Orton did not think that the reading disorder was caused by faulty development of the angular gyrus, as Hinshelwood had proposed. Seeking a more plausible neurological explanation, Orton proposed that the reading problem was caused by a failure of one of the cerebral hemispheres to develop dominance over the other.

In view of the fact that some of the pioneer investigators of reading disability have been physicians, who naturally tended to view the disability from a medical perspective, it is easy to see why neurological explanations have been advanced to explain the disorder. These explanations, however, have failed to appeal to the sentiments of educators in general. There are several reasons for this. First, the concept of brain dysfunction is viewed as a circular and empty term because all cognitive functions are mediated by the brain and learning failure of any kind can be attributed to brain dysfunction. Second, investigative studies that have been undertaken to examine the validity of the neurological basis of developmental dyslexia have produced mixed results. Finally, a neurologically based etiology of dyslexia leaves the educator in a state of helplessness because traditional instructional procedures can be of little help in "fixing" the brain.

No one will question the fact that there are some individuals who experience a great deal of difficulty in learning to read; nor would many challenge the veracity of the observation that among those who experience difficulties in learning to read, there are some individuals who have normal or even superior intelligence. The term *dyslexia* refers to this latter group of individuals and so does the term *specific reading disability;* the only difference between these two terms is that the latter does not carry any additional neurological baggage. We believe that, expunged of its neurological encumbrances, the concept of dyslexia will be acceptable to most educators.

The incidence of SRD among school children may not exceed 2% (see figure 2.1). The occurrence of SRD is even less frequent among college students. Studies that claim that nearly 10% of the school children have dyslexia usually fail to apply strict psychometric criteria in subject selection and, therefore, include a large number of borderline cases who are actually low ability readers. Inclusion of these "garden variety" poor readers in the dyslexia category is responsible for the frequently reported inflated figures.

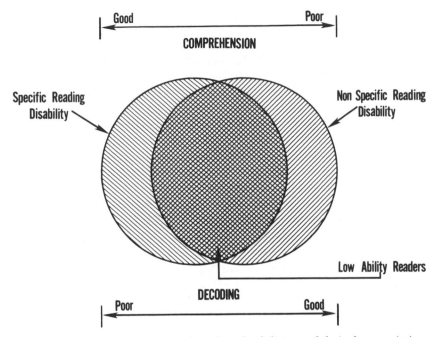

Figure 2.1. The three varieties of reading disabilities and their characteristics.

Symptoms of Specific Reading Disability The most fundamental deficit that characterizes SRD is a phonological processing deficit. The phonological deficit manifests itself in the form of more than one symptom. These symptoms include: slow reading, erratic oral reading, spelling errors, incorrect use of suffixes and function words in reading and writing, and below average comprehension on timed reading tests. As will be seen later, all these symptoms can be accounted for by poor phonological skills.

Research shows that a deficit in any particular process of reading results in greater reliance on other knowledge sources. In agreement with this finding, individuals with poor decoding skills, in addition to presenting the above symptoms, tend to compensate for poor phonological skills by relying on other strategies for reading. One such compensatory strategy is to rely excessively on context for recognizing written words. Any viable explanation of SRD should, therefore, be able to account for the constellation of these symptoms, including the compensatory strategies, not simply one or the other. Because individuals with SRD differ in the degree of their phonological deficit, past reading experience, and the amount of remedial instruction they might have received, a certain amount of variation in the extent of symptoms can be expected among disabled readers. In the following section the symptoms that characterize SRD are described.

Slow Reading Speed: A number of studies show that the speed with which words are recognized is a major factor that contributes to individual differences in reading skill. Even though written words can be understood without resorting to phonological recoding, poor readers are held back when they encounter unfamiliar words as well as function words. Indeed, a large number of words are unfamiliar to students with reading disabilities. Individuals with SRD tend to remain slow readers relative to others of their age, in spite of a number of years of schooling. This was demonstrated in a study of college students in which information regarding reading speed and comprehension was collected by administering the Stanford Diagnostic Reading Test (Aaron and Phillips 1986). It was found that the mean reading speed of 18 of the 20 subjects was considerably lower than their comprehension scores. The reading speed of poor readers with NSRD as well as subjects who can be described as having an impulsive cognitive style are usually within the normal range.

Errors in Oral Reading: Poor decoding skill leads to an overdependency on sight-word reading strategy. Because poor decoders tend to identify words on the basis of minimal cues, usually the first few letters of the word, they tend to misread a large number of words and commit reading errors. Oral reading errors committed by subjects with SRD involve the misreading of content words and the omission and substitution of function words. Normal readers also tend to commit reading errors that involve function words, but the magnitude of errors committed by SRD subjects exceeds normal limits. When such errors are committed, the substituted function word invariably belongs to the same grammatical category as the target word. For example, the article *a* may be substituted for *the*, the verb *is* for *was*, and the preposition *on* for *above*. Because such errors do not alter the meaning of the sentence substantially, it may be concluded that despite oral reading errors, subjects with SRD are monitoring their comprehension. Furthermore, because the target word and the substituted word do not visually resemble each other, defective visual perception cannot be used as an explanation of the misreading; nor can lack of familiarity with the word be used to account for the reading error because function words occur more frequently in text than do content words. In addition to these errors, omission and substitution of suffixes also are seen frequently in the oral reading of students with SRD. Even though these misreadings give the superficial impression of errors of grammar, they may really be a manifestation of the underlying phonological problem. The fact that function words and suffixes are semantically empty and, therefore, have to be kept in the working memory in the phonological form may be used as an explanation of the misreading of such common words.

The misreading of content words by readers with SRD generally results in contextually appropriate substitutions. Furthermore, these errors are as prevalent when these subjects read a list of isolated words as when they read sentences or passages (Aaron 1987). The fact that subjects with SRD commit a significant number of errors when they read isolated words suggests that their problem can be traced to the word recognition level. Students with SRD often, but not always, make an equal number of errors when they read "regular" words and "exception" words. Because good decoding skill is expected to provide an advantage in the oral reading of "regular" words over "exception" words, an absence of differences in these subjects' reading of both lists of words indicates that they use the same strategy for reading both lists. This strategy, probably, is whole-word reading and retrieving the pronunciation of the word as a single unit.

Poor Spelling: Many studies of developmental dyslexia suggest that poor spelling is a concomitant of poor reading. This should come as no surprise, since it appears that spelling-to-sound relational rules are used both in reading and spelling and that readers with SRD are deficient in grapheme-phoneme conversion skills. Without exception, all the college students with SRD studied by the authors are poor spellers. Even though some adults with SRD manage to acquire adequate reading skill—probably by using a whole-word reading strategy and by building up a substantial sight vocabulary—they fail to make similar progress in spelling. The reason for this difference between spelling and reading may be due to the fact that reading is primarily a recognition task, whereas spelling is a recall task. As noted earlier, these so-called "good readers but poor spellers," nevertheless, have residual reading deficits.

There have been attempts to classify spelling errors into subcategories such as "phonologically acceptable" and "phonologically unacceptable." For example, spelling *girl* as "gal" and *blue* as "bloo" would be considered phonologically acceptable whereas spelling *girl* as "gril" and *stop* as "spot" would be considered as phonologically unacceptable. It appears, however, that instead of representing two distinct subtypes of spelling and reading disabilities, these errors represent two substages of spelling acquisition. Very young and immature readers tend to commit numerous phonologically unacceptable spelling errors, whereas older individuals who have mastered many of the spelling rules, but not all of them, tend to make phonologically acceptable errors. A number of investigators have observed that spelling-to-pronunciation rules are progressively acquired by children as they

grow older. The progressive mastery of the spelling rules and their relationship to spelling errors was demonstrated in a study by Phillips,
Taylor, and Aaron (1985). In this study a spelling test consisting of 38
words was administered to 41 normal readers and 26 poor readers from
grades 2 through 6. Analysis of the reading errors revealed that normal
readers committed significantly fewer spelling errors than poor
readers. More importantly, the spelling of poor readers from grades 2
and 3 contained predominantly phonologically unacceptable errors,
whereas the spelling errors committed by poor readers from grades 5
and 6 were mostly phonologically acceptable. This developmental interpretation of spelling errors also suggests that phonologically unacceptable spelling errors would seldom be seen in the writings of mature students. This prediction appears to be correct; we have not come
across any college student with reading disability who produces many
phonologically unacceptable spelling errors. In summary, spelling errors indicate an accompanying poor phonological skill. An excessive
number of spelling errors in a student's writing should alert the instructor to the possibility of an associated reading deficit.

Errors of Syntax in Written Language: The written work of readers
with SRD usually contains errors in the proper use of suffixes even
though among college and senior high school students there are considerable differences in the quantity of such errors. Confusion of
"homophonic words" (e.g., were—where; there—their; won—one)
can also be seen in the written work of these students. It should be
noted that some of these words are not homophones in a strict sense
and that there are subtle differences in the pronunciation of these
homophonic pairs. Consequently, confusing the spellings of these
homophonic pairs may indicate the presence of subtle phonological
deficits. A sample of one dyslexic college student's spontaneous writing that contains errors of suffix and spelling is shown in figure 2.2.
Even though these errors could be considered errors of grammar, they
could, as noted earlier, also be considered products of an underlying
phonological deficit. This conclusion is partly supported by a study in
which the knowledge and use of grammar of five college students with
dyslexia were assessed. Even though their written work contained
spelling and suffix errors, their knowledge of grammar was found to
be normal (Aaron, Olsen, and Baker 1985).

Excessive Reliance on Context for Word Recognition: One of the college
freshmen we had the opportunity to assess read the sentence "Baseball is a game played by many in America" as "Basketball is a game
played by men in America." He then went on to "read" the remaining
sentences in the passage entirely by fabricating basketball related
phrases as he went along. The errors he made when he read the open-

The Bloomberg Conference

I went to a one leture where a special ed teacher was talking. She was a teacher of learnig disablity She gave a spech on how she works in the classroom. She tolds) us about how she has a goup session with her children.

She ask her children their opion on some of the subject in the classroom. But she said that their opinion is taken in consideration. Also she does not ask question about everything— some things she decide your hirself.

After she talk for a while she show us a film. The film show us how she work with the children on their opinion.

One of the children was ready to leave them and go to a normal classroom. She ask the girl that is ready to leave what she thought about leaving. The girl said she was ready to go the normal clasroom. The teacher ask the other children

After the film was over the teacher begin speaking aguin to us. She said that the group clasroom may not work with everyone.

Figure 2.2.   Spontaneous writing of a college student with reading disability

ing sentence suggest that he did not decode the word *baseball* correctly but probably recognized correctly words such as *game* and *play* and guessed from context that the word was *basketball*. This case serves as an example of how subjects with SRD tend to rely on their stored knowledge and depend on contextual cues to recognize words. As noted in Chapter 1, reading is an interactive process wherein both *top-down* and *bottom-up* processes operate simultaneously. Readers with SRD, being weak in decoding, depend excessively on context; those with NSRD, being deficient in higher level cognitive processes, depend much on print and use *bottom-up* processes excessively. This results in the former making contextually acceptable errors. The latter frequently commit contextually inappropriate errors.

There is some controversy about the extent to which good and poor readers make use of context. Some reading experts have claimed that good readers make use of context while poor readers are unable to make optimum use of context. But a substantial body of research indicates this is not true. One of the reasons for this controversy is a misunderstanding about the stage of reading in which context is thought to play a role.

Context probably is important for the proper understanding of sentences. For instance, consider the following pair of sentences:

(1) Jane's parents were very poor. They always fed her dog biscuits.
(2) Mary's parents were very rich. They always fed her dog biscuits.

In these sentences, whether the girl or the dog was fed dog biscuits depends on the context in which the phrase occurs.

While context may facilitate sentence comprehension, its role appears to be minimal in word recognition. Mitchell (1982), after reviewing the relevant literature, concludes that word recognition is not guided or helped by contextual information, the main reason being that word recognition is simply too fast an operation to rely on context. Several studies also show that poor readers rely on context for word recognition more than do normal readers (e.g., Juel 1980; Allington and Strange 1977; Allington and Fleming 1978).

Before closing this section on specific reading disability, we have to mention one symptom that is often mistakenly thought of as an identifying feature of SRD or dyslexia. Many individuals who are concerned with children's education, including some elementary school teachers, associate dyslexia exclusively with letter and word reversals in writing. We noted at the beginning of this chapter that Orton was one of the earliest investigators to draw attention to the disabled readers' tendency to reverse letters and words. Orton, however, noted that a tendency to produce reversals in writing was by no means a reliable and consistant symptom of specific reading disability. Systematic investigations undertaken since that time have indicated that Orton essentially was correct in noting the variability of reversal errors in poor readers. It has also to be added that reversals in the writing and reading are seldom seen among adult poor readers, suggesting that a maturational phenomenon might be responsible for the reversal errors seen in children. One possible explanation is that many children, having not mastered the print-to-phonology conversion skills, tend to rely on visuo-spatial information and to treat letters and words as though they are pictures. Visuo-spatial information quickly decays from memory, whereas verbal and semantic information has a much longer life. This can easily be demonstrated. Without looking at any of the real coins try to pick out the "counterfeit" shown in figure 2.3 by detecting which head is pointed in the wrong way. The chances are good that you failed this simple test because information about the right-left orientation is not retained in the LTM as part of our visual memory about coins. In other words, we can recognize any of these four coins regardless of its left-right orientation. Children who tend to process written words as visual information rather than as phonological information also may disregard the orientation of letters and words and, therefore, commit reversal errors. If this is true, these children may not reverse letters and words consistently, but may do so on a random basis. This, indeed is borne out by observations.

Below-Average Reading Comprehension in Timed Reading Tests: We wish to stress the point that the reading comprehension of college students with SRD tends to be substantially below average only on timed reading tests and tasks; when comprehension is assessed by untimed reading tests such as the Woodcock Reading Mastery Tests, comprehension tends to be normal or close to normal. In fact, the difference in performance between timed and untimed tests can be used to differentiate SRD from NSRD and LAR, since students with NSRD and LAR perform poorly on tests of reading comprehension whether they are timed or not. In the Learning Skills Center at Indiana State University

Figure 2.3.   Which one of these is a reversed drawing of a coin?

we often use the difference in the performance of under-achieving college students on timed and untimed tests as one of the means of identifying cases of SRD. In an unpublished dissertation Hill (1984) reports that college students without LD performed better than college students identified as having LD on the comprehension part of the Nelson–Denny reading test. When the test was administered as an untimed test, however, there was no difference between the two groups in reading comprehension.

The fact that the reading comprehension of students with SRD tends to be close to normal on untimed tests indicates that the poor reading comprehension seen in these subjects under certain conditions is more apparent than real. It is highly probable that in these subjects, the phonological processing factor becomes a bottle-neck during reading and operates as a limiting factor. In skilled readers, decoding has become an automatized task thus releasing attention to be directed at comprehension. In the case of subjects with SRD, decoding remains an attention-demanding operation, preventing them from directing attention entirely to comprehension. This may be why subjects with SRD tend to do much better in tests of listening comprehension (which do not require the grapheme–phoneme transformation) than in tests of reading comprehension. Thus, poor reading comprehension is not a primary deficit but is secondary to the phonological processing deficit. Studies of dyslexic children that have failed to find comprehension deficits in dyslexic children (Frith and Snowling 1983; Mann 1986) lend support to this view. In two studies of college students similar results were obtained. In the first study (Aaron, Olsen, and Baker 1985) the syntactic and semantic competencies of the oral language of five college students who presented symptoms of SRD were assessed with several tests. It was found that, but for phonological deficits, the linguistic competence of these subjects was as good as that of a control group. In the second study (Aaron 1989c, table 2.1), the listening comprehension and reading comprehension of six adult dyslexics were tested. Listening comprehension of these subjects was found to be at college level. Their reading comprehension was assessed under timed and untimed conditions by administering the Stanford Diagnostic Reading Test (timed test) and the Woodcock Reading Mastery Tests (untimed test). On the timed test, the reading comprehension of all the six subjects was below the 12th grade level; on the untimed test, five subjects performed at college level. The one subject who failed to perform at college level, nevertheless, obtained higher scores on the untimed test than on the timed test.

Taken together, these studies show that the reading comprehension deficit seen in students with SRD is a secondary symptom that is a by-product of the primary phonological deficit.

Table 2.1. The Performance of Six Adult Dyslexics in Different Tests

	Subject					
	1	2	3	4	5	6
CA	20.7	22.0	25.6	31.8	41.3	49.2
Educational level	3rd yr.	3rd yr.	1st yr.	3rd yr.	B.S.	Ph.D.
Major	Engng	Educn.	. . .	Nursg.	Art	Engng
IQ (WAIS-R, full-scale)	114.0	104.0	93.0	98.0	116.0	110.0
Total Rdg. achievement	Grad.	Grad.	Grad.	8.7	11.3	Grad.
Rdg. comprehen'n (Woodcock)	Grad.	Grad.	Grad.	9.9	Grad.	Grad.
Rdg. comprehen'n (Stanford)	10.3	11.0	8.1	9.0	10.0	10.3
No. of words wrong (List 1)*	0.0	0.0	0.0	1.0	3.0	1.0
No. of words wrong (List 2)**	0.0	2.0	5.0	5.0	2.0	3.0
No. of nonwords wrong	6.0	12.0	15.0	26.0	11.0	7.0
Word attack (Woodcock)	8.0	7.9	3.8	4.4	4.1	Grad.
Spelling errors (list 1)*	0.0	1.0	8.0	2.0	8.0	2.0
Spelling errors (list 2)**	2.0	11.0	20.0	14.0	11.0	4.0
No. of function words wrong (20)	0.0	0.0	2.0	2.0	0.0	0.0
No. of content words wrong (20)	0.0	0.0	0.0	1.0	2.0	0.0
No. of errors in reading standard passages	2.0	4.0	10.0	11.0	3.0	2.0
No. of errors in reading context-free passages	2.0	20.0	25.0	21.0	4.0	3.0

*Number of words in list 1 is 36.
**Number of words in list 2 is 43.

Nonspecific Reading Disability (NSRD)

The most important feature of nonspecific reading disability is poor comprehension with relatively intact decoding skills. As noted in Chapter 1, individuals with hyperlexia present an extreme form of this condition. It should, however, be noted that hyperlexic individuals present additional symptoms such as autistic tendencies and social aloofness; they also have a unique early childhood history of having started "reading" in a compulsive, ritualistic manner at a very early age. The existence of children who can pronounce words and read sentences aloud rather well but fail to comprehend what they read has been well documented in reading research. Harris and Sipay (1980) note that there are some children who can read rather fluently but do not pay attention to the meaning of the sentence and make no effort to remember what they were reading. They call such mechanical, thoughtless reading "word calling." The number of children who can be considered to have NSRD is much smaller than those with SRD. This is more true of college students than children in elementary school. The existence of the NSRD condition is not totally unexpected because decoding is a component that is independent of comprehension and, therefore, can be expected to show a developmental trend that is different from comprehension.

Individuals with NSRD appear to be able to pronounce written words by both assembling the pronunciation and addressing the whole word pronunciation lexicon. A study of two subjects who could read aloud far better than they could understand (Aaron, Frantz, and Manges [1990] described in Chapter 1) showed that one of the subjects, the 19-year-old girl, read familiar words fluently but did very poorly in reading nonwords. This performance, in addition to her having read "regular" and "exception" words equally well, led to the conclusion that she was not able to use spelling–sound rules to pronounce a word, but pronounced by associating the whole word with its pronunciation. This process, however, imposed severe limitations because she could not read any word with which she was not familiar. The second subject, the 11-year-old hyperlexic girl, however, could read nonwords quite well but showed better performance in reading "regular" words than "exception" words. It appears that she could use spelling–sound rules for pronouncing words.

The most outstanding symptom seen in students with NSRD is their poor reading and listening comprehension that is in striking contrast to their oral reading skill. These subjects do not commit errors while spelling words with which they are familiar. The "word class effect," namely a difference seen between the reading of function words, suffixes on the one hand and content words on the other, frequently seen in subjects with SRD, is also not seen among these subjects.

Low Ability Readers

By far the largest group of poor readers seen in high schools belong to this category. This statement is also true of post-secondary institutions that are not very selective and have an open admission policy. As noted earlier, this group of students also constitutes the largest proportion of those labelled as learning disabled in elementary schools and is marked by deficits not only in reading but in all aspects of learning.

In contrast to students with SRD and NSRD, low ability readers are deficient in both decoding *and* comprehension; their listening comprehension and reading comprehension are below their age and grade level. They tend to be slow readers and when comprehension is required, their reading rate becomes even slower. They are poor in decoding skill, and because of their limited vocabulary and background knowledge they cannot rely much on context to recognize a word. As a result, while reading aloud they often produce words that are contextually inappropriate and some of these responses could be non-sense words. They seldom correct their own reading errors, thus indicating weak metacognitive skill.

Many of these symptoms are also exhibited by students whose past academic history is marked by frequent absences, poor motivation, and limited reading experience. It was noted earlier that such reading failure that is environmentally induced is not genuine reading disability but is referred to as reading difficulty. Procedures that will be helpful in differentiating reading difficulty from the different kinds of reading disabilities are presented in the next chapter.

Reading Disability And Metacognition

While it is possible that many disabled readers also have poor metacognitive skills, it is uncertain whether deficient metacognitive skill alone can produce reading disability. In a study of fourth grade good and poor readers, Paris and Myers (1981) found that poor readers were deficient in their knowledge about the adverse effect of negative strategies on comprehension. In a similar study Garner and Kraus (1982) compared good and poor readers from grade 7 for their knowledge about reading. Important differences were found between these two groups. For instance, to the question "If you are given something to read, how would you know if you were reading it well?", good readers gave answers such as "if I could understand it without reading it over and over again," whereas poor readers gave answers such as "if I read fluently loud" and "if I didn't pause much." It is the authors' experience that many college students who are average readers are also deficient in metacognitive skills and show improvement in test performance after receiving information about metacognition.

Reading Disability and Cognitive Styles

In Chapter 1, the term *cognitive style* was defined as consistent individual difference in ways of organizing and processing information and experience. It was also noted that cognitive style is more concerned with the process than the product, with style than content. Nearly 20 cognitive styles have been identified, but three have been more thoroughly investigated than others. These are, *reflectivity–impulsivity*, *field independence–dependence*, and *successive–simultaneous processing*. Even though cognitive style is concerned with the manner in which behavior occurs rather than with the level of performance, studies that have investigated reading in light of cognitive styles indicate that some cognitive styles are not conducive to reading. For instance, impulsive subjects are known to commit more oral reading errors than reflective subjects. A weakness in successive processing style and an overdependence on simultaneous style has also been proposed as an explanation of developmental dyslexia.

A new cognitive style that has implications for reading has been reported recently (Aaron and Whitefield 1990). This has been named *dysfluency* and is marked by extreme slowness in the processing of symbolic information such as the written and spoken language. Subjects who are dysfluent show no other signs of reading problems. Because they are very slow in reading they tend to perform poorly on timed tests. Consequently, their grades are not consistent with their level of intelligence and with the time they spend in preparing for tests. Because of their slow processing tendency, they also do poorly on tests of STM such as the digit-span subtest of WISC-R.

Cognitive styles are considered to be stable and enduring and do not appear to be modified easily by special training. Consistent with this, the dysfluent reader remains a slow reader even after years of reading experience. Such persons, however, experience success when sufficient time to complete tests and assignments is allowed.

It is important to distinguish dysfluent readers from poor readers who, for want of sufficient reading experience, also tend to be slow readers. The latter group, however, tends to have poor vocabulary and a mediocre academic history. Careful examination of the verbal skills as well as the academic history of students can be used to separate dysfluent readers from this type of poor reader.

Chapter 3

Differential Diagnosis of Reading Disabilities

INTRODUCTION

The objective of a diagnostic procedure is to identify instructional needs of the student with a reading disability and to target appropriate instructional and management procedures for the reading problem. The primary intent of a diagnostic assessment is not necessarily to classify a student into one of the three categories of poor readers described in Chapter 2 but to identify the weakness of an individual student and to provide appropriate instructional guidance. Because many students with reading disabilities tend to adopt compensatory processes by excessively utilizing one or the other strategy, the diagnostic procedure also attempts to identify such "strengths" of a reader with a disability. Sometimes, such compensatory strategies can be utilized to help the student circumvent the weaknesses and, at other times, a student may be encouraged to avoid them. Diagnostic testing, therefore, is not an end in itself but a means to help a student reach his or her academic potential. Placing a reading-disabled student in one of the three categories, however, can provide a broad orientation for the learning skills specialist as to the general principles to be incorporated in corrective instruction and management procedures as well as help set up realistic academic goals for students on an individual basis. For example, students with SRD, in spite of their reading and spelling problems, may be expected to succeed in courses that deal with concrete information but an equal degree of success may not be hoped for in social science courses that deal with abstract materials. Conversely, students diagnosed as having LAR may be expected to do better in courses that impart information through hands-on experiences than in courses that rely solely on lectures as a means of instruction.

Information needed to reach diagnostic conclusions is based on quantitative and qualitative measures. Quantitative measures are in the form of numerical data and are obtained through two procedures: formal assessment and informal assessment. Formal assessment utilizes standardized tests, and a student's performance on these tests is compared against national norms. Informal assessment is based primarily on information collected regarding errors committed during oral reading, impromptu writing, and spelling. The informal assessment is accomplished with the help of locally developed instruments that can contain test items from curriculum material a student is likely to encounter. Informal assessment also generates numerical data that are compared not with preset national norms but with informal criteria established by the reading disability specialist.

Qualitative assessment of a student is carried out primarily through interviews and observations in which information regarding a student's academic history, educational experience, level of motivation, and biological and genetic characteristics can be obtained. A schematic outline of this form of testing procedure is shown in table 3.1.

One important consideration in the development of this assessment procedure is that the time needed to administer diagnostic tests and the specialists needed to administer standardized tests are in short supply. Consequently, the number of tests and tasks that are used for diagnosis has to be kept to a minimum; the administration of the tests should not require extensive training of personnel or the services of specialists.

The assessment procedure described in this book is based on the "componential view" of reading and, therefore, differs in several important ways from the traditional procedures used in the diagnosis of LD in children. Because some experts advocate the use of diagnostic methods in colleges that are modeled after the traditional LD procedure, it is important to know the differences between the diagnostic procedure presented in this book and the traditional ones.

TRADITIONAL METHODS OF DIAGNOSIS
VERSUS COMPONENTS-BASED ASSESSMENT

The traditional diagnostic procedure that deals with learning and reading disabilities is almost exclusively meant for children at the elemen-

Table 3.1.   A Schematic Outline of the Assessment Program

Quantitative measures		Qualitative measures
Formal assessment:	Informal assessment:	Interview and observation:
Standardized tests of reading comprehension, listening comprehension, decoding, and vocabulary.	Locally developed tests of decoding, spelling, reading speed, context dependency, errors of syntax in writing, metacognition, and cognitive style.	Information about academic history, level of motivation, biological factors, genetic background, and family background.

tary and junior high school levels. The population dealt with in this book comes from senior high schools and post-secondary institutions and, therefore, differs from that encountered in traditional LD programs. The most important difference between these two populations is that children in early primary grades are "learning to read," whereas mature students "read to learn" (Chall 1979). When young children fail to learn how to read, teachers usually adjust their instructional objectives and procedures to help them learn to read. Consequently, the mechanics of reading acquisition, such as decoding, segmenting, blending, and word recognition skill are given precedence over the learning of subject matter. In contrast, in high school and college classes, the emphasis is on "reading to learn," and the subject matter becomes more important than the mechanics of reading. Consequently, when these students fail to learn, the focus of the academic skills program is on efficient acquisition of information by improving comprehension and other skills, such as note taking, summarizing, and test taking.

It also has to be remembered that poor readers in high schools and colleges, barring some unusual circumstances, have been exposed to many years of reading instruction, which obviously has failed to produce satisfactory results. Many of these students also have received remedial instruction, which invariably includes some form of phonics training. A number of studies report that in many individuals, symptoms of dyslexia linger on through adulthood in spite of these subjects having received "conventional remedial instruction" when they were young. Bruck (1987), for instance, tested 101 reading-disabled children with average or higher IQ and retested them when they were about 21 years old. She found that, compared to a control group, the reading-disabled subjects performed poorly in tests of single word decoding and spelling. In another study of reading-disabled subjects, Scarborough (1984) also reported that individuals with a history of specific reading disability as children were found to be deficient in word reading, phonic analysis, reading speed, and spelling. DeFries (1988), in his longitudinal study, observed that a deficit in symbol processing speed remained as one of the most important differences between dyslexic and normal readers. Considering the chronic nature of decoding and spelling deficits and their persistence into adulthood, it is naive to expect that the decoding and spelling problems of older students could be "fixed" by subjecting the students to more phonics. It should be noted, however, that certain new forms of remedial procedures such as phoneme awareness training (Bradley and Bryant 1985) and teaching segmenting and blending skills with the aid of the computer seem to be more promising than conventional procedures. These new procedures appear to be particularly effective with very young children and may not produce positive results in the case of adolescents and adults with a long history of decoding problems.

These observations should not be interpreted to mean that subjects who have SRD have a dismal prognosis as far as reading is concerned. Dyslexic readers investigated in these studies lagged behind their peers only in processes associated with the first component of reading, namely decoding. Many poor readers with deficient decoding skills do attain adequate reading comprehension skill, probably by developing a good sight vocabulary. For instance, in the study mentioned above, Bruck (1987) found that reading comprehension was the most intact skill in the adults she studied. The six adolescents described in the previous chapter (Aaron 1989c) were deficient in nonword reading and spelling but demonstrated normal comprehension when tested by an untimed test of reading comprehension.

Not only is there a paucity of evidence regarding the effectiveness of conventional methods of improving decoding skills with older disabled readers, but the demands of academic work in college also leave very little time to devote to the remediation of the decoding deficit. It is not uncommon to hear from students with SRD that phonics training was not only of little use to them but also boring. For these reasons, the most pragmatic approach is not to invest time in trying to remediate decoding and spelling deficits but to put efforts into practices that improve vocabulary, reading comprehension, and other academic skills. Because of the difference in instructional goals set for young readers and mature readers (i.e., learning to read versus reading to learn), the objectives of assessment are also different.

The traditional LD assessment is based on the rationale that LD is a form of learning disorder that is different from the one associated with general cognitive retardation. Whereas a child with LD is performing below his or her learning potential, the child who is classified as a low ability reader reads and comprehends at a level that is in line with his or her below-average intellectual ability. Furthermore, identification of these two groups of children is motivated by administrative policies that require data that are necessary for placing these two groups of children in different learning environments. The learning potential of the child is traditionally estimated from the IQ obtained by administering an intelligence test such as the Wechsler Intelligence Scale for Children (WISC–R) or the Stanford Binet test of intelligence. The use of IQ tests in separating children with specific reading disability from children who are low ability readers, however, has been criticized for several reasons. First, the validity of the assumptions that underlie the use of IQ in defining learning disabilities has been questioned (Siegel 1989). In addition, IQ score is not able to account for a large amount of variance seen in reading performance because the correlation coefficients obtained between IQ and scores of reading achievement are rather low and range from .4 to .6. Furthermore, a lack of consensus as to the extent of the discrepancy between reading achievement and the potential estimated with the aid of IQ that marks LD is a major problem in the use of IQ-based diagnosis. A more serious problem, which is not of theoretical but utilitarian nature, is that diagnosis based on IQ may satisfy administrative and fiscal expediencies but it does not lead to recommendations regarding remediation, instruction, and management.

In the place of IQ tests, a test of listening comprehension is used in the diagnostic procedure that is advocated in this book. As a diagnostic tool, listening comprehension does not have many of the limitations of IQ. The advantages of using listening comprehension are that it is an integral component of the reading process, is simple to administer, and more importantly, the diagnostic findings based on the components of reading lead to recommendations regarding corrective instruction.

DIAGNOSTIC PROCEDURE BASED ON THE COMPONENTIAL VIEW OF READING

Rationale

The diagnostic procedure described in this book is based on two propositions: (1) decoding and comprehension are the two major components of the reading process and (2) beyond the differences that can be attributed to the modalities of input, reading comprehension and listening comprehension are mediated by the same cognitive mechanisms. These propositions lead to the following expectations: (a) decoding skill and comprehension skill can be developmentally arrested independent of each other, resulting in the following three different kinds of poor readers—those with deficient decoding but adequate comprehension skills, those with poor comprehension but adequate decoding skills, and those with deficient decoding and poor comprehension skill; and (b) listening comprehension can be utilized to estimate the reading comprehension potential. It was noted in Chapter 1 that a substantial body of psychological evidence exists to support the two-component view of the reading process. There is also an impressive body of literature to support the second proposition, namely, that reading comprehension and listening comprehension are highly correlated. For instance, Duker's (1965) review of 23 studies that compared reading comprehension and listening comprehension and another review of an additional 12 studies (Kennedy 1971) report correlation coefficients that range from .45 to .82. In a more recent review Danks (1980) reported similar data. Kintsch and Kozminsky (1977) administered reading and listening tasks to college students and found surprisingly small differences in the production of structural elements and propositions that led them to conclude that reading and listening involve identical comprehension skills. Stanovich, Cunningham, and Feeman (1984) compared the reading performance of children from grades 1, 2, and 5 with measures of intelligence, listening comprehension, and decoding skill. Consistent with other studies, the correlation coefficient between reading comprehension and listening comprehension rose from .37 in grade 1 to .59 in grade 5. At all levels, listening comprehension was found to be a better predictor of reading achievement than were measures of intelligence. Wood, Buckhalt, and Tomlin (1988) obtained a higher mean correlation coefficient of .78 between reading and listening comprehension for a group of children classified as learning disabled and mildly mentally retarded. In an unpublished study of 180 children from grades 3 through 8, Aaron and Simurdak obtained correlation coefficients that ranged from .58 to .71.

The high correlation coefficient obtained between listening comprehension and reading comprehension makes listening comprehension a viable means of estimating reading comprehension. The idea of using listening comprehension as a predictor of reading comprehension is not an entirely new one. Several years ago, Ladd (1970) noted that listening comprehension is one of the most important indicators of reading ability. Durrell and Hayes (1969) noted that listening comprehension is more directly related to reading than are most tests of intelligence. Carroll (1977) was explicit in advocating the use of listening comprehension for assessing reading comprehension potential. In their study of college students Palmer et al. (1985) obtained a correlation coefficient of .82 between reading comprehension and listening comprehension, which led them to state that reading comprehension can be predicted almost perfectly by a listening measure.

The facts that the major components of reading are comprehension and decoding and that listening comprehension is well correlated with reading comprehension lead to certain consequences. One of them is the expectation that once the contribution of listening comprehension to reading is factored out, the remaining deficit could be attributed to decoding deficit. There is evidence to support such a proposition. In a study of 172 dyslexic children Conners and Olson (in press) found that printed word recognition and oral language comprehension each contributed independent variance to reading comprehension and that reading comprehension of the dyslexic children was higher than their word recognition. Reading difficulty of a student who has good listening comprehension but poor reading comprehension can be attributed to poor decoding skill. Conversely, the intrinsic cause of the reading disability of a student with poor listening comprehension can be attributed to suboptimal comprehension skill. In other words, in low ability readers, both listening comprehension and reading comprehension are low. In addition to poor comprehension skills, these students may also have decoding deficits. Studies that investigated such "garden variety" poor readers, in fact, confirm such an expectation. For instance, Curtis (1980) found that, among third and fifth grade poor readers, there was much common variance between word recognition and listening comprehension that accounted for poor reading comprehension; she also found that these children were poor in both listening and reading comprehension. A study of poor readers from fifth grade by Berger (1978) and a study of adult poor readers by Sticht (1979) produced similar results. In contrast to this condition, readers with SRD have normal listening comprehension but poor reading comprehension.

The proposition that once the contribution of listening comprehension to reading is factored out, the remaining deficit can be attributed to poor decoding skills is advocated by investigators who subscribe to the componential view of reading. For instance, according to Gough and Tunmer (1986), reading (R) equals the product of decoding (D) and comprehension (C). That is, $R = D \times C$. It follows that if $D = 0$, then $R = 0$; and if $C = 0$, then also $R = 0$. They conclude that the linear combination of decoding and listening comprehension predicts reading so well that there is no room for improvement.

Separation of the three different types of poor readers is based on this rationale. In addition to aiding in the identification of the three types of poor readers, this procedure also provides guidance for corrective instructional measures that are to be adopted.

Procedure

Quantitative Measures: Formal Assessment

Reading Comprehension: This is assessed with the aid of two tests —the Passage Comprehension Subtest of *Form G* of the Woodcock Reading Mastery Tests–Revised (WRMT–R; Woodcock 1987) and the Reading Comprehension Subtest of the Stanford Diagnostic Reading Test (SDRT), Blue level (Karlsen, Madden, and Gardner 1977). The WRMT battery has nine subtests, passage comprehension being one of them. This is an *untimed* test and is in a cloze format that assesses inferential skill of the reader by requiring the subject to furnish the missing word. The reading comprehension subtest of the SDRT is a *timed* test and assesses the comprehension and recall of factual information and inferential comprehension. The raw scores obtained on the WRMT are converted into grade equivalents and standard scores; the raw scores obtained on the SDRT are converted only into grade equivalents because there is no simple way to convert the raw scores into standard scores. Comparison of the subject's performance on these two tests of reading comprehension provide useful diagnostic information.

Listening Comprehension: This skill is assessed by administering the Passage Comprehension Subtest from WRMT–R, *Form H* as a test of listening comprehension. The examiner reads each sentence aloud and the subject is required to furnish the missing word. If the subject requests, the sentence is read again one more time only. A good test of listening comprehension should be valid in the sense that the obtained results should be free from contamination by variables such as memory, attention, and motivation. Furthermore, when listening comprehension is being compared with reading comprehension, the level of difficulty of the vocabulary, complexity of the sentences, and the cohesiveness of the sentences should be equivalent under both listening and reading conditions. Good tests of listening comprehension that satisfy these requirements are simply not available. Taking these constraints into account, researchers have used equivalent forms of the same test for assessing reading and listening comprehension.

Because the two forms of the WRMT (Form G, which is used to measure reading comprehension, and Form H, which is used to measure listening comprehension) are similar in the number of inferential questions, length, and difficulty level, both forms of the test provide comparable data. In an unpublished study, Aaron and Simurdak administered the two tests to 180 children from grades 3 through 8 and obtained a correlation coefficient of .73 between reading comprehension and listening comprehension. Even though a similar study was not carried out using mature students, there is reason to expect a similar relationship to exist between listening and reading comprehension because the correlation between these two measures increases as the age of the subjects increases. The listening comprehension test has a test/retest reliability of .67. The raw scores obtained in this test are also converted into grade equivalents and standard scores.

Vocabulary: Reading vocabulary of the subject is measured with the aid of three subtests from the WRMT–R. These are: Antonyms, Synonyms, and Analogies. The raw scores obtained by the subject can be converted into standard scores and grade equivalents.

Decoding: The decoding skill of the subject is assessed with the help of the Word Attack Subtest from the WRMT–R. This test requires the subject to read either nonsense words or words with a very low frequency of occurrence in text. The raw scores obtained by the subject can be converted into standard scores and grade equivalents.

Initial Diagnosis: The objective of the formal assessment procedure is to identify the component(s) in which the student is weak and to make an initial judgment as to which one of the three categories of reading disabilities (SRD, NSRD, LAR) the subject belongs. This initial diagnosis is made on the basis of the student's performance in the tests used in the formal assessment procedure. As a first step, the student's performance in the WRMT reading comprehension is examined. The manual provides grade equivalent (GE) up to 16.9 level, which is roughly equivalent to the college senior level. The grade equivalent is the most readily interpretable metric and indicates whether the student's reading comprehension is at or below the grade he or she is in. Freshmen entering college are expected to score equivalent to the 12th grade. The confidence interval for the grade equivalent score can then be calculated by using the Standard Error of Measurement (SEM) provided in the WRMT test manual. The confidence range obtained by adding and subtracting 1 SEM to the obtained grade equivalent score indicates that the chances are 2 to 1 that the true score of the student falls within this range; the range obtained by adding and subtracting 1.96 times the SEM to the obtained score provides a range that reduces errors of measurement and chance factors to a 5% level. For example, in the Passage Comprehension Subtest, a college freshman obtained a score equivalent to 7.4 grade. There is nearly 66% chance that his true score falls between 6.5 and 8.4 grades (i.e., ± 1 SEM) or, there is 95% chance that his true score falls between 5.3 and 10.7 (i.e., ± 1.96 SEM). Clearly, the student has comprehension deficits. In the WRMT, these statistics are somewhat cumbersome to calculate, but a microcomputer scoring program called ASSIST can make computation much easier.

What degree of discrepancy should indicate reading disability? There is no simple answer to this question and the decision is largely left to the learning skills specialist. The test scores can tell if the student's reading comprehension is at grade level or lower and what degree of confidence we can attach to this number. In our view any degree of discrepancy found in a student who wants to improve his or her reading performance deserves attention. College students with SRD, in general, score at grade level or above on the WRMT reading comprehension test. This is because this is an untimed test, and given sufficient time, students with SRD can decode the printed material and comprehend it. A timed test such as the SDRT, however, tells a different story.

The reading comprehension subtest of SDRT is a timed test and provides grade equivalents and stanine scores. The GE ranges from 1 through 12.9, and the Blue level is standardized on high school and junior and community college students. SEM for grade equivalents is not provided and, therefore, confidence intervals cannot be established. Nevertheless, a direct comparison of reading comprehension GEs obtained on the WRMT and SDRT can provide useful diagnostic information. In general, students with SRD do less well on SDRT than on WRMT because they have adequate comprehension but are slow readers; students with NSRD and LAR do poorly on both tests.

The next step is to compare a student's reading comprehension score with the listening comprehension score, both obtained from WRMT. The raw scores obtained in these tests are converted into standard scores for the purpose of comparison. The logic involved in this form of comparison is that if a student has a listening comprehension score that is at grade level and a reading comprehension score that is lower, his or her reading difficulty is due to poor decoding skill. In contrast, if a student has below average scores in both forms of comprehension, the deficit is not limited to the written language but includes spoken language as well. But what should be the extent of the difference between these two comprehension scores for it to be considered as indicative of a genuine difference? At a very basic level, if there is no overlap between the confidence limits set up by 1 SEM, then it can be inferred that a true difference exists. For instance, a college sophomore obtains a raw score of 52 on listening comprehension and a score of 45 on reading comprehension on the WRMT. The corresponding standard scores are 98 and 87 and the GE are 12.9 and 6.9 respectively. When the confidence range is computed by adding and subtracting 1 SEM to each of the standard scores, we obtain the following data:

Listening comprehension: 91 ——————— 100;
Reading comprehension: 73 ——————— 83.

Because there is no overlap between these two estimates, we can conclude with approximately 68% confidence that a true difference exists between the listening comprehension and reading comprehension of this subject. The student is poor in reading comprehension but not in listening comprehension. The source of his or her reading disability is likely to be poor decoding skill. The student's performance on the two remaining subtests of the WRMT, viz., vocabulary and word attack, can be used to confirm the initial diagnosis.

As we saw earlier, reading is a major means of vocabulary acquisition. Because of their poor reading habits and limited reading experience, poor readers of all kinds tend to have a limited vocabulary. This condition is much more evident in the case of students with NSRD and LAR. These students, therefore, may need intense instruction in vocabulary development. The student's vocabulary level is determined by combining the raw scores obtained on the three WRMT subtests, viz., Antonyms, Synonyms, and Analogies. These can then be converted into grade equivalents or standard scores. Before these tests are given to a student and after the sample items in each test are demonstrated, a measure of metacognitive ability can be secured. This can be accomplished by telling the student how many questions there are in each subtest and then asking her or him to estimate how many items he or she thinks can be answered correctly. This number should be recorded and then compared with the number of questions subsequently answered correctly. The discrepancy between the estimate and the achievement is a measure of the accuracy of a student's self-evaluation, which in turn, is one aspect of metacognitive skill.

The Word Attack Subtest from the WRMT is used to assess a student's decoding skill. The raw scores obtained are converted into grade equivalents or standard scores.

Quantitative Measures: Informal Assessment   Information obtained through the informal assessment procedure is used for validating the initial diagnosis that was made through the formal assessment procedures. The tests and tasks used in the informal assessment procedure are developed locally and can be used only to see if a student has met locally established criteria. These tests are shown in the appendix. The informal assessment procedure is used to evaluate a student's decoding skill, spelling, reading speed, dependency on context, metacognition, and cognitive style. It is also used to see if a student's written language contains errors of syntax.

Decoding: A list of 36 pronounceable nonwords is used for evaluating a student's decoding skill. The list is based on selected spelling-pronunciation rules. The ability to pronounce the written word is progressively acquired by children, and it is believed that pronunciation of written words goes hand in hand with the progressive acquisition of a knowledge of the spelling-to-sound relationship, even though a reader may not make conscious use of such rules. The list of 36 pronounceable nonwords used in this test was developed after examining the literature and identifying these rules (Calfee, Venezky, and Chapman 1969; Venezky 1976; Wijk 1966). In an unpublished study we found (Aaron and Simurdak 1989) that the mean number of nonwords correctly read by a group of eighth graders was 30. At the high school and college level, an error of 5 or more, therefore, can be considered as indicative of decoding difficulty. By the time they reach sixth grade, a majority of children have mastered the decoding skill and should be able to pronounce almost all the words in this list.

Spelling: It was noted that one manifestation of decoding deficit is poor spelling. In individuals who have compensated for some of their reading deficits, poor spelling remains as the only readily identifiable residual of the reading problem. These individuals, however, continue to be rather slow readers. Consequently, poor spelling should alert the instructor to the possibility that a student may have associated reading problems, perhaps in an attenuated form.

A list of 42 common words is used to evaluate a student's spelling skill. These words were selected on the basis of the same rules as was the list of nonwords. The examiner says each word, follows it up with a sentence using the word, and says the target word again. The student writes the word down. There is an impressive degree of similarity between an individual's performance on the nonword reading task and on the spelling task. An error of 5 or more on the spelling test is a strong indication of an associated decoding deficit.

Reading Speed: The speed with which words are recognized and passages are read is an important correlate of reading skill. The ability to read fast and to skim and scan passages rapidly is an important skill required for success in high school and college. Poor decoders are slow readers because they take more time to identify words than do good decoders. Thus, students with poor decoding skills tend to be slow readers regardless of their comprehension skills. Reading speed is traditionally expressed in terms of words read per minute. However, passages tend to contain a variety of words of varying frequency and familiarity. This introduces a confounding factor because there could be individual differences in the word knowledge of readers. Some readers tend to spend an unusually long time when they encounter an uncommon word that they cannot readily decode even though they can read most other words in the text at normal speed. Thus, the presence of one or two uncommon words in a passage can give a distorted view.

In order to avoid this problem, we use a list of 20 function words for estimating reading speed. The 20 words in this list occur frequently in written text (more than 500 times per 5,088,721 words of running text; Carroll, Davies, and Richman 1971). Because function words lack meaning, they cannot be pronounced by first apprehending their meaning. The mean reading speed of eighth graders in reading aloud this list of 20 words is about 12 seconds and the SD is 2. Any departure from this figure is an indication of slow reading speed.

Context Dependency: McClelland and Rumelhart (1981) have provided a detailed exposition of reading within the framework of their Interactive Activation Model, which holds that top-down or conceptually driven processing works simultaneously and in conjunction with bottom-up or data driven processing. When the reader encounters difficulties with the bottom-up process, decoding becomes difficult. Under these circumstances, the reader tends to rely more on previous knowledge, as well as on the contextual cues found in the text, than on print. Conversely, the disabled reader who has poor comprehension ability and insufficient background knowledge is likely to depend more on print than on context. Removal of the context from the material to be read will, therefore, have greater negative impact on the performance of a poor decoder than on NSRD or LAR subjects. The effect of context removal therefore, can provide a measure of context dependency. Context dependency is measured in the following manner: a student is asked first to read aloud two passages that match his or her grade level, and the oral reading errors made are noted. After a day or so, the student is asked to read aloud the same words that made up the passages but which are arranged randomly in the form of a columnar list (see appendix for examples). Taking the words out of the sentential context eliminates contextual cues. The number of errors committed while reading the word list minus errors made in reading the passages is a measure of context dependence. The passages selected for reading come from a list of 24 graded passages that have been calibrated for syntactic density and readability (Aquino 1969; Miller and Coleman 1967). In our standardization study (Aaron and Simurdak 1989) we found that normal readers from grades 1 through 8 tend to make fewer errors when they read lists of words than when they read the passages.

The passage-reading task also provides an opportunity to examine the nature of errors made while reading aloud. Students with SRD tend to make context-appropriate errors, whereas students with LAR make errors that are meaningless; these students occasionally produce neologisms. In addition, if the student shows evidence of a tendency to self-correct errors made during oral reading, it is an indication that the student is monitoring his or her own comprehension. On-line monitoring of the comprehension process is considered to be one aspect of metacognition.

Metacognition: Knowledge of one's own cognitive processing and the ability to undertake deliberate corrective actions when comprehension fails are aspects of metacognition. The two corresponding features of metacognitive skills that can be assessed during the testing process are accurate self-evaluation and comprehension monitoring. The metacognitive aspect of self-evaluation is evaluated in terms of the accuracy of a student's perception of his or her own ability or weakness. It may be recalled that when the vocabulary subtests of WRMT were administered, students were asked to predict how many questions they thought they could answer correctly and this figure was subtracted from the actual score they obtained. A striking discrepancy between these two figures is an indication of poor self evaluative skills. Similarly, an absence of a tendency to correct the mistakes committed during oral reading of the passages described in the previous section also indicates that the student is not actively monitoring his or her own comprehension.

Cognitive Style: Cognitive style is defined as consistent individual differences in the ways of organizing and processing information, and it is more concerned with the process rather than the product. In a way, SRD or dyslexia can be viewed as a product of a unique cognitive style wherein, in order to recognize the written word, the individual relies more on meaning than on the phonological features of the word. Even though nearly 20 cognitive styles have been identified in the psychological literature, the impact of only a few cognitive styles on reading has been studied. It seems that children who are described as impulsive make many more errors while reading aloud than those who are described as reflective. What appears to be an important cognitive style that affects reading performance has been reported by Aaron and Whitefield (1990). This cognitive style is labelled as *dysfluency—fluency*. *Dysfluency* is described as extreme slowness in the processing of symbolic information such as reading. Fluency is described as the speed of processing symbolic information that is typical of an age group or faster than is normal for that population. Even though both dysfluent readers and SRD readers do poorly on timed reading tests, dysfluent readers are not weak in decoding and spelling. They do not show any of the symptoms seen in SRD students other than slow reading. A subject is considered dysfluent when he or she reads the list of 20 function words very slowly but does well on tests of comprehension, decoding, and spelling. The dysfluent reader does well on untimed tests of reading but not as well on timed tests. In contrast to students who have had a mediocre academic history, a dysfluent reader usually has a reasonably good academic record and presents evidence of a high level of motivation and sustained work. A dysfluent reader's digit span, as measured by intelligence tests such as the Wechsler Adult Intelligence Scale–Revised (WAIS–R) is also very small. It may be recalled that the number of digits recalled in short-term memory tests is a function of the speed with which information is processed rather than the capacity of the STM store.

Syntax In Written Language: It was noted that errors of omission and substitution of suffixes seen in the writings of SRD poor readers may be indicative of a weakness of phonological skill. These errors can be detected if an informal sample of a student's writing can be obtained. A student is asked to write a paragraph on a prescribed topic, and the written material is then analyzed for errors of syntax.

Qualitative Measures Information that is of a qualitative nature is obtained through informal observation of the student's behavior and an interview. In the United States it is possible to get a high school diploma without passing public examinations, and it is even possible to enter a college without demonstrating sufficient academic skills. Students who have never bothered to open a book or prepare for an exam, of course, are most likely to be poor readers. These poor readers are not necessarily reading disabled in the real sense. There is no test to separate students whose poor reading is environmentally induced from those with real reading disability. Information gathered about a student's previous academic history during the interview will provide perhaps the only basis for making a diagnostic decision in this regard.

Dyslexia or SRD is associated with certain biological characteristics, and information regarding these can be useful in separating SRD from the other forms of reading disabilities. There is evidence that there are more left-handers who are dyslexics than right-handers and the incidence of immune related health problems such as allergy is higher among dyslexic subjects than in a normal population (Geschwind and Behan 1982). It has also been known for nearly a century that dyslexia has a genetic predisposition. However, the presence of relatives who are poor readers does not ensure that a student has SRD. Extreme caution should be exercised before a genetic history of dyslexia can be assumed to exist in a family; there is always the possibility that some parents and siblings are poor readers not because they have a reading disability but because either they had limited education or they do not have a habit of reading. A life style in which reading is not given much importance can mimic reading disability in the family. Under these circumstances, the reading deficit seen in the family members can be environmental in origin. Qualitative information, when obtained and carefully analyzed, can provide additional information for the differential diagnosis of reading disabilities. The following set of questions can be used to obtain information regarding these conditions during interview.

1. Would you describe yourself as a serious student while in elementary school? In high school? What kind of grades did you receive? (If a student claims to have tried hard to learn to read, the accuracy of such a statement can be checked by asking him or her to name a few favorite books and a few authors.)
2. While in elementary school: Were you interested in reading? Did you receive special help in reading or were you placed in a LD class? If so, what kind of remedial teaching did you receive? Were you interested in reading outside school? If so, can you name one or two books you read on your own? How were your grades in math?
3. What can you say about your parents' reading habits? Do you consider them good readers? How is their spelling? Do your father and mother read newspapers, magazines, and books?
    What are their occupations? Do they involve reading and writing? How much education have they had? Do you have siblings? Do they or did they experience reading difficulties at school?
4. Are you left-handed? What are the things you do with your right

hand and with your left hand? Are any of your close relatives left-handed?

5. Are you allergic to any substance?
6. Do you think you have some special talent in art or music? Are you mechanically inclined?

CASE HISTORIES THAT ILLUSTRATE THE DIAGNOSTIC PROCESS

Before we present case histories that are representative of the different types of reading disabilities, it will be helpful to review the cognitive profiles of the three types of poor readers shown in table 3.2.

Case 1: Specific Reading Disability

Background Information: K.B., a 20-year-old male, was referred to the psychology clinic by one of his professors. At the time of testing he was a sophomore majoring in education. During the interview, he informed us that his academic performance in elementary and high school ranged from average to poor and that he received special training in speech. He also is attending the writing lab at the University. He has a middle class background; his father works as a plumber and mother as a cashier in a department store. His parents reportedly do

Table 3.2.   Diagnostic Profiles of Different Types of Reading Disabilities

	SRD	NSRD	LAR
Reading comprehension: untimed test	Close to normal	Poor	Poor
timed test	Low	Poor	Poor
Listening comprehension	Normal	Poor	Poor
Decoding skill	Poor	Normal	Poor
Spelling	Poor	Normal	Poor
Reading speed	Slow	Normal	Slow
Context dependency for recognizing words	Yes	Rarely	Some
Oral reading errors:	Many, errors fit context	Few, mechanical pronunciation; Many do not fit context	Many, some are nonwords; Do not fit context
Self correction of errors in oral reading	Often	Rarely	Rarely
Suffix dropping and substitution in writing	Often	Not often	Not often

not do much reading at home. He has three older brothers and could not recall any of them having had difficulty at school. All the brothers went to college and are successfully employed. K.B. is right-handed and has a good health history except for the fact that he is allergic to certain kinds of foods. His responses to questions that are relevant to his study habits and motivation gave the impression that he has been and is serious about school work.

The following data were obtained by administering the diagnostic tests.

Formal assessment:

Reading comprehension WRMT : Raw score = 52; W score = 520; GE = 12.9; SS = 91; 1 SEM range = 86–96*

SDRT : GE = 7.0

Listening comprehension WRMT : Raw score = 55; W score = 525; GE = 14.7; SS = 95; 1 SEM range = 90–100

Decoding (WRMT Word Attack): GE = 6.7
Vocabulary (WRMT Word Comprehension): GE = 13.7

Informal assessment:

Nonword reading: 25 correct out of 36
Spelling: 31 correct out of 42
Reading speed: 22 seconds
Context dependency: No. of errors in reading passages 12 A and B = 2
                             No. of errors in reading list of words = 4
Oral reading errors
(Passage 12 A)
    First in the procession came willing (wailing) men. Finally came the nobels (nobles) . . . who rode in a barrel (barrow) covered with gold disks.
(Passage 12B)
    Then (when) the men pulled themselves into the boat by these lines. All this is (was) provided to make sure that they would keep afloat.

Errors of syntax and spelling in written English: (Excerpts from K.B.'s writing)
    Bush had an over welling way to convay his personal life to the people. Dukakis had a sence of waring a mask will he was in public.

---

*GE, SS, and SEM are Grade Equivalent, Standard Score, and Standard Error of Measurement, respectively.

Bushes managar play very well with it. Bush would carry out the prosparity of the Reagon years.

Performance on Intelligence test: K.B. was also administered the WAIS–R and the following results were obtained. Verbal IQ = 91; Performance IQ = 131; Full scale IQ = 110; Vocabulary, scaled score (S.S.) = 8; digit span, (S.S.) = 6.

Diagnosis: K.B.'s reading comprehension as assessed by WRMT, which is an untimed test, is within normal limits. His listening comprehension is also appropriate to his grade. There is an overlap between the reading and listening comprehension standard scores. He obtained average scores on the WRMT word comprehension subtest. These findings suggest that K.B. does not have a comprehension deficit. There, however, is a striking difference between his reading comprehension as assessed by the WRMT and the SDRT which is a timed test. This indicates that *time* is an important factor that influences his performance on tests. In other words, he is a slow reader. This may be due to his poor decoding skill as revealed by his poor performance in the WRMT Word Attack Subtest. The low digit-span score he obtained on the WAIS indicates that he processes information at a slow rate. The initial diagnosis, therefore, is that K.B. has specific reading disability.

Results of informal assessment confirm this initial diagnosis. For instance, his performance on the nonword reading and spelling were extremely poor, and he took 22 seconds to read the list of 20 function words. These show that K.B. is a poor decoder and a slow reader. His oral reading errors fit the general context suggesting a dependence on top-down processing. The fact that he made more errors while reading the lists of words than while reading the two passages can also be taken as evidence of context dependency. His tendency to self-correct oral reading errors indicates that he is capable of monitoring his comprehension as he reads. Even though slow, he cannot be considered a dysfluent reader because he is a also poor decoder.

Information gathered during the interview indicates that K.B. had been a reasonably well motivated student throughout his elementary and high school years. At present he is working hard to get through his academic courses successfully. Family history does not portray a hostile or negligent environment. All this information leads to the conclusion that his reading problems are intrinsic in nature and not environmentally generated. The test results converge on the diagnosis of SRD.

Case 2: Nonspecific Reading Disability

Background Information: C.L. is a 19-year-old female enrolled in a two year college program for business secretaries that leads to an associate degree. She was referred to the psychology clinic by her professor, who noticed that C.L. had to struggle to keep up with the other students in the class. C.L. is a neat-looking, earnest individual who was much concerned about meeting her academic goals. During the interview C.L. informed us that her performance in elementary and high school was not spectacular but that she managed to get at least Cs in the classes she had taken. While in elementary and high school she did not receive any special remedial help. C.L. comes from an upper-middle class family and is the only child. From her reports, it appeared that her parents valued intellectual pursuits and, if necessary, were willing to sacrifice material comforts in order for their daughter to attain her academic goals. C.L. is right-handed and has a good health history except for the fact that she had some "neurological problems" while in elementary school. The following data were obtained from the tests.

Formal assessment:

Reading comprehension	WRMT :	Raw score = 46; W score = 510; GE = 7.4; SS = 87; 1 SEM range = 82–92
	SDRT :	GE = 6.9
Listening comprehension	WRMT:	Raw score = 48; W score = 514; GE = 8.4; SS = 91; 1 SEM range = 86–96

Decoding (WRMT Word Attack): GE = 13.1
Vocabulary (WRMT Word Comprehension): GE = 8.6

Informal assessment:

Nonword reading: 34 correct out of 36
Spelling: 40 correct out of 42
Reading speed: 11 seconds
Context dependency: No. of errors in reading passages 12 A and B = 2
                   No. of errors in reading list of words = 2
Oral reading errors
(Passage 12 A)
    Many years ago (before), the wife of an Indian chief had thrown herself in (into) a lake to escape punishment.
(Passage 12 B)
    The (their) airplane had been forced down at sea. All this was proved (provided) to make sure that they could keep afloat.

Errors of syntax and spelling in written English: (Note: there are only a few errors)

My goal in life is to be a good secretary and a good role model. — make people look inward instead of outward. I see if the person is good by deeds not necessary by words. Action speak louder than words.

Performance on Intelligence test: C.L. also was administered the WAIS–R and the following results were obtained: Verbal IQ = 85; Performance IQ = 81; Full scale IQ = 82; Vocabulary, scaled score (S.S.) = 7; digit span, (S.S.) = 11.

Diagnosis: C.L.'s reading comprehension as assessed by WRMT is well below that which is expected of a college student. Her listening comprehension, as assessed by the WRMT, is equally low. There is a large overlap of the reading comprehension and listening comprehension standard scores suggesting that C.L. has a general comprehension deficit. This means that she is poor in comprehending language whether it is written or spoken. Her vocabulary, as assessed by the Word Comprehension Subtest of the WRMT as well as the WAIS, is in line with this interpretation. Time does not appear to be an important factor in her reading because her comprehension was more or less the same whether assessed by timed or untimed tests. The speed with which she read the list of function words is typical of a college student.

Her good decoding skill, as seen in her performance on the Word Attack Subtest of the WRMT as well as on the nonword reading task, is in striking contrast to her poor comprehension skill. Her spelling skill is also well developed. Her good digit-span score indicates that she can process information rapidly. The initial diagnosis, therefore, is that C.L. has nonspecific reading disability.

Results of informal assessment support this initial diagnosis. For instance, her performance on the nonword reading, spelling, and reading speed test was good. She committed very few errors in the oral reading task, but the ones she committed do not fit the general context (e.g., *the* for "their", *prove* for "provided"). She seldom corrected her oral reading errors, which indicates that she is not monitoring her comprehension as she reads.

From the information obtained during the interview and from her response to questions that are relevant to her study habits and motivation, one can conclude that she is a serious and hard-working student. Her family background and her past school history indicate that she has an intrinsic reading problem and that environmental factors might not have contributed to her reading problems. The fact that a comprehension deficit exists in the presence of adequate decoding skills and that the comprehension deficit includes both written and spoken language confirm the diagnosis that C.L. has nonspecific reading disability.

Case 3: Low Ability Reader

Background Information: M.G., a 25-year-old male, came to the psychology clinic partly of his own volition and partly because his brother, who also had a reading disability and had received assistance from the clinic, encouraged him to do so. M.G. is a junior in college majoring in industrial technology. He comes from a middle-class family, and his only brother, as mentioned earlier, also has reading problems. Two years ago, the brother successfully graduated from college with a degree in fine arts and has gone on to graduate school. M.G. has had learning problems since the first grade and received speech therapy while in elementary school. His current problem is that he has to read over and over again in order to understand the textbook and, even then, forgets what he has read. Reading and spelling continue to be problems for him. From the information obtained during the interview and from his family background there is no reason to suspect that his reading problem is environmental in origin. Since childhood he has suffered from allergies resulting in sinus-related problems for which he has been under medication. M.G. is right handed. The following data has been obtained from the several tests.

Formal assessment:

Reading comprehension   WRMT : Raw score = 49; W score = 515;
                                       GE = 9.0; SS = 91; 1 SEM range =
                                       86–96
                          SDRT : GE = 8.1
Listening comprehension   WRMT : Raw score = 50; W score = 517;
                                       GE = 9.8; SS = 92; 1 SEM range =
                                       88–98
Decoding (WRMT Word Attack): GE = 4.2
Vocabulary (WRMT Word Comprehension): GE = 7.5

Informal assessment:

Nonword reading: 26 correct out of 36
Spelling: 22 correct out of 42
Reading speed: 18 seconds
Context dependency: No. of errors in reading passages 12 A and B = 24
                     No. of errors in reading list of words = 22
Oral reading errors
(Passage 12 A)
     When the Spaniards came to Columbia, they were told of a terrible (tribe) of Indians who posed (possessed) famous (fabulous) wealth. First in the possession (procession) came walking (wailing) men, who bore signs on (of) mourning the chief who had died.

(Passage 12 B)

They barely had time to inlet (inflate) the yellow rubber . . . (dinghies) and climb into them before the plane sank. To the surprise of the anxious watcher(s), they saw a boat coming (hanging) under it.

Errors of syntax and spelling in written English: (Excerpts from M.G.'s writing)

My incounter with Halley comet. I have always been interested in Halley comet; sents (since) I was a boy. I frist tried to see it on December 15. Makeing sure I was seeing Halley comet I decited to watch it movement through the different constilation (constellation). It was five degree above the horizing (horizon). Finally I had to saw (say) good by in April not to see it till 2062.

Performance on Intelligence test: WAIS–R Verbal IQ: 89; Performance IQ = 101; Fullscale IQ = 93; Vocabulary = scaled score 9; digit span = 6

Diagnosis: M.G.'s performance in tests of reading comprehension and listening comprehension are substantially below average, suggesting that his poor reading comprehension is not an isolated deficit. His reading comprehension is several grades below expectation whether assessed by the timed or untimed test. There is also an overlap between his reading and listening comprehension standard scores, suggesting that the comprehension deficit is a pervasive one. His decoding skill as assessed by the Word Attack Subtest of the WRMT is also extremely poor. Unlike K.B., his word comprehension is also poor. The initial diagnosis, therefore, is that M.G. is a low ability reader.

Results of informal assessment further support this conclusion. For instance, his performance in tests of nonword reading and spelling were very poor. He is a rather slow reader also. He does not appear to depend much on context to decode words because some of the oral reading errors he committed do not fit the context. In fact, some of the errors are neologisms (e.g., "horizing," "sents"). During oral reading, he did not attempt to correct his own errors, which indicates that he is not monitoring his own comprehension.

Information gathered during the interview and analysis of his past history indicates that M.G. had been a reasonably well motivated student during all of his elementary and high school years. At present he is working hard to get through his academic courses successfully. Family history does not portray a hostile or negligent environment. All this information leads to the conclusion that his reading problems are intrinsic in nature and not environmentally generated. The test results converge on the diagnosis of LAR.

Diagnostic information obtained by evaluating these three cases should be helpful in selecting the appropriate instructional procedures for them. The cognitive profiles of these three students differ from each other, and thus, we cannot expect all of them to profit to the same degree from the same instructional program. K.B., the student diagnosed as having specific reading disability, needs to improve his word recognition skill and speed of reading, whereas C.L., the student with NSRD, has to improve her vocabulary and comprehension skill and may, in addition, require tutorial help in the subject matter areas. A comprehensive instructional program that focuses on improving word recognition skill, vocabulary, study skills, and subject matter knowledge may be required for M.G., who is a low ability reader. Correspondingly, the prognosis of success in college also may vary among these three students; while we can be optimistic about the future of K.B., similar expectation is not warranted in the case of M.G.

Chapter 4

The Academic Support Program

INTRODUCTION

In this and the following chapters we describe the most important aspect of the reading disability program, namely, procedures that may enhance the academic achievement of students with reading disabilities. The reading disability program has two components: an academic support program and an academic skills program. The academic support program is concerned with the management of reading disabilities, whereas the academic skills program is designed to teach strategies of learning that will be helpful in optimizing the academic performance of students with reading disabilities. This chapter deals with the first component, namely management of reading and writing problems. The academic skills program, in which strategies that are specifically aimed at improving study skills such as note taking, listening comprehension, reading comprehension, essay writing, and vocabulary building, is described in the next chapter.

A distinction is made between academic support and remediation, the former being the focus of this book. A distinction is also made between reading disability and learning disability, again the former being the subject of this book. The differences between management and remediation, on the one hand, and reading disability and learning disability, on the other, are elaborated in the subsequent sections of this chapter.

MANAGEMENT OF READING DISABILITIES

Management Versus Remediation of Reading Disabilities

The primary goal of the reading disability program at secondary schools and colleges is to enable students with reading disabilities to achieve their potential in the academic areas. The program has two components: providing support services and teaching academic strategies. It is hoped that the academic performance of these students can be improved through a combination of strategic management of the reading difficulties and proper use of certain learning strategies. These are modest but pragmatic goals as compared to efforts to *remediate* reading deficits, which may be ideal goals to strive for but which often yield nothing more than paltry dividends. There exists no compelling evidence that leads us to believe that the chronic decoding deficits of mature students can be overcome with available remedial methods. Some of the studies that report persistent decoding problems in mature students were described in Chapter 3. It was also noted in that context that the demands of academic work in college and high school leave very little time for remediation efforts.

Because a full-scale application of remedial efforts is not feasible in high school and college, the academic support program should be aimed at providing students with management strategies that will help them cope with academic problems and at teaching them learning skills that will facilitate academic achievement. The focus, therefore, is on reading to learn rather than learning to read. Coping or management techniques include assisting students in the selection of proper courses and instructors, providing help with written assignments, and providing tutorial assistance. The management component also includes provisions for psychological counseling for the student.

Reading Disabilities Versus Learning Disabilities

It is necessary to draw a distinction between RD and LD because many authors who write about learning skills programs tend to use the term *learning disabilities* rather than reading or writing disability. Throughout this book, we have preferred to use the term *reading disability* and, whenever possible, avoided the use of the term *learning disabilities*. When the term *learning disabilities* is used, it denotes reading disabilities. The preference for the former terminology is deliberate, the reason being that reading disability can be much more clearly defined than learning disability. In a discussion of the issue of defining learning disabilities, Hammill (1990) has presented 11 popular definitions. These definitions of learning disabilities include, in addition to difficulties in reading and writing, a wide variety of symptoms that range from poor perceptual motor skills to inadequate social skills. In addition to this absence of precision, learning disability as a concept lacks specificity because it also is often used as a catch-all term to describe all kinds of problems seen in students. For example, in a list of problems manifested by adults with LD, Vogel (1985) includes poor mathematic computation and reasoning, memory problems, sequencing problems, poor problem-solving ability, time management difficulties, poor social-interpersonal skills, and auditory and written language problems. In their list of characteristics of LD at the college level, Mangrum and Strichart (1984) include difficulties in acquiring information about

the world, understanding abstract concepts, distinguishing the important from the unimportant, reasoning, perceiving the correct orientation of complex visual figures, perceiving spatial attributes, fine-motor
coordination, organizing and budgeting time, social relationships, and
maintaining appropriate family relationships. These authors are non-
committal about the intellectual ability of learning disabled students
but make a general statement that the IQ of college students with LD is
not usually lower than 85. Johnson and Blalock (1987), in their book on
learning disabilities in adults, include problems in reading and writing, comprehension, personal appearance, keeping track of one's own
belongings, and finding one's way around the campus. Many authors
include attention deficits in this inexhaustible list of symptoms. As a
result, descriptions of LD include every conceivable problem.

Not only is the list of LD symptoms endless, but the validity of
most of these putative symptoms is debatable. The status of a percep-
tual-motor deficit as a form of LD is not clearly established. Furthermore, a number of studies indicate that perceptual deficits, if they can
be identified, do not contribute to reading disability. It is possible that
some apparently bright individuals may encounter difficulties with
math, but it has not been shown that math difficulty can exist indepen-
dently of reading disability. Indeed, a decoding deficit and poor computation skill may have a common origin. It should also be noted that
an attention deficit is a causal factor that can affect learning and is not a
learning disability by itself. This unrestrained conceptualization of LD
renders every student on campus a viable candidate for learning disability and makes diagnosis of LD meaningless. It is not reasonable to
expect colleges and high schools to be willing to set up programs that
will provide assistance to such an overwhelming number of students
and deal with such a limitless number of "deficits."

It is ironic that in spite of a lack of specificity in defining LD, it is
almost always diagnosed with the help of standardized reading
achievement tests. Consequently, regardless of how LD is defined, in
reality, it almost always refers to reading disability. Limiting the learning problems faced by students to difficulties associated with learning
to read and write reduces the number of students who require help
and renders the problem manageable. In essence, this means teaching
the appropriate strategies to students who experience difficulties in
reading and writing.

The academic skills program described in this book is concerned
with teaching students with reading disabilities strategies that are necessary for successful reading. According to Alley and Deshler (1979),
the learning strategies approach seems to be most effective with LD
adolescents who can deal with symbolic language and have normal IQ.

SRD, NSRD, and LAR

Should the principles of management and the learning skills that are taught to the students with different kinds of reading disabilities also be different? The principles of management and study skill strategies taught to these groups of disabled readers are the same, but the degree of emphasis placed on different strategies can vary from group to group. Generally speaking, in the case of the student with SRD, the management principles center around making choices in course selection by recommending courses that deal with concrete concepts rather than with abstractions. Courses in visual arts, technology, drafting and design, and architecture are examples of courses that might be recommended. The students' strengths and interests are also important in course selection. The instructional techniques focus on improving word recognition skills and on forming and writing grammatically correct sentences. Counseling should include opportunities for pointing out each student's strengths, and the avenues those strengths open up for the student.

Students with NSRD and those who are identified as LAR need to improve their comprehension skills as well as study skills. These students need to build adequate background information and schemata in subject matter areas and, therefore, require more tutorial help in the subject matter areas than SRD students. They need training in almost all skills required for success in the classroom including practice in effective listening, note-taking techniques, and test-taking techniques. Because these students may not reveal any area of particular strength, they may be expected to do best in courses that provide hands-on experiences. Compared to students with SRD, the academic prognosis for those with NSRD and LAR is much less optimistic.

Who Enrolls in the Reading Disability Program?

The management techniques described above and instructions in strategies for academic skills to be described in the next chapter make up the reading disability program. Enrollment in the reading disability program has to be mandatory for students who, once being admitted, are found to be backward in reading. We recommend that college freshmen who enter with an SAT verbal score below 400 *and* who fall below the 40th percentile in their graduating high school class take the Stanford Diagnostic Reading Test. Students whose reading comprehension is at or below the 10th grade should be required to enroll in the RD program. The reading comprehension subtest of SDRT is a timed test and takes 35 minutes to administer. Because many students with reading disabilities are also slow readers, they hardly ever complete

the test within this prescribed time. A differential diagnosis can be
made by asking the students to make a mark on their test sheets at the
end of the 35 minute period and then to complete the test. Students
who have good comprehension skill but poor decoding skill (SRD)
achieve satisfactory comprehension scores if they are allowed sufficient
time whereas students with poor comprehension skill (NSRD and
LAR) do not show appreciable improvement even when additional
test-taking time is provided. Thus, calculating the difference in the *inferential* comprehension scores achieved under timed and untimed condition can be useful in making a differential diagnosis. In high school,
students can be admitted into the program on the basis of recommendations made by the teachers as well as on the basis of their performance on the Stanford Diagnostic Reading Test.

Traditionally, the battery of tests used for identifying learning disability includes an intelligence test. Many experts advocate the use of
intelligence tests in college as well. The use of IQ tests in the diagnosis
of learning disability, however, is associated with numerous problems,
some of which were discussed in Chapter 3. A serious problem in the
use of intelligence tests arises in the context of instruction and management. As Salvia and Ysseldyke (1985) observed, a good assessment
practice should extend beyond making identification decisions, and
there should be continuity among screening, eligibility decision making, program planning, student progress monitoring, and program
evaluation. The intelligence test, as an assessment tool, does not lend
itself to such a continuity. In the field of learning disability, decisions
regarding eligibility, diagnosis, and remediation are treated as separate
issues, and the use of IQ is often limited to making eligibility decisions
about remedial services. Deno (1989) draws a parallel between the current LD diagnostic practices wherein there is little relationship between procedures that determine eligibility for services, treatment,
and program evaluation on the one hand and third party reimbursement systems concerned with insurance and welfare payments on the
other. But even in the health-care field, which is closer to psychology, a
discontinuity of this magnitude does not exist. For example, investigative procedures that are used for diagnostic purposes and procedures
that are used for Medicare reimbursement decisions are not different
from each other. Using two different sets of procedures for these purposes is a waste of time and money.

Using tests of reading and instruments related to reading provides
an economical and practical continuity between diagnosis and treatment. Decisions regarding eligibility for services in the LD field are
constrained by administrative and fiscal factors and are not made on
the basis of psychological needs. Such a situation is unfortunate and
need not exist in the case of reading disability. Having admitted stu-

dents with below-average reading skills, institutions of higher education have an obligation to extend help to all students who need it.

PRINCIPLES OF MANAGEMENT

Suggestions regarding management of reading disabilities are provided to the student in counseling sessions held before the start of the academic year. These suggestions are based on information obtained from formal testing and informal assessment procedures. Management strategies are not aimed at improving students' learning skills themselves but are designed to create conditions and circumstances that will enhance students' academic achievement. In essence, these are coping strategies. Management strategies can be classified into two broad categories: self-help strategies that are instituted by the student and those extended to the student from outside sources.

Self-Help Strategies

Some self-help strategies include a judicious selection of courses and instructors, sound management of time, the use of aids such as a tape-recorder to record lectures, and the use of a computer as an aid to writing essays. College freshmen can find the academic workload overwhelming. This is even more true in the case of the student who is not a proficient reader. The overwhelming demands of academic requirements can be minimized by taking a minimum number of required courses and by avoiding taking too many courses at once that require an excessive amount of reading. A semester course load of 12 hours appears to be ideal, but the student may start with a 15-hour load, which allows him or her to drop one course should it prove to be difficult and still maintain a full-time student status. It is also desirable to keep the number of courses that deal in abstractions to a minimum.

Many students with RD are diffident and, whenever possible, would prefer to remain anonymous by avoiding any interaction with their instructors and teachers. This tendency hardly benefits students with reading disabilities. It will work to the advantage of the student to perceive the instructor as a "coach" rather than as an antagonist who is out there "to get you." It is recommended that the student meet with the instructor during the first class meeting or even before that to explain the nature of the reading disability. Students with SRD may wish to divulge that their spelling is not the best, but that it is not for want of effort and that it does not reflect their general scholastic ability. During this first meeting with the instructor students may add that SRD, in addition to poor spelling, also means slow reading and explore the possibility of being given additional time for taking tests. This certainly is a reasonable request because, after all, most tests are intended to see whether students have mastered the required information and not how fast they can put it down on paper. Students with reading disabilities will be surprised to see that a majority of instructors are sympathetic towards them. To be fair to all students, the instructor can extend this privilege to any student who requests additional test-taking time. If the student needs to tape the lecture, the permission of the instructor to do so may be sought at this time. Students should avoid any instructors who are resistant to the idea of extending assistance to those with reading disabilities.

Help From External Sources

This form of help includes tutorial assistance, audio-taping of text books, and correcting the written essays for grammar and spelling errors.

Tutorial assistance   Almost all students classified as NSRD and LAR will require tutorial assistance in subject matter areas. The extent of tutorial assistance required by students is not uniform and varies depending on the student and the nature of the course. Tutorial help, when needed, is provided by the academic skills center. The following general principles are to be observed in providing tutorial assistance.

One of the most successful tutoring systems for students with reading disabilities is the mentor system. Rather than having many different tutors, a student with RD is assigned a mentor tutor, one with whom the student will meet daily to discuss his or her lessons, assignments, and exams. This does not mean that a student will never have other tutors who can help in specific subject matter areas. When the tutoring needs go beyond the capabilities of the mentor, it will be necessary to assign a subject matter specialist as a tutor. A knowledge of a student's needs and abilities, as well as the trust and development of positive interrelationships, cannot be brought about successfully by having numerous tutors.

Once a student and a mentor tutor have been paired, the tutor must begin by becoming familiar with the student's background, strengths, and weaknesses. One of the best sources of this information is the student.

High school seniors and college students can provide this information to the mentor tutor because they often recognize what they can do and cannot do and also are able to recognize the situations when they need help. The tutor can obtain additional information about a student by becoming knowledgeable about the student's test performance. Thus the tutoring process is not limited to discussions of academic matters alone but requires an understanding of the tutee as a student and a person.

Once the tutor has gathered such information about the student, it is necessary to design a program tailored to that student's needs. In so doing, a number of services and techniques can be employed. One of the services rendered by the tutor is audio-taping of textbooks. Students with SRD particularly are helped by listening to "taped books" or having the book read to them by a tutor or a reader. The use of "taped books," however, is not recommended by some authorities (e.g., Pauk 1983). The reason for this opinion is that textbooks contain too many anecdotes and examples that are interesting and illuminating but not always pertinent to the main topic. Textbooks also contain information that is redundant. Consequently, listening to a chapter that is taped verbatim can be very time consuming even though the repetitions and examples help reinforce the information the student has to learn.

Some of these problems, however, can be overcome by omitting, during taping, redundant information and parts of the text that are not relevant to the main topic. In essence, this amounts to summarizing information contained in the textbook and paraphrasing statements, when necessary. This requires that tutors who tape textbooks have a sound background knowledge of these particular subjects. According to Deshler and Graham (1980), instead of reading the text verbatim, the learning skills specialist can record a special version of the text by adopting certain principles. The following recommendations are adapted from suggestions made by these authors for handicapped secondary students.

1. With advice from subject matter experts, identify the most important content of the text and record only those sections that relate to the course objectives. If a tutor in the subject matter area is available he or she can do the taping.
2. Begin each chapter with an overview of the contents of that chapter.
3. Stress or repeat important points.
4. Explain briefly abstracts and concepts as well as technical terms.
5. Repeat key concepts.
6. Include a summary of the chapter and questions.

The student listening to the tape should simultaneously follow the corresponding passage in the textbook. This multisensory input can improve the retention of information.

Often students with RD need to have exams read aloud to them and this service can be rendered by a tutor. This procedure, of course, requires the consent of the instructor. In order to avoid embarrassment to a student, the place for this reading should be somewhere other than the classroom. Often an instructor's office offers privacy and is relatively free from interruptions. When reading tests, it is imperative that the tutor, who may know the material, be objective and careful not to allow voice inflections or other physical clues to divulge answers. Sometimes it may be necessary to rephrase a question in order to ensure that the student understands the question correctly.

Another service tutors often provide is helping a student with written work. One of the goals of education is to develop in students adequate written communicative skills. Students with reading disabilities, therefore, are expected eventually to learn to organize their thoughts and express themselves clearly and correctly through written language. For this reason, tutorial help with written work does not involve writing or rewriting essays for a student but is kept to a minimum. Instructions for writing good quality essays are provided in the academic skills program.

One of the tasks of a mentor tutor is to help students with RD learn gradually to proofread their own work. In our program, when students bring written assignments in for proofreading, the tutor asks the student to read the work aloud. Often, a student can detect some of the errors of omission and so is able to correct these mistakes even before turning the paper over to the tutor. Wong and Wong (1986) report that the COPS strategy improves the proofreading skills of students with reading disability. The acronym COPS stands for capitalization, organization, punctuation, and spelling. Being sensitive to COPS errors gives the student a sequence of things to check when proofreading his or her own compositions. As noted in Chapter 2, students with SRD are prone to commit numerous errors of spelling and syntax. They may need help in these areas also.

By using a personal computer, a reading-disabled student can minimize dependency on the tutor. Students, therefore, need to acquire word-processing skills as soon as possible because the spell-check program is an invaluable tool for students with reading disabilities. If the student has no keyboard skills, they can be learned in the academic skills course.

While students who make spelling and grammatical errors are relatively easy to help, those with comprehension difficulties are faced with a much more serious problem. Consequently, students who are identified as having NSRD and LAR require much more tutorial assistance. These students need in-depth instruction in subject matter areas in addition to training in comprehension monitoring. The need for in-depth instruction in subject areas arises for two reasons: an inability of a student to focus on the main idea of the text and a lack of sufficient schema pertinent to the material in the text. The first reason is that the student is not able to understand what must be known for a specific assignment or academic task. This problem is closely related to the inability to identify the main idea in a text and differentiate it from supporting ideas. Everything seems to be equally important. Students are given special training in developing these skills in the academic skills course described in the next chapter. Tutoring sessions offer an excellent opportunity to practice the techniques presented in that course. The tutor and the student can carry out these steps together, thinking through the content matter of the text. This also provides an opportunity for the tutor to model his or her own cognitive processes so that the student can see how the tutor thinks about the subject matter and the project at hand.

One method of modeling reportedly helpful in improving comprehension is a form of role-playing called Reciprocal Teaching (Palincsar 1986). In this approach, tutor and student take turns leading a dialogue on sections of a text. The steps in Reciprocal Teaching are these: clarification of task demands, activation of background knowledge, focusing on the main idea, evaluation of content *via* background knowledge, monitoring comprehension, and drawing and testing inferences and conclusions. One of the most salient features of this technique is that the roles of the tutor and student are periodically reversed so that the student learns the cognitive processes without always being the follower. In this manner, the student is encouraged to develop some independence and self-confidence that will ultimately lead to freedom from dependence on the tutor.

The second reason for comprehension failure is that the RD student does not possess sufficient background information to comprehend the subject matter. This problem arises partly from lack of reading experience and partly from RD students not having the relevant schema. In tutoring sessions it is essential for the tutor to find methods to activate the schemata relevant to the academic task at hand. If a student does not have the necessary background information, the tutor will have to provide it. Students often do not have sufficient historical and scientific knowledge and are, therefore, unable to relate the concepts and ideas presented in class to the relevant schema. The following case is an example.

> P.R., one of our students, came to see the tutor about a story he had been assigned to read for freshman English class. An average student, he had been retained in elementary school and still resents the fact that he was not provided with help there. In college, he was determined to succeed and took advantage of every opportunity for help. In his weekly meetings with his tutor, he discussed each of his courses and what he needed to do for the week. With this particular story, however, he was quite frustrated. "It was real long, but I've read every bit of it," he said, and he could recite

the names of all the characters. When asked about the setting, however, he was not so sure. "It's way back in the Middle Ages, or something like that," he replied. When asked about the plot, he said that nothing made sense; it was just about a party. The story was James Joyce's "The Dead." But P.R. had no concept of early twentieth century Dublin or of the manners and attitudes of the people who lived there, a fact that made comprehension of the story almost impossible.

As noted earlier, students with NSRD and LAR are also deficient in comprehension monitoring and, therefore, require specific training in this skill. As discussed in Chapter 2, comprehension monitoring is one of the two aspects of metacognition, the other being correct self-evaluation. Some comprehension monitoring training can be provided during tutorial sessions. As the student or the tutor reads aloud from a text or class notes, the tutor stops periodically to ask the student questions about what has been learned or heard up to that point and also about what the student expects to hear in the next few paragraphs. If the student does not remember sufficient information, the tutor provides prompts until the student is able to respond correctly. If rereading is necessary, then they must go over some of the material that already had been read. The goal is to teach the student to monitor comprehension and to become aware when he or she does not understand the text.

The following general psychological principles should be observed by tutors while they are engaged in tutorial work:

1. The main goal of tutors is to help students with reading disabilities do well in their academic courses. While tutors should assist students to attain this goal, they should not do the students' work.
2. Tutors must maintain an attitude of respect and not superiority toward their tutees. While a student may not read fluently, he or she may possess other skills and may be quite intelligent. In other words, tutors should be knowledgeable enough to separate decoding and spelling skills from general intellectual ability.
3. If a student makes errors while reading aloud, the tutor should ignore them unless such errors will interfere with comprehension. It is good to remember that a tutor's main goal is to improve comprehension and not word recognition skills. If a student is an extremely slow reader and has great difficulty in recognizing words, the tutor will have to read the text aloud so the student can listen.
4. A tutor should try to avoid using terms such as *no, don't, not like that,* and *you are wrong*. Positive feedback and attention are necessary for success.
5. A tutor should be a good listener.
6. A tutor must understand that there are different kinds of reading problems. Some students may be able to pronounce words well but

not be able to grasp the meaning; some can understand the meaning of words but cannot pronounce them well. In other words, a tutor should have sufficient background knowledge about different kinds of reading disabilities.

7.   Finally, a tutor should remember that tutoring is a cooperative venture; it is not helpful when a tutor sends a student alone to a room with instructions to outline chapters or answer questions found at the end of a chapter.

In fact, the job of the tutors, especially that of the mentor tutors, is both more varied and more important than almost any other because it is with these persons that the students actually spend the most time. In many cases, the program administrators only see students as they enter or exit the program or when crises arise. Tutors, however, see students for years, often on a daily basis, and it is with the tutors that long and close relationships usually develop. These relationships are extremely valuable to the RD student, for out of them grow feelings of confidence and self-worth as well as a sense of not fighting the battle alone. And frequently, RD students have never experienced these feelings in an academic setting before. Thus, the tutorial component of an academic support program must be organized carefully and supervised because tutors can teach and model study skills, metacognitive skills, task-approach behaviors, and survival techniques. They, indeed, are the heart of the academic support program, and as such, they are concurrently teachers, counselors, confidants, and friends.

Chapter 5

The Academic Skills Program

I.   INTRODUCTION
II. SYNOPSES OF LECTURES
     A. Note Taking
     B. Listening Comprehension
     C. Vocabulary
     D. Spelling
     E. Reading Comprehension
     F. Metacognitive Skills
     G. Writing Skills
     H. Test-Taking Skills
III. THE USE OF COMPUTERS IN THE ACADEMIC SKILLS COURSE
     A. Criteria in Selecting Software Programs
     B. Summaries of Selected Software
         1. *Grammar and Punctuation*
         2. *Vocabulary*
         3. *Reading Comprehension*
         4. *Writing Skills*
         5. *Readability Estimation*

INTRODUCTION

Teaching the strategies necessary for success in academic courses is a service for students with reading disabilities and is, therefore, an integral part of the reading disabilities program. The extent to which any student utilizes the opportunities provided in such a course depends, to a large extent, on the motivation level of the student. Because of past failures, many students with reading disabilities lack the motivation needed for the maximum utilization of opportunities available in college and high school. For this reason, basic academic skills are best imparted to students with reading disabilities through an academic skills course in a highly structured format.

The academic skills course provides training in the use of several strategies required for academic success. These include note-taking and test-taking techniques, writing skills, and strategies to improve listening comprehension, reading comprehension, vocabulary, and meta-cognition. The basic principles that underlie these skills are introduced in a lecture format and students are provided with hands-on experience in the classroom to try out what they learned from the lectures. The content of these lectures and exercises are presented in this chapter.

In our institution we offer the academic skills course as part of the general education curriculum as a 3-hour credit course and not as an extra-curricular activity. We believe that the course should be mandatory for students who are in the reading disability program and for those who are thought to be at risk. This includes entering freshmen with an SAT verbal score below 400 and those who fall below the 40th percentile in their graduating high school class. In high school all students identified as having a learning disability and those recommended by teachers can be accommodated in the course. Optimal results can be expected from the academic skills course if it is taken when students enter college or during the summer that precedes college entry in the case of those who have graduated from high school. Many colleges offer such a preparatory course and require students who are thought to be deficient in academic skills to take it. There is some disagreement as to whether or not a "remedial" course should be part of the regular college curriculum and offered on a credit basis because college students are expected to have mastered the basic academic skills before they enter college. There are, however, some advantages in offering it as a regular course for credit. When it is offered as a non-credit course, much of the seriousness that is associated with a regular course is lost, and this usually results in poor attendance. Eventually the objectives of the course are compromised. Another reason to offer credit is that a course in study skills is not necessarily a remedial course. It is designed as a self-improvement course that is open to all students. Even though a majority of students enrolled in an academic skills course might have experienced learning difficulties in the past, students with no previous history of reading disability also frequently express a desire to enroll in the course. As a matter of fact, students who are maintaining a C or B grade gain the most from such a course. A grade of C or B, of course, does not mean an absence of a reading disability. In fact, many students with SRD maintain a decent grade-point average. This is not only our impression but is also documented by research studies. For instance, Cordoni (1982) reports that of the 46 students enrolled in Project Achieve at Southern Illinois University during the years 1980 and 1981, a majority maintained a B average in their chosen field. Four of these students were able to make the Dean's list.

At Indiana State University the course is offered as a 3-hour credit course under the title *The Psychology of Effective Study* by the Department of Educational and School Psychology. The skill level and needs of the students who enroll in this course vary a great deal. Upon entering the course, nearly one third of the students are maintaining a B grade; nevertheless, they wish to improve their grade point averages. Almost all of them attain this goal.

The academic skills course is designed to provide a good deal of hands-on experience for the students. Usually, each class begins with a lecture that introduces the basic techniques and strategies relevant to the topic. This is followed by students' completing exercises and reporting back to the entire class, at which point both the instructor and other students in the class react to the report. Several books on study skills improvement are available, and most of these books also contain exercises that can be used both in the classroom and given as take-home assignments. We have used the following books and found them to be satisfactory.

1. Cortina, J., Elder, J., and Gonnet, K. 1989. *Comprehending College Textbooks: Steps to Understanding and Remembering What You Read.* New York: McGraw Hill.
2. Fry, E. 1986. *Vocabulary Drills, Advanced Level.* Providence, RI: Jamestown Publishers.
3. Sotiriou, P. 1989. *Integrating College Study Skills: Reasoning in Reading, Listening, and Writing,* (2nd Edition). Belmont, CA: Wadsworth.

4. Pauk, W. 1986. *Six-Way Paragraphs, Advanced Level.* Providence, RI:
    Jamestown Publishers.

The following books are recommended by Scheiber and Talpers (1987):

1. McWhorter, T. 1983. *College Reading and Study Skills.* Waltham, MA:
    Little, Brown and Co.
2. Fitzpatrick, E. M. 1982. *College Study Skills Program Level III.* Reston,
    VA: National Association of Secondary School Principals.
3. Pauk, W. 1983. *How to Study in College,* 3rd ed. Burlington, MA:
    Houghton Mifflin Co.
4. O'Brien, L. 1985. *S.O.S. Strengthening of Skills.* Rockville, MD: Spe-
    cific Diagnostics, Inc.
5. Turkel-Kesselman, K., and Peterson, F. 1981. *Study Smarts: How to
    Learn More in Less Time.* Chicago, IL: Contemporary Books, Inc.

Students discuss completed take-home assignment exercises in subsequent class meetings. During each class meeting, students are required to complete some lessons and assignments on the personal
computer. Satisfactory execution of all these activities, including the
lecture, requires more than two hours of class time. We have found that
a class meeting of three hours, once per week, is a satisfactory arrangement. The three-hour meeting is not fatiguing to the students because
the class time is filled with a variety of activities and the students are
kept active most of the time. Because the instructor often has to interact on a one-to-one basis with the students, the enrollment has to be
kept within reasonable limits, not exceeding 15. The students' overall
performance in the course is determined on the basis of their attendance, completion of take-home assignments, and participation in the
classroom activities.

A course outline that shows the topics covered along with the exercises and assignments is shown in table 5.1.

The computer has become an important instructional aid. Even
though much of the educational software that is available is designed
for children in elementary and junior high schools, a few software programs are aimed at older students. Some of these software programs
are described at the end of this chapter.

During the first meeting of the class, the nature and requirements
of the course are described and the Stanford Diagnostic Reading Test
(*Form A*) is administered as a pretest to those who have not taken it
before. Form B of the test is administered at the end of the course as a
posttest, and the difference between the performance in the two tests
provides a measure of the effectiveness of the course.

The first lecture is on note taking and listening comprehension.
Students are asked to take notes during the lecture. At the end of the
lecture, some of the students are asked to read their notes aloud, and

Table 5.1. Course Outline

Educational and School Psychology 200: The Psychology of Effective Study
Credit: 3 Hours. Spring, 1990
Prerequisites: None Mon. 6:15–9:00

Date	Topic	Assignment
Jan. 15	Introduction; pretest; note-taking; listening comprehension.	Read Sotiriou, Ch. 9. Assignment: Sotiriou, Ch. 9.1 & 9.2.
Jan. 22	Lecture: The reading process; vocabulary and spelling. Exercise: Fry, Unit 1. Software: Bearings (Spelling).	Read Sotiriou, Ch. 10 & 11. Assignment: Sotiriou, Ch. 10 & 11.
Jan. 29	Lecture: Reading comprehension (main idea, topic sentence). Exercise: Pauk, Units 48–50. Software: Grammar Gremlins.	Read Sotiriou, Ch. 3. Assignment: Sotiriou, Ch. 3; Fry, Unit 2.
Feb. 5	Lecture: Reading comprehension (major and minor details). Exercise: Pauk, 51–54. Software: Vocabulary Devt., (Hefte and Doody).	Read Sotiriou, Ch. 4. Assignment: Sotiriou, Ch. 4; Fry, Unit 3.
Feb. 12	Lecture: Reading comprehension (inferential comprehension). Exercise: Pauk, 55–57. Software: Vocabulary Adventure.	Read Sotiriou, Ch. 6. Assignment: Sotiriou, Ch. 6; Fry, Unit 4.
Feb. 19	Lecture: Reading comprehension (organizational pattern of the text). Exercise: Fry Unit 4; Pauk, 56–60. Software: Skills Bank II.	Read Sotiriou, Ch. 5; Read Cortina et al., Ch. 6. Assignment: Sotiriou, Ch. 5 & Cortina et al., Ch. 6.
Feb. 26	Lecture: Reading comprehension (summarizing and paraphrasing). Exercise: Fry, Unit 5; Pauk, 61–63. Software: Skills Bank II.	Read Sotiriou, Ch. 8 and complete exercises.
Mar. 5	Lecture: Cognitive style; metacognition. Exercise: Pauk, 64–70. Software: 88 Passages.	Assignment: Fry, Units 6 & 7.

continued

Table 5.1. *continued*

Date	Topic	Assignment
Mar. 12	Lecture: Writing skills development. Exercise: Pauk, 71–75; Fry, Unit 8. Software: 88 Passages.	Assignment: Read Sotiriou, Ch. 12 and complete exercises.
Mar. 19	Lecture: Writing skills development. Exercise: Pauk, 76–80; Fry, Unit 9. Software: 88 Passages.	Exercise: Analyze the organizational pattern of the article supplied to you and provide a summary. Construct sentences using 20 words from the list provided.
Mar. 26	Lecture: Writing skills. Exercise: Discussion of the take-home assignments; Pauk, 81–85. Software: Bank Street Writer II.	Write a two-page article on the topic provided. Construct sentences using 20 words from the list provided.
Apr. 9	Lecture: Writing skills. Exercise: Discussion of the take-home assignment; Pauk, 86–90. Software: Bank Street Writer II.	A two-page article on the topic provided. Construct sentences using 20 words from the list provided. Use the computer and compute the readability index of your essays.
Apr. 16	Lecture: Writing skills. Exercise: Pauk, 91–95. Discussion of the take-home assignment.	Complete the assignments missed.
Apr. 23	Lecture: Test-taking strategies Exercise: Pauk, 96–100; Fry, Unit 10. Software: 88 Passages	Read Sotiriou, Ch. 14 & 15. Assignment: Construct a 50 item multiple choice and a 20 item T/F test from chapters in your subject matter textbooks; complete exercises in Sotiriou, Ch. 14 & 15.
Apr. 30	Review of the course; Posttest.	

the instructor uses this opportunity to point out the good features, comment on the mistakes made in note taking, and offer constructive suggestions as to how to improve note-taking skill.

In the following pages, basic principles concerning the different academic skills to be mastered by students are presented in the form of synopses. The instructor can explain the ideas presented in the synopses to the students with the aid of examples and demonstrations. Each synopsis is preceded by a brief introductory remark that is addressed to the instructor. The synopses appear in italics.

NOTE TAKING

Even though taking notes from lectures appears to be a relatively easy skill to master, many students with reading disabilities are deficient in this skill. Experienced instructors can quite readily spot those students in the classroom who are likely to perform poorly on examinations by observing their note-taking behavior. Some students fail to write down those points considered to be important by the instructor, which may be potential test questions; instead they write down relatively unimportant information presented in the lecture. Other students display the opposite form of behavior by indiscriminately taking down everything they hear. Both kinds of students can profit by following the principles presented in the following synopsis.

An important thing to remember while taking notes is that one cannot and should not take down everything the teacher says. You should write down only what is important and disregard the unimportant. In order to separate the important from the unimportant, you should know the main idea that is to be covered during the lecture. Every good lecture has at least one main idea in addition to several details that are presented to support the main idea. Some lectures may contain more than one main idea. Lectures also contain anecdotes, jokes, and stories that are used as devices to hold the attention of the listener. Good teachers also use numerous illustrations and examples to clarify the main idea. These are often superfluous as far as note taking is concerned. Often, lecturers express the same idea in different forms, a practice that results in redundant statements. If you focus on the meaning of such statements, you should be able to reduce the amount of note taking by not recording repetitive statements.

Most instructors state the main idea explicitly at the beginning of the lecture. It is, therefore, important to pay close attention to the opening remarks made by the instructor. The main idea also can be surmised by reading the course outline that lists the dates of class meetings along with the topics to be covered during those meetings. Instructors usually provide such outlines for the courses they teach. It is also helpful to preview the chapter in the textbook that corresponds to the topic before attending class. Such previewing does not involve critical reading but can be accomplished by a quick reading of the chapter summary and a cursory examination of the subtopics. Once the main idea is identified, it can be kept at the back of the mind and can be used as a point of reference to evaluate incoming information for its relevancy to the topic presented.

Notes taken should be in a reasonably well organized format so that they can be read easily later. When they start the lecture, many instructors describe the organizational pattern they will use in the lecture. For instance, the instructor may say, "Today, I am going to introduce three theories of personality and discuss their relative strengths and weaknesses." Such an opening remark gives the important information that the lecture has three major ideas; it also provides an overall framework of the lecture that can be used to organize information that is presented. You can construct a skeleton outline, like the one shown in table 5.2, leaving plenty of space between subtitles and filling in details as they are delivered. Even three separate notebook pages can be used to take down information about the three main ideas.

If an organizational pattern is not readily discernable from the lecture, then you will have to provide your own. Learning-skills experts have developed several note taking formats such as "laddering," "mapping," and "the Cornell system," and you can follow any one of these systems in developing your notes (see Sotiriou 1989 for a description of these systems). Notes also can be organized in such a way that major points can be written on the left-hand page and the supporting ideas on the facing right-hand page of the notebook.

An important function of classnotes is that when read again they arouse your memory of facts and ideas heard during the lecture. For this reason, listening to the lecture is more important than taking notes. One common weakness seen in many students is that they invest more attention to the note taking activity and thereby miss important points covered in the lecture. If it is thought that note taking is a hindrance to listening, the possibility of audiotaping the lecture should be explored. This requires prior permission from the instructor. Taping the lecture, however, is not a substitute for note taking; the important points covered in the lecture should still be noted carefully and systematically. The gaps in classnotes can be filled in later by replaying the tape. This is an important point that is worth repeating. That is, high priority should be given to listening to the lecture and understanding the topic; note taking should be considered only as an aid to memory.

Table 5.2. Outline for a Lecture

Lecture 1: Psychology of Personality. Jan. 15.	
Theory of personality No. 1.	
	Strengths:
	Weaknesses:
Theory No. 2.	Strengths:
	Weaknesses:
Theory No. 3	Strengths:
	Weaknesses:

LISTENING COMPREHENSION

Perhaps the most important single factor that determines what students learn in the classroom is their listening comprehension skill and the extent to which they make use of this skill. A failure in listening comprehension can affect note taking considerably. Students who are deficient in listening comprehension skill are equally poor in reading comprehension also. Poor listening comprehension can be the result of two factors: lack of motivation or interest in the subject matter of the lecture or the student's inability to relate what he or she hears to what he or she already knows. Development of adequate background knowledge and schemata can minimize the influence of these factors.

Note taking is recording information on a sheet of paper whereas listening is recording information in the mind. For this reason, many of the strategies that enhance note-taking skill also facilitate listening comprehension. It is much easier to remember information that is meaningful than bits of isolated information that do not make up a coherent theme. Information becomes meaningful when what one hears can be related to what one already knows. The background information or schema one has is helpful in molding isolated bits of information into meaningful units. Such a "chunking" process reduces the cognitive load. The main idea contained in a lecture activates the appropriate schemata and acts as a cementing material to integrate isolated bits of information into a unified theme. Once the main idea is identified, the minor details presented in the lecture can be latched on to it. Identifying the main idea and keeping it in mind as you listen to the lecture promotes listening comprehension. If the lecture contains more than one main idea, pay attention to all of them.

Being cognizant of the organizational pattern of a lecture also facilitates comprehension, retention, and the subsequent recall of information presented. Information is stored in a systematic fashion in our minds and this storage is referred to by psychologists as the mental lexicon. *Because information is stored in an organized format, efficient storage and recall of information is facilitated when the input information is also organized. That is, when you listen to a lecture or read an essay, try not to memorize isolated facts, rather arrange or group the information to be learned in meaningful units.*

Because instructors routinely use tests and examinations to see whether or not students have learned what has been presented in the lecture, a major goal of the academic skills course is to enable you to become proficient in test-taking strategies. Preparation for tests does not begin a day or a week before the test; it begins the first time the lecture is delivered. It will be helpful to keep the following questions at the back of your mind as you listen to a lecture: "Can this statement be a question? Is this statement important enough to appear as a test question?" Lecturers often provide clues that indicate that a statement is a potential question. They do so by repeating the statement, changing the stress pattern of their expression, by altering the speed of delivery, or even by explicitly stating that the particular statement is very important.

The lecture on listening comprehension is followed by completing textbook and computer exercises assigned for that date.

During the next meeting the instructor lectures on the reading process, vocabulary, and spelling. The lecture on the reading process is essentially a simplified version of the information presented in Chapter 1 and is not repeated here.

VOCABULARY DEVELOPMENT

Vocabulary is an important correlate of reading ability. Vocabulary and comprehension have a reciprocal relationship in the sense that students with a larger vocabulary comprehend more than students with a limited vocabulary; the more students comprehend, the more they know; and the more they know, the more they comprehend. As noted in Chapter 1, students who have been avid readers know more words than those with a history of poor reading. Many students with reading disabilities have a history of poor reading, and for this reason, a certain amount of direct teaching of vocabulary is necessary in the academic skills course. Bringing the vocabulary of reading-disabled students up to a level that is necessary for comprehending subject matter areas is a basic goal of the academic skills program. Some authorities believe that the best way to acquire new words is to meet them in context. They believe that rote memorization of individual words is not usually a very effective means of building vocabulary because it is difficult to remember isolated bits of information. Words become meaningful when they are encountered in sentences and are, therefore, easier to remember. This makes the teaching of vocabulary by pairing a word or list of words with their respective dictionary meaning less effective than presenting those words embedded in sentences. Meeting words in books also provides an opportunity for repeated encounters with the same word and thereby facilitates retention. This means that extensive reading is an effective way to improve vocabulary.

Words also become meaningful when their linguistic origins and etymology are appreciated. They gain meaning also when presented in association with their antonyms, synonyms, and in the context of a group of words belonging to the same semantic family. Efforts to teach words with reference to their etymology, synonyms, antonyms, and the family to which they belong is referred to as *direct teaching of vocabulary.* Many experts recommend this method of teaching vocabulary because they believe encountering new words in texts is fortuitous and slow. Three different approaches are recommended for the direct teaching of vocabulary. They are: *semantic mapping, cluster analysis,* and *morphological analysis.*

The academic skills course offers an opportunity to carry out exercises on semantic mapping, cluster analysis, and morphological analysis. Some textbooks on study skills contain such exercises (e.g., *Vocabulary Drill,* by Fry 1985). These books, however, contain a limited number of words and may not have words that are usually encountered in college-level textbooks. The instructor, therefore, will have to prepare special exercises that incorporate vocabulary from college textbooks.

The computer provides an excellent opportunity to build students' vocabulary. Unfortunately, many of the currently available software programs are not aimed at college-level students. Some of the available computer programs are described at the end of the chapter.

Words that are encountered in context are more readily understood and retained in memory than words that are read in isolation. Words become meaningful when they are encountered repeatedly in sentences. Such words are, therefore, quite readily learned. This type of encounter, however, is largely determined by chance and, therefore, cannot be relied upon entirely as a means of building vocabulary. You have, therefore, to make some special efforts to learn words by creating the context. Experts recommend three ways of making words meaningful by creating context. These are: semantic mapping, cluster analysis, *and* morphological analysis.

Semantic Mapping: *This is a process whereby the relationship between a word and related words and concepts are portrayed by constructing a visual display. Such a diagram is assumed to match the organizational format of the semantic lexicon.*

Johnson and Pearson (1984) have provided guidelines for teaching vocabulary through the semantic mapping procedure. The steps recommended for the construction of semantic maps presented here is in a slightly modified form. Students can follow this procedure and construct semantic maps for words and concepts found in their textbooks. Procedures that can be useful in constructing semantic maps along with illustrations are provided also by Heimlich and Pittelman (1986).

Following are the steps you should follow when constructing a semantic map.

1. *Choose a word or topic from the textbook.*
2. *Write the word or concept on a large sheet of paper.*
3. *Think of as many words or concepts as possible that are related to the word and put them on the paper and connect them to the target word in some*

systematic way. For example, synonyms of the target word can be placed on one side of the paper, and antonyms on the other side.

Semantic mapping also can be used as a study skill device while reading the textbook or during note taking. Under such circumstances, the main idea becomes the pivot and the major and minor supporting details are organized as separate categories and then connected to the main idea with lines. Such a graphic representation of information can be helpful to many of you who complain of difficulties in remembering verbal materials.

Cluster Analysis: *This is similar to semantic mapping but is limited to the development of a family of related words or concepts. The process includes identifying words that are related to a single concept or idea and then learning these words by noting the similarities and subtle differences among them. For example, the basic concept is* mental activities. *Words that are related to this concept include common words such as:* think, forget, remember, guess, wonder, *or* solve, *and unusual words such as* ponder, perceive, *and* cognize. *Related concepts such as intelligence, artificial intelligence, and subconscious can also be introduced in this context. These groups of words and concepts are referred to as category lists.*

The similarity between category lists and the "set model" of the mental lexicon is obvious. The above example is taken from Marzano and Marzano (1988).

Morphological Analysis: *A large number of words encountered in texts are combinations of root morphemes and affixes. Sometimes two words are combined to make a compound word. Psychologists and linguists think that root morphemes and suffixes are stored in separate mental lexicons; experts have also noted that errors in the proper use of suffixes are quite common in the oral reading and writing of disabled readers. Analyzing words into root morphemes and their affixes is, therefore, likely to increase your awareness about the morphological structure of words.*

It is also thought that morphological analysis of words enables the reader to capture the meaning of some unfamiliar words even though some experts question the usefulness of such training as a method of increasing vocabulary. However, Henry (1989) reports that dyslexic students who were taught the structural nature of words and trained to use structural analysis showed significant gains in both reading and spelling. In her training program Henry required elementary school children to identify structural and morphemic patterns (consonants, diagraphs, prefixes, suffixes, etc.) of words of three etymological origins, namely, Anglo-Saxon, Romance, and Greek.

A knowledge of the origins of English words can also help you comprehend many words. Most English language words are of Anglo-Saxon, Romance, or Greek origin. Anglo-Saxon words are the common, everyday words, and most of them have a consistent pattern of pronunciation (e.g., cap, stand, sister, forbidden*). Several words, however, do not conform to the common spelling-sound pattern, and these have to be memorized by rote. Many Romance words are technical words and primarily of Latin and French origin. Many of these words also follow simple letter-sound correspondences even though the stress pattern can be complex (e.g.,* excellent, direction*). Suffixes such as* tion, tious, tial, sion, cial, cious *are common in Romance words. Knowing that many affixes are of Latin origin can be helpful in realizing the meaning of many words (e.g.,* aud = *"hear" as in audience, audible;* dict = *"speak" as in predict, verdict;* fac = *"make" as in factory, facsimile). Greek words are generally compound words (e.g.,* microscope, hemisphere, physiology*). A knowledge of Greek root-words can facilitate understanding the meaning of some uncommon words (e.g.,* ast = *"star" as in aster, astronaut;* phon = *"sound" as in phonics, phoneme;* andr = *"male" as in androgynous, polyandry;* gyn = *"female" as in misogynist, monogyny;* morph = *"shape" as in amorphous, morphology).*

Lists of words along with descriptions of the nature and origins of these words can be found in these books: *Words, Tutor I and Tutor II* by Henry (1990) and *The New Reading Teacher's Book of Lists* by Fry, Fountoukidis, and Polk (1985).

Despite the fact that a large number of words have come into the English language from other languages, words tend to change their meanings over a period of time. Some of these changes are: generalization, *wherein the word acquires additional meanings (e.g.,* chair, grass*);* pejoration, *wherein a word takes on a negative connotation (e.g.,* maverick; machiavellian*);* amelioration, *wherein a word takes on a positive connotation (e.g.,* cowboy; black*); and* euphemism, *wherein a somewhat negative meaning is expressed by neutral words (e.g.,* revenue enhancement *instead of* tax, patient outcome negative *instead of* the patient died*).*

Very often you will encounter unfamiliar words that do not lend themselves to easy analysis and whose meanings, therefore, remain obscure. The meaning of some of these words can be inferred by examining the context in which the word occurs. Writers use several types of context cues to elucidate their writing, including the following: restatement *(e.g.,* The point he was making was banal and commonplace*);* definition *(e.g.,* Altruistic behavior, or sacrificing one's own interest for the weflare of others, can be seen even in animals*);* contrast *(e.g.,* John was brusque in his behavior, but his wife was more agreeable*); and* comparison *(e.g.,* John can be described as an ingenuous person, but his wife is shrewd and clever*).*

SPELLING

The ability to spell a word correctly and the ability to decode it and pronounce it accurately are highly related to each other. Sometimes the only symptom that can be seen in mature students with reading disabilities is their poor spelling. It was noted in Chapter 2 that these students have acquired adequate word recognition skills by developing a substantial sight vocabulary but that careful testing reveals subtle reading difficulties and that they are somewhat slow readers. If this were not so, the so called "good reader but poor speller" should be able to read his or her own writing and correct the spelling mistakes. In these students, the spelling deficit stands out more than the reading deficit because spelling is a recall task that requires the reproduction of all the graphemes in a word in the correct sequence, whereas reading is primarily a recognition task that can be accomplished on the basis of partial cues. For this reason, spelling is a more difficult task to master than reading.

Some investigators have analyzed the spelling error patterns of poor readers and have attempted to classify poor spellers into subtypes. This is based on the expectation that if phonological skill and visual memory are involved in the spelling process, deficiency in either process can result in defective spelling of two different kinds. If the validity of spelling subtypes can be unequivocally established, it means that one type of spelling error is caused by a deficit in the phonological process and the other by a deficit in the visual-orthographic process. For example, spelling *city* as "sity" and *girl* as "gal" is claimed to be a weakness of visual-orthographic process and an overreliance on phonological process, whereas spelling *city* as "ctiy" and *girl* as "gril" is indicative of the opposite pattern. Research, however, suggests that these "subtypes" really reflect different stages in the acquisition of spelling skills rather than differences that are enduring and qualitative in nature (e.g., Phillips, Taylor, and Aaron 1985). This interpretation of spelling errors is further supported by the observation that the spelling errors committed by college students are almost exclusively phonetic (e.g., *city*—"sity") and a substantial number of errors committed by children in early primary grades is nonphonetic (e.g., *city*—"ctiy"). A more appropriate interpretation of the two types of spelling errors would be that they both reflect a basic weakness of phonological process, nonphonetic errors reflecting a failure to master even the most elementary spelling–pronunciation rules and phonetic errors reflecting a failure to master the more advanced rules.

Being an automatized skill, spelling is also independent of comprehension skill. In other words, an individual can be a poor speller but still intelligent. Many teachers and college instructors, unfortunately, equate poor spelling with intellectual obtuseness. Considering the close relationship between decoding and spelling, it is not surprising that the spelling skill of mature students with reading disabilities, like decoding skill, hardly improves. The instructor should be careful not to expect significant improvements in the spelling skills of students with reading disability and not to expend much time and energy in exercises that are designed to improve spelling skill. It is also worth remembering that the spelling checks that are part of word-processing programs for the computer have considerably enhanced our ability to produce documents that are virtually free of spelling errors.

There is an intimate relationship between reading and spelling because phonological skill plays an important role in both these processes. Pronunciation of the written word is governed by certain rules and it is thought that these rules are stored in a specialized mental lexicon, called the phonological lexicon. *Experts also believe that there may exist an orthographic lexicon in which visual representations of words are stored. Our ability to correctly spell homophones such as* read—reed, meet—meat, *or* there—their *is often cited as evidence for the existence of such a lexicon because members of the homophone pairs can be distinguished from each other only on the basis of their visual features. Nevertheless, there is a considerable amount of uncertainty regarding the nature of visual memory, and visual representation of words may be a necessary, but not sufficient, condition for spelling words correctly in alphabetic languages. In other words, poor spelling cannot be attributed to poor visual memory. This view is confirmed by the findings of several studies that reveal that a knowledge of spelling—pronunciation relationships (grapheme—phoneme rules) is essential for correct spelling.*

Production of the correct spelling of a word involves three stages: correct analysis of speech sounds and identifying the constituent phonemes in the word, conversion of phonemes into graphemes, and selection of the conventionally correct graphemes from all the phonetically plausible graphemes (Frith 1980). This shows that there is a close relationship between decoding and spelling because pronunciation of the written word also involves phoneme identification and phonological analysis. As a matter of fact, the correlation coefficient between performance of children on nonword reading tests and their performance on spelling tests is as high as .75 (Aaron 1989a).

Can anything at all be done to improve spelling skills? Available evidence suggests that rote memorization of spelling patterns and spelling—pronunciation correspondence rules does not bring about appreciable results. The most frequently encountered spelling errors seen in mature students arise because of confusion among similar-sounding words or between a word and a similar-

looking nonword (e.g., there–their, piece–peace, elicit–illicit, disease–decease; separate–seperate, necessary–nessesary*). Under such circumstances, correct spelling depends on making the right choice, thus making spelling almost a multiple choice test. A knowledge of the word's meaning, its origin, and its structure can increase the probability of selecting the correct spelling and produce some positive results, but even here the expectation should be modest.*

Word Meaning: *Spelling patterns of the English language are more conducive to the extraction of meaning of many words than to the execution of their pronunciation. As stated by Venezky (1980), English spelling is a phonemically based system that preserves morphemic identity wherever possible. For example, the silent letter /k/ in the word* know *is helpful in quickly identifying it as different from the word* no *even though the pronunciation of the two words is similar; the words* disease *and* decease *facilitate the quick extraction of the corresponding meanings, "not at ease" and "cease." This psychological advantage, in addition to the fact that, unlike spoken language, printed language is formal and resistant to change, has helped to preserve the spelling pattern over a period of time. Even if by some miracle a reform that makes English spelling into a "one letter, one sound" system is brought about, it will not bestow any additional advantage to the reader; in fact, the quick extraction of meaning, an advantage of the present orthographic system, will be lost. This idea can be illustrated with the help of a few examples. The word "separate" comes from apart, therefore, it is not spelled "seperate;" "negative" comes from negation, therefore, it is not spelled as "negitive;" "there" comes from "ere" which means before, therefore, it is different from "their."*

Word Origin: *English language has borrowed many words from other languages. A knowledge of the origins of words can be helpful in avoiding common spelling errors. For example, "bacteria" (not bakteria) comes from the Latin word* bacillus; *"necessary" (not nessary or nesessary) comes from the Latin words* ne cesse; *"aerobatics" (not arobatics) comes from the Greek morpheme* aer; *"clear" (not cleer) comes from the latin word* clarus; *"calendar" (not calender) comes from the Latin word* calendra; *"quiet" (not quite) comes from the Latin word* quiescens. *Information regarding word origin can be found in any standard dictionary.*

Word Structure: *When a word is stripped of its suffix or prefix and the root morpheme identified or segmented into its constituent syllables, the spelling ambiguity can sometimes be resolved. It has to be noted that the root morpheme represents a unit of meaning. Some examples are: "decease" =* de/cease *versus "disease" =* dis/ease; *"definite" =* de/finite *(not defanite); "bargain" =* bar/gain *(not bargen); "noticeable" =* notice/able *(not noticable). There are several exceptions to the above principles and English orthography abounds with these exceptions. Sometimes, application of these principles can lead to misspellings.*

In spite of all these efforts, you may not be able to improve your spelling skill dramatically. It should also be noted that we have a tendency to spell phonetically those words with which we are not familiar. For this reason, efforts to improve spelling should go hand in hand with vocabulary building. The severity of spelling problems in written essays can be considerably minimized by using spell-check programs that come with word processors.

READING COMPREHENSION

The psychological processes underlying reading comprehension were described and discussed in Chapter 1 and will not be repeated here. It may be recalled that beyond the input modality level, reading comprehension and listening comprehension are mediated by the same cognitive processes and that students who experience difficulty in comprehending spoken language are likely to experience similar difficulty when they read. The converse, however, is not true. In other words, students with adequate listening comprehension skill, but who, nevertheless, encounter difficulty in comprehending written language are likely to have specific reading disability. The instructor may, therefore, have to adapt the reading comprehension training program according to the needs of individual students.

Reading comprehension is facilitated when a reader (1) can identify the main ideas in the text and separate them from major and minor details, (2) is aware of the organizational pattern of the chapter or essay, and (3) is able to summarize and paraphrase the information in the text. Reading comprehension also involves critical reading of the text whereby a reader is able to evaluate the information presented, accept what is valid, and reject what is questionable. The three subskills that facilitate reading comprehension and the mechanics of critical reading will now be described.

Identifying Main Ideas and Major Details: *Comprehending a written passage involves relating the content of the passage to previously acquired knowledge and then retaining the relevant information so that it can be recalled on a subsequent occasion. This means that first the gist of the passage has to be identified and then related to the relevant knowledge. Second, the many details present in the passage have to be reduced to a manageable number so that they can be retained in memory. This is accomplished by relating these details to the background knowledge the reader has so that relevant details can be organized into a "gestalt" and irrelevant information discarded. These two goals can be accomplished by identifying the main idea, major details, and minor details contained in the passage. If the main idea is not quickly identified, you may be forced to retain the main details and supporting details in the form of numerous bits of unrelated information. That is why identifying the main idea in a passage is considered the most important single act necessary for proper reading comprehension. It should be noted that what is true of listening comprehension is true of reading comprehension as well. As will be seen later, the same principles apply to writing; that is, written work also should contain a clearly identifiable main idea to which the main details and supporting details should be tied.*

The most important thing in reading comprehension is to be aware of the concept of a main idea and actively try to identify it in the passage you read. It is generally thought that each paragraph in a chapter contains one main idea that is usually stated in one sentence. Often, the opening sentence of the chapter and the first sentence of the paragraph contain the main idea. Of course, there are exceptions to these statements. Sometimes a paragraph may be a continuation of the previous paragraph; sometimes the main idea may not be explicit, the author deliberately avoiding a direct statement. Such writing is frequently encountered in literary prose.

The following tips can be helpful in identifying the main idea. As a first step, it is good to keep in mind that the chapter title and the subtitle tell you the general area from which the main idea comes. It is expected that you have some background knowledge about the subject matter under discussion. If not, the necessary background knowledge should be acquired through tutorial help or other means. For example, a chapter in a book on child psychology may deal with the genetics of developmental disorders. In order to identify the main idea of the text, the reader should have the background necessary to understand the genetics of developmental disorders. If the reader does not have the background, he or she will have to learn the fundamental principles of genetics.

A general notion about the main idea can be gained by reading the title, subtitle, and headings and subheadings. You should also scan the pages for words printed in boldface. Often a summary of the chapter is provided at the beginning or end of the chapter, and it is a good idea to read the summary before starting to read the chapter. It is also helpful to read the questions that accompany the chapter. The main idea of a paragraph usually answers the "what" question. Because the main idea is often straightforward and important, instructors may draw a large number of questions from it.

Sentences that elaborate on the main idea are referred to by several descriptors such as major detail and minor idea. We will use the phrase major detail *to refer to these descriptive statements. Authors make a number of statements in order to support the main idea presented in the paragraph. These statements generally are descriptive and answer the "who," "how," "how many," and "when" questions. According to Sotiriou (1989), sentences that present major details come in four different forms. They are sentences that present examples, a sequence of steps, description of characteristics, and cause-effect relationships. Often sentences that contain major details are prefaced with phrases such as "for example," "after that," "subsequently," "furthermore," or "because." Identifying major details helps the reader understand the main idea more fully and remember it better.*

In addition to major detail, there are sentences with minor detail. Sentences of this type are used to qualify, embellish, or elaborate upon major details. Sentences that contain minor details often start with words or phrases such as "incidentally," "in other words," "as an aside," or "a corollary to this statement." The following passage illustrates the relationship between main idea, major details, and minor details.

Freud's psychoanalytic interpretation of the personality of Leonardo aroused a great deal of interest, as well as violent criticism, because the deductive procedures involved in the analysis were novel and the conclusions daring. In order to support his controversial interpretation, Freud relied heavily on three sources of information: Leonardo's recollection of a childhood fantasy about a vulture, the nature and composition of his paintings, and slips and errors found in his writings. Viewed from a psychoanalytic perspective, these phenomena inevitably led Freud to conclude that Leonardo had the characteristics of a neurotic obsessional personality. In other words, Leonardo's personality should be considered as deviant from the normal (Aaron and Clouse 1982).	*Main idea; answers the questions "what" and "why."* *Major detail; elaborates on the main idea, answers the question "how many."* *Minor detail; rephrases the previous statement; is prefaced with the phrase "in other words."*

In many passages, particularly ones that deal with literary material, the intended message is not explicitly stated, but the author assumes that the reader possesses the knowledge necessary to construct the implied message by making inferences. For example, the sentence "Jack and Jill went to McDonald's and had a great time" expects the reader to have a knowledge about McDonald's and make the inference that Jack and Jill had a meal there.

Generally speaking, inferential comprehension of textbook material requires a sophisticated background knowledge or schema of the subject matter. When the intended information is not explicitly stated, identifying the main idea can become a difficult task. Under these circumstances, readers are expected to make inferences regarding the main idea based on their background knowledge. Sometimes inferential comprehension is encouraged by authors who want readers to arrive at their own conclusions. The same device could be used to enliven the essays you write.

Organizational Pattern of the Essay: *An awareness of the organizational pattern of the text promotes reading comprehension. Writers usually present information they want to communicate in a systematic and coherent manner that facilitates comprehension and retention of what is read. Written material that does not follow an organizational pattern makes identification of the main ideas difficult and creates an additional cognitive load that makes retention impossible. Conversely, the reader who is insensitive to the organizational pattern of the text finds comprehension difficult. The conclusion is supported by experimental evidence. For instance, a study by Marshall and Glock (1978) shows that children who are good readers are sensitive to text organization and are able to recall more information than children who lack this awareness.*

Reading specialists have identified the following patterns of organization:
1. *Taxonomical listing*
2. *Sequencing, chronology or process based*
3. *Compare–contrast*
4. *Cause–effect*
5. *Expository–explanatory.*

Taxonomical listing usually contains information about different items that are classified according to some criterion. Sometimes the listing can be narrow, and at other times it can be quite broad. The description of the three means of improving comprehension in the section on reading comprehension is an example of a narrow list, whereas the chapter as a whole is an example of a broad listing. Text that follows an organizational pattern of taxonomical listing can be recognized by phrases such as "there are many principles" or "the three theories discussed are."

Sequential patterns of organization present chronological progression of events or successive stages of some process in the form of narratives. Most of the information presented in history books is organized chronologically, whereas information found in science books about physical, biological, and psychological phenomena usually is organized sequentially.

The compare–contrast pattern is followed when two objects, ideas, or events are compared. Comparison focuses on the similarity between items, whereas contrast deals with the differences between them. Phrases such as "similarly," "likewise," "contrary to," and "unlike" are indicative of the compare–contrast pattern.

The cause–effect pattern is utilized when an attempt is made to relate two phenomena to each other and one of them is thought of as the consequence of the other. Be careful in interpreting two events happening at the same time as having a cause–effect relationship. For example, the rather free life-style and frequent earthquakes seen on the west coast do not have a causal relationship with each other. A good deal of caution has, therefore, to be exercised when trying to understand statements that contain phrases such as "due to," "because of," or "it follows then." A similar critical attitude is necessary when you write essays.

The expository–explanatory format of organization is used in presenting a large portion of the material found in textbooks. In expository writing, ideas simply may be listed and not be linked to each other with the aid of any of the devices presented above. This makes remembering such information relatively difficult. Linking the separate ideas with the aid of a "semantic map" described earlier in this chapter can be a useful device that can facilitate retention of such information.

Summarizing and Paraphrasing: *Summarizing and paraphrasing are activities that involve both reading and writing. They are important means of promoting comprehension. Summarizing usually requires that the contents of a textbook chapter be expressed in the form of a single paragraph. Lectures also can be summarized. Summarizing is not simply retelling what is in the text but requires the identification of the main ideas and major details and regrouping and presenting them in a brief, coherent, meaningful manner. Consequently, summarizing requires the reader to focus on these essentials and thereby improves comprehension of the passage.*

One procedure that will make summarizing a relatively easy task is to underline the main idea in each paragraph and then rewrite each main idea in your own words making certain that a meaningful gist emerges. The following principles can be helpful in preparing summaries:[1]

1. *All of the author's main ideas should be included in the summary.*
2. *Only those major details that clarify the main idea are to be included.*
3. *Do not include any of your own views or opinions in the summary.*
4. *Unless they affect the meaning of the summary, main ideas should be presented in the same sequence as in the textbook.*
5. *Sentences that express similar ideas should be grouped together and redundant statements should be deleted from the summary.*
6. *General terms and higher order concepts should be substituted for lists of words and items.*

Reading specialists have often remarked that summarizing is a difficult skill to master and requires much practice before one acquires proficiency in it.

Paraphrasing involves an accurate restatement of a sentence or sentences, in the reader's own words. In contrast to summarizing, condensing the information present in the original passage is not an essential feature of paraphrasing; in fact, a paraphrase can be longer than the original statement. Usually, paraphrasing involves a sentence or a few sentences rather than an entire chapter. Two important points to remember while paraphrasing are that the original statement is to be recast in your own language and that a long sentence can be broken down and expressed in the form of many short sentences.

Critical Reading: *The development of critical thinking is one of the goals of education. By becoming a critical reader, you will learn to reach your own conclusions, you will be able to separate fact from opinion, and you will not be unduly influenced by authors and the printed page. Critical thinking, as far as*

---

[1]These principles are taken from Cortina, Elder, and Gonnet (1989).

reading is concerned, involves at least four abilities: distinguishing facts from opinions, distinguishing an author's interpretation of facts from the facts themselves, recognizing the author's attempts to persuade the reader, and realizing when the author arrives at conclusions based on insufficient data. The following examples illustrate these aspects of critical thinking. Working with similar examples can sensitize you to the importance of critical thinking.

Distinguishing facts from opinion:

So far as I know, not a single author has clearly recognized the regular existence of a sexual instinct in childhood; and in the writings that have become so numerous on the development of children, the chapter on Sexual Development is as a rule omitted. The reason for this strange neglect is to be sought, I think, partly in considerations of propriety, which the authors obey as a result of their own upbringing and partly in a pyschological phenomenon which has itself hitherto eluded explanation (Freud 1925).

(What is the fact and what is the opinion in the above section?)

Author's interpretation of facts:

Although the study of dream-symbols is far from being complete, we are in a position to lay down with certainty a number of general statements and a quantity of special information on the subject. There are some symbols which bear a single meaning almost universally: thus the Emperor and Empress (or the King and Queen) stand for parents, rooms represent women and their entrances and exits the openings of the body . . . Sharp weapons, long and stiff objects, such as tree-trunks and sticks, stand for the male genital while cupboards, boxes, carriages or ovens may represent the uterus (Freud 1911).

(In the above passage identify the facts and their interpretation.)

Recognition of the author's attempt to persuade:

The tendency of biological research to-day is to explain the chief features in a person's organic constitution as being the result of the blending of male and female dispositions, based on chemical substances. Leonardo's physical beauty and his left-handedness might be quoted in support of this view. We will not, however, leave the ground of purely psychological research. Our aim remains that of demonstrating the connection along the path of instinctual activity between a person's external experiences and his reactions. Even if psychoanalysis does not throw light on the fact of Leonardo's artistic power, it at least renders its manifestations and its limitations intelligible to us (Freud 1910).

(How does Freud try to persuade the reader to think that psychoanalytic theory can explain human personality?)

Conclusions based on insufficient data:

To-day we know that neurotic symptoms are structures which are substitutes for certain achievements of repression that we have to carry out in the course of our development from a child to a civilized human being . . . It seems at any rate as if only a man who had had Leonardo's childhood experiences could have painted the Mona Lisa and the St. Anne, have secured so melancholy a fate for his works and have embarked on such an astonishing career as a natural scientist . . . (Freud 1910). (Does Freud provide sufficient data to support his psychoanalytic explanation of Leonardo da Vinci's artistic and scientific achievements?)

METACOGNITIVE SKILLS

It was noted in Chapter 1 that metacognition involves the ability to accurately appraise one's own skill level and to monitor the ongoing process of comprehension. Self-appraisal includes preceptions about one's own reading speed, cognitive style, the ability to comprehend, and an awareness about the nature of the task at hand. It is not unusual for instructors to come across students who cannot pinpoint the reason for their poor performance on tests. These students might have studied hard for the examination, and until the papers are returned, entertain a vision of success. When the test is returned they are surprised at their poor performance. These students are deficient in metacognitive skills. There is some evidence that children can be trained to use metacognitive skills and that such training improves their reading comprehension.

Metacognition can be described as the ability to know what one knows and to know what one does not know. Metacognition involves two subskills: having a reasonably correct estimate of one's own abilities and being aware of whether or not one is comprehending what is read or heard.

Good readers have a more or less accurate view of their own ability regarding their reading speed, cognitive styles, and memory capabilities. There is a great deal of variation in the speed with which students read. The average reading speed of a college student can vary from 300 to 500 words per minute. This rate, of course, depends a great deal on the type of material read and on the purpose for reading. Slow readers are handicapped because the amount of material that is to be read and comprehended in high school and college is quite vast. Increasing reading speed can, therefore, be of tremendous help in improving academic performance. There is, however, little evidence that the reading speed of those who are slow can be substantially increased. Claims have been made about the effectiveness of speed reading training, but most of these appear to be extravagant. When excessive speed is achieved, it is done so at the expense of accuracy. The speed-accuracy trade-off has been fairly well demonstrated.

For instance, after carefully comparing "speed readers" with normal readers, Just and Carpenter (1987) concluded that speed readers had a comprehen-

sion advantage only on familiar topics; speed-reading skill is not perceptual but conceptual; and speed readers do more top-down than bottom-up processing. In other words, one can read fast only the material with which one is already thoroughly familiar. The value of speed-reading training for comprehension of new and difficult material, such as textbooks, is not established. This leaves the slow reader with only one option. That is, he or she can allocate more time for reading and cover the material to be read. This adjustment, however, is possible only if you are aware of the fact that you are a slow reader. This metacognitive skill is, therefore, essential for the student with reading disability who, invariably, is a slow reader.

A problem common to many students is that they assume that they are reasonably fast readers simply because they have no way of assessing their own reading speed. They usually compare the amount of time they spend with books with the time spent by their normally achieving peers and feel that they read as fast as others do. If you suspect that you may be one such student, the academic skills course instructor or the tutor can provide you with accurate information regarding your reading speed. Inspection of the number of questions attempted within the allotted 35 minutes in the passage comprehension subtest of the Stanford Diagnostic Reading Test also can provide a reasonably accurate measure of your reading speed. If you happen to be a slow reader, once you know your reading speed you can allocate more time for reading and cover the same amount of material that normal readers do in less time.

Cognitive styles are defined as consistent ways of organizing and processing information. The term learning style *is sometimes used interchangeably with cognitive style, even though some educators claim there are subtle distinctions between these two terms. The metacognitive aspect of cognitive style involves recognizing your own cognitive style and taking actions if a modification is necessary. However, it has to be cautioned that while it is possible to evaluate one's cognitive style, it is uncertain as to what extent such styles can be modified.*

Cognitive styles are thought to be enduring personality traits and resistant to instructional change. Nevertheless, it is also claimed that techniques such as cognitive behavior modification have a positive impact on children who are identified as being impulsive (Kirby and Grimley 1986).

Cognitive styles relevant to the reading process are: impulsivity–reflectivity; scanning–scrutinizing; and dysfluency–fluency. Even though, theoretically, within any given pair, one style is not preferred over the other, in reality cognitive styles such as "reflectivity" and "fluency" are preferable to "impulsivity" and "dysfluency." Readers who are impulsive tend to respond quickly without considering all aspects of a problem. For this tendency they pay a penalty, particularly when taking multiple-choice tests. Students who are scanners also tend to overlook important details and take information in huge chunks. Dysfluent readers are extremely slow in reading even though they do not have a reading disability. They tend to perform poorly in timed tests, not because they do not know the subject matter, but because they simply do not have sufficient time to complete tests.

An awareness of your own cognitive style can be of some help to you. If you happen to have an impulsive style, you may remind yourself that you have to be slow, deliberate, and careful while carrying out academic tasks such as writing an essay or taking a multiple-choice test; if you happen to have a scanning style, you may remind yourself that you should scrutinize the material you read and look for details; if you are a dysfluent reader you can ask your instructors for extra time to complete assignments and tests.

Being aware of the nature of the task at hand is also one aspect of metacognitive skill. The nature of the reading task can vary from situation to situation; under some circumstances the text may only need to be scanned for main ideas while disregarding details; at other times, careful reading of even minor details may be necessary. Essay type exams require the identification of main ideas and major details, whereas multiple choice exams often require the careful reading of sentences that contain the main idea or major and minor details. Being unaware of the requirement of the reading task can result in treating all the reading material in the same way; on the one hand, you may spend an excessive amount of time reading what might be trivial and on the other hand, you may miss important details. You can increase your sensitivity about the nature of the task by frequently asking yourself what is the purpose of your reading.

Another metacognitive skill is comprehension monitoring, recognized by reading specialists as a useful metacognitive process. There are times when you read an essay and may not be able to comprehend the material. If, however, you are aware of the fact that you are not comprehending what you are reading, you can take appropriate measures to remedy the comprehension failure. For example, you may read the material again or you may use a dictionary to help you understand the meanings of difficult words. In contrast, if you are not aware of the fact that you are not comprehending what you are reading, then you are not monitoring your comprehension process. Understandably, if you are not monitoring your comprehension, you do not have an opportunity to take corrective actions.

There are some informal means of assessing one's own comprehension monitoring skill. You may ask the following questions of yourself: "When I read the textbook, how often do I go back to a passage or sentence and reread it so as to clarify things?"; "How often do I ask a fellow student or the instructor for clarification of ideas?"; "Am I not able to get the main idea of some passages that I have read?"; "How often, after an exam, do I feel I have done well only to find out when the exam is returned that I was in for a big disappointment?". If the answer is "rarely" to the first three questions and "often" to the last question, you may not be good at monitoring your own comprehension. Comprehension monitoring during reading can be improved by continuously asking yourself whether the passage being read can be remembered and recalled without difficulty.

WRITING SKILLS

Teachers of English have noted that good writing accomplishes three things: it communicates the ideas of the writer clearly; it convinces the reader of the writer's view-point; and it clarifies the writer's own thoughts on the subject he or she is writing about. These constitute the three C's of writing. Good writing should strive to communicate effectively, and through logical presentation of ideas, should convince the reader. In order to produce writing of good quality, the writer must have a clear idea of the subject matter he or she is going to write about.

Many of the subskills that have been presented with reference to reading are equally applicable to the writing process. In fact, writing is often advocated as a means of improving reading skills. A knowledge of key concepts such as the organizational pattern, identification of main idea and major details, format of the passage such as cause–effect, compare–contrast, or expository, is also useful in improving writing skill. There is, however, one important difference between writing and reading; in writing, information is created, whereas in reading, it is recognized. Writing is, therefore, more demanding than reading.

Critiques of written composition are essential for proper revision. Most students put their best efforts into their work and believe they have written the best essay they can; they also may believe that others share this opinion as well. An objective evaluation of the writing skill of students with reading disabilities, therefore, is an important feature of the acdaemic skills course even though such feedback has to be carried out in a way that will not discourage the student or dampen his or her enthusiasm.

There are two ways of assessing the written work of students: quantitative and qualitative. Quantitative measures are provided by the number of sentences, words, and clauses used in the written sample, and the ratio between the total number of words and the variety of words used. A relatively objective measure of this kind can be obtained by using readability formulas. There, however, is no objective way of evaluating the quality of an essay for its originality, creativity, organization, and humor. This form of assessment, therefore, can be done only by the instructor.

Writing is not just spoken language put down on paper. Spoken communication is often informal and spontaneous, whereas writing tends to be formal and to adhere to rules of grammar. While the speaker and listener interact in person, the writer and reader are separated by space and time. The writer, therefore, has the obligation to anticipate the reader's questions and write with-

out ambiguity. This is an important feature of good writing and can be accomplished to some extent by the writer switching roles from writer to reader. This does not mean that written language is rigid, sedate, and lifeless. In fact, many noted authors have used conversational and even colloquial styles and have achieved success in their writing. Spoken language contains prosodic features such as pause, stress, and elongation that are useful in highlighting certain aspects of the information conveyed. These features are absent in written language even though punctuation is a limited means of attaining a similar effect. For this reason, punctuation plays an important role in written language.

Another difference between written and spoken language is that idea units in spoken language contain, on an average, seven words, whereas idea units in written language contain an additional two or three words. These words are used primarily to embellish and adorn the language. Consequently, written language provides an opportunity to use a wider vocabulary.

The three essential steps for writing a good essay are planning, writing, and revising–reviewing.

Planning: *Good planning starts with writing a summary even before starting to write an essay. While planning and writing an essay, you should keep in mind the three C's of good writing mentioned earlier. In addition, at this time, it is important to determine the format on which the essay is to be based. As discussed earlier, the format can be expository, taxonomical listing, or may be based on a cause–effect or compare–contrast model. Planning also can include creating a rough sketch on the basis of the main ideas and major details. Both the summary and the sketch should take into account the principle of story grammar, namely that every essay has a beginning, a body, and a conclusion. Before putting an idea on paper, it will be helpful to visualize the subject matter of the essay. Scenes, settings, and events become lively when they are visualized first and then described with words.*

Writing: *When writing, it will be necessary often to refer to the summary and the diagram developed during the planning stage. It is important to keep in mind that each paragraph should contain a main idea that is stated clearly in a straight-forward manner. All major details in the paragraph should relate to the stated main idea. A writer should be aware of whether he or she is communicating facts or his or her own opinion to the reader. Statements that reflect opinion can be qualified by phrases such as "perhaps," "probably," "according to some authors," or "in my opinion." Facts should be authenticated by quoting their sources. It is also important not to plagiarize by quoting clauses and sentences verbatim from books and other material without using quotation marks and indicating the source. Preparing a set of prompts beforehand and incorporating these in the writing at suitable intervals introduces variety to the writing. Examples of such prompts are: "A new idea is," "No one would have thought of," "Another way to put it would be," "The reason I think so," or "Even though it is generally believed that" (Bereiter and Scarmadalia 1987).*

An excessive concern about the correctness of the essay, which robs the essay of creative elements, is a problem experienced by many students. Errors of grammar and spelling can be corrected when the essay is reviewed. If you think that concern about spelling and grammar impedes the free flow of your ideas, you may dictate your essay into a tape recorder and correct these errors when transcribing them.

Revising and reviewing: *Revising the essay that has already been written can also be seen as part of planning because revising may involve improving or changing some of the ideas or even the overall plan and format of the essay. Revising is different from reviewing in the sense that the latter involves checking the essay for errors of grammar and spelling. Reviewing, therefore, is the last step in the production of an essay. While reviewing, it is desirable to focus on one type of error at a time. For instance, during the first review, you should check for spelling errors and during the subsequent review, you can check for errors of grammar.*

It helps to be aware of some of the weaknesses commonly found in the written compositions of high school and college students. The following list of problems in writing[2] is followed by a brief explanation of each problem.

1. *Lack of coherence in text organization.*
2. *Conclusions do not flow from the body of the essay.*
3. *Opening sentence and main idea are vague.*
4. *Main idea too narrow and specific.*
5. *Main idea too broad to be recognizable.*
6. *Sentences too simple as indicated by short T-units and short clause length.*
7. *Fragmented and run-on sentences.*
8. *Syntax errors relating to conjunctions and errors of agreement among words that represent the same object in successive phrases and clauses.*
9. *Overuse of terms such as* and *and* rather.
10. *Inappropriate use of personal pronoun by using* you *and* I *interchangeably.*

Problem: Lack of coherence in text organization. This problem arises because the writer does not have a clear overall view of the yet to be written essay. Nor has he or she given serious consideration to the format of its organization (viz., cause–effect, expository, temporal–sequential).

Solution: Develop a summary and outline of the essay to be written; depict the organizational plan of the essay in the outline.

Problem: Conclusions do not flow from the body of the essay; conclusion has no logical relationship to information presented in the essay.

Solution: Paying close attention to the outline sketch can eliminate this problem.

Problem: Opening sentence and main idea are vague or too narrow. Main

---

[2]The list of problems was selected from a review article by Scott (1989).

idea too broad to be recognizable. The opening statement does not inform the reader what the passage is all about because it is too broad or too narrow.

Solution: You should have a clear conception of what is meant by main idea, major detail, and minor detail. Trying to state the main idea in the opening sentence in unambiguous terms and relegating major and minor details to subsequent sentences can minimize this problem.

Problem: Sentences too simple. Sentences are simple structurally and in terms of vocabulary.

Solution: Try to connect choppy sentences to make them into a longer sentence. Use the thesaurus to avoid redundancy in word usage but make sure the meaning is preserved while using synonyms.

Problem: Fragmented and run-on sentences. These sentences are the result of a lack of effort to read and comprehend the sentence that is written. They also reflect a lack of sensitivity to grammar or a lack of knowledge of punctuation rules.

Solution: It is more desirable to write short and understandable sentences than long and incorrect sentences. If each clause is constructed to represent a unit of meaning, this problem can be minimized.

Problem: Errors of syntax and anaphora.

Solution: While reading the essay, look for suffix errors. Relate the subject to its verb and grammatical morphemes to their anaphoric representations and make sure they agree with each other.

Problem: Overuse of certain words. This problem indicates that one writes colloquially—the way one speaks. It also indicates that sufficient attention is not given to the ideas represented by the essay. The conjunction and *reflects agreement between two clauses or ideas and ignores other possibilities such as disagreement and conditional situations. Overuse of the term* rather *indicates uncertainty.*

Solution: Examine carefully the relationship between ideas and explore the possibility of using other relationships and corresponding conjunctions such as because, since, but, *and* although.

Problem: Inappropriate use of personal pronouns you *and* I: *This is one of the common mistakes committed by students in higher grades and reflects a colloquial style. An example is: "They try to make things look bigger in shape and size to trick* you, *but* I *think they should keep them like they are. . . ." This also indicates that the writer uses a conversational, colloquial style.*

Solution: Realize that you are not speaking to a person but that you are writing to someone who is removed in space and time.

TEST-TAKING SKILLS

In order to achieve success in academic areas, the student, in addition to knowing the subject matter, should also have a knowledge of the nature of the test (multiple-choice, essay), and the nature of the instructor (stresses concepts, stresses minute details). The student should also be familiar with certain strategies that can enhance his or her performance on tests. Usually instructors explain the type of test they have made up and give sample questions in advance. If they do not, it is to the advantage of the student to elicit this information from the instructor. It is also desirable to go over a sample test or a copy of a previous test, if one is available.

Like any other skill, test-taking skill also improves with practice. The instructor of an academic skills course should, therefore, provide frequent opportunities for students to take different forms of tests. This is particularly true of competitive examinations such as the SAT, performances on which have been shown to improve with practice.

Preparation for examinations is a continuous process starting, not just the day before the exam, but the moment you attend the first class meeting. Tests come in different forms, but the most frequently administered ones are in the form of essays, and multiple-choice and true/false questions.

The Essay Test: *The essay test is less objective than the multiple-choice test in the sense that the examiner's biases, likes, and dislikes influence the score. For this reason, while taking the essay examination, you should be aware of the opinions of the examiner. Essays should be well organized and easy to read so that the examiner understands them readily.*

The principles described under the writing section apply to the essay examination as well. You may recall it was recommended that you have a summary and the organizational pattern of the essay in mind before starting to write. It helps both the examiner and you to have a diagrammatic outline of the essay drawn at the beginning of the essay. This ensures that the essay is logical and coherent; it also prevents you from leaving out any important point inadvertently while you write. Before beginning to answer the question, you should decide whether the essay calls for opinions or facts. If it is a discussion question, it is desirable to state your stand at the beginning of the essay. It is desirable to break the essay into paragraphs, with each paragraph containing a main idea and supporting details. If possible, state the main idea in the opening sentence of the essay. A relatively simple way to test if your essay is coherent and well organized is to read the first sentence of each paragraph in the essay and see if you have a summary of the essay.

Multiple-Choice and True/False Questions: *In contrast to essay questions that require recall of information, the multiple-choice and true/false tests require recognition of information. Because recognition is easier than recall, test makers employ many ruses to mislead or confuse the test-taker. The following are some tips that will be helpful in answering multiple-choice and true/false questions:*

1. *Read all the options in each question because test-makers include, among the options, distractors that are true statements but may not be the best answer.*
2. *Answer just those questions of which you are sure you know the answers. If after answering these questions, time is available, other questions can be attempted.*
3. *Be watchful for phrases such as "all but one," "none of the following," and double negatives such as "not unlikely." Be particularly careful in reading options that contain words with prefixes such as "incorrect" and "unlikely." The difficulty caused by these "ringers" can be minimized to a certain degree by matching the stem and one option at a time and seeing if the combination can be a true statement.*

There are occasions when you lack the information necessary to choose the correct answer. Under these circumstances, being aware of some of the following clues may be of help in choosing the correct answer. These tips may not work to your advantage when there is a penalty for wrong answers.

1. *Options with absolute qualifiers such as "all," "always," "only," or "never" are likely to be incorrect answers.*
2. *General statements with phrases such as "often," "most of the time," "almost always," tend to be correct.*
3. *When two similar-looking options are present, one of them is likely to be the correct answer.*
4. *When two options contain synonyms or words with identical meaning, both are likely to be incorrect.*
5. *When two options contain antonyms or are opposite of each other, one of them is likely to be correct.*
6. *In true/false questions, for a statement to be true, each of its parts must be true. For example, in the statement "Freud was a leading psychoanalyst France has produced," the first part of the statement that Freud was a leading psychoanalyst is true whereas the remainder of the sentence is wrong, making the statement a false one.*
7. *As it is in the case of multiple-choice questions, statements that contain absolute terms such as "all" or "always" are likely to be false.*
8. *In contrast, statements that contain qualifiers such as "often" or "most of the time" are usually true.*

Many colleges use SAT scores as one of the criteria for admission, and consequently, many high school students who plan to attend college take the SAT test. The Educational Testing Service and the American College Testing Program provide special conditions under which the SAT (and the ACT test) can be taken. These special conditions provide additional time for test taking that usually is of some help to high school students with reading disabilities. When the test has been taken under special conditions, this is noted in the score report. The few studies that have examined whether or not additional time improves the test performance of students with reading disabilities show that it does (e.g., Centra 1986; Hella 1988; Hill 1984). The study by Centra compared the test performance of reading-disabled students on the SAT with the performance of students without reading disabilities. It was found that disabled students gained an average from 30 to 38 points when the test was given under extended time; 15% of the students increased their scores over 100 points, and another 26% gained from 60 to 100 points. About 7% of the reading-disabled students also lost as many as 50 points. The control group of nondisabled students, however, did not show a similar gain because of the extra time, which indicates that providing extra test-taking time allows the disabled students to read and respond to many more items than they would have under standard administration.

The advantages gained by the extended time provision can be increased by additional practice and direct instruction in test-taking skills. Several software programs on how to take the SAT are also available. An article by Rothschild (1987) provides some useful tips about SAT preparation.

THE USE OF COMPUTERS IN THE ACADEMIC SKILLS COURSE

In recent years computers have become a major instructional tool. Software programs that are helpful in organizing and conducting computer-assisted instruction in elementary and junior high school grades are available. New software programs intended for improving language skills in older students are beginning to appear on the market. In the following section we present some of the basic principles to be observed for incorporating computer-assisted instruction in the academic skills program and subsequently describe some of the software programs that are available for use in high school and college.

There are five important criteria to be considered in making decisions regarding software program selection. These are subject matter to be taught, appropriateness for the ability level of the student, interest level, ease of use, and cost of the program.

Criteria in Selecting Software Programs

Subject Matter to be Taught: In the academic skills course we are primarily concerned with the improvement of reading and writing skill, and therefore, other subject matter areas such as math and science are not considered. Within the area of reading and writing, software programs are available for improving grammar, spelling, decoding skills, writing skills, and the development of vocabulary. As noted earlier, mature students with SRD make little progress in decoding skill and spelling, and for this reason, the value of software programs intended to improve word recognition and spelling skills is questionable. In the academic skills course, software programs can be expected to produce gratifying results in the areas of vocabulary, comprehension, and writing skills.

Appropriateness for the Ability Level: It is our experience that even though many software programs claim to be appropriate for high school and beyond, most are suitable only for the 9th or 10th grade levels. This, however, may not be a serious problem if the students enrolled in the course are poor readers with NSRD or LAR. Such programs, however, may not be challenging to students who do not have reading disabilities, but are enrolled in the course for general improvement. Thus, the anticipated composition of the class is a factor in program selection.

Interest Level: Closely related to the appropriateness criterion is the interest level of the students. One of the common criticisms against mechanized devices used for teaching is that they are boring to the learner. This is true of tutorials presented through the computer as well. Software program developers are aware of this problem and have incorporated several motivating devices in their programs. These include presenting the lessons in game or problem-solving formats. By and large these software programs are able to hold the attention of students and challenge them and are preferable to those that present information in a matter-of-fact format. A good software program should also be interactive with the student and not simply a one-way information-providing source.

Ease of Use: In spite of the fact that personal computers have become commonplace, some students are leery of them and have reservations about their use. Software programs with simple instructions are likely to alleviate the fears of the student with RD. A software program installed on a hard-disc drive is preferable to the one that comes in the form of two floppy discs. Programs installed on the hard-disc drive eliminate the need for frequent swapping of the program disc and the data disc.

Software programs that provide immediate feedback and are able to summarize data regarding the performance of the learner will enhance learning. Another important feature is the availability of a provision for skipping those sections the student has already gone over or considers too simple. If a program does not have this feature, the student is forced to repeat the same steps before she or he reaches the point where the needed section begins. In their book on computer applications in reading, Blanchard, Mason, and Daniel (1987) describe several criteria for software selection and cite pertinent articles. Articles that evaluate currently available software are periodically published in the following journals: *Computers in the Schools; Computers, Reading and Language Arts; Creative Computing; Educational Computer Magazine; Educational Technology; The Computing Teacher; Electronic Education;* and *Electronic Learning.*

SUMMARIES OF SELECTED SOFTWARE

Grammar and punctuation

Software: Grammar Gremlins.   Available from Cambridge Developmental Laboratories, 214 Third Ave., Waltham, MA 02154. This software program has a pretest and a posttest and provides drill and practice in the use of plurals, possessives, subject-verb agreement, parts of speech, and capitalization. A print-out option provides feedback to the student about his over-all performance. The teacher can add additional grammar rules and questions. Even though intended for Grades 3 through 6, the information in this program can sensitize an older reading-disabled student to punctuation and grammar.

Software: Essential Punctuation.   Distributed by Cambridge Developmental Laboratories. This program provides instruction in the correct use of punctuation, capitalization, and quotation marks. Feedback is provided at the end of each lesson.

Software: Skills Bank II, Language Series.   Available from Softwriters Development Corporation, 4718 Harford Road, Baltimore, MD 21214. The entire set of software programs in the language series is on 16 discs and contains lessons on the proper use of grammar, suffixes, and punctuation. It contains quizzes and tests.

Vocabulary

Software: Word Attack Plus.   Available from Davidson, 6069 Groveoak Place No. 12, Rancho Palos Verdes, CA 90274. This new version of Word Attack is intended to build vocabulary by introducing nearly 700 words through activities such as multiple-choice quizzes, sentence completion, words matched with meaning, and an arcade-style word attack game. The program is flexible enough to allow the instructor to add his or her own list of words. It has 10 levels with the highest being suitable for high school and college students with limited vocabularies.

Software: Vocabulary Adventure II.   Available from Queue Inc., 5 Chapel Hill Dr., Fairfield, CT 06432. This program introduces nearly 750 words in context and in a game format that requires the reader to select the correct word from a choice of four words. Presentation of words in context is an advantage of this program that also makes it interesting. It is suitable for college students with reading disabilities.

Software: Vocabulary Development.   Available from Weekly Reader Family Software, 245 Long Hill Rd., Middletown, CT 06457. This program contains exercises in the use of synonyms, homophones, antonyms, suffixes, and prefixes. The program does not provide feedback data and does not permit skipping of exercises.

Software: Skills Bank II, Reading Series.   Available from Softwriters Development Corporation. The entire series consists of 12 discs that include lessons of root words, affixes, synonyms, and antonyms. The reading series also includes lessons on literal and interpretive comprehension as well as quizzes and tests.

Reading Comprehension

Many of the programs that are intended to promote reading comprehension do so by combining book reading with computer presented exercises. Some programs also attempt to increase the speed of reading.

Software: 88 Passages.   Available from College Skills Center, 320 West 29th St., Baltimore, MD 21211. This program is intended for grades 6 through college. Students choose an area that interests them and after reading the passage presented by the computer, answer comprehension questions. If the answer is incorrect, the program explains why the answer is wrong, and the student is directed back to the text. The program also tells why an answer is correct. Strickland, Feeley, and Wepner (1987) report that college instructors who have used this program are enthusiastic about it.

Software: Comprehension Power.   Available from Milliken Publishing Co., 1100 Research Blvd., St. Louis, MO 63132. This program, which is meant for grades 4 through college, comes in a set of 12 discs. The program is intended to build inductive comprehension skills by focusing on major comprehension skills.

Software: Skills Bank II, Reading Series.   This program was discussed in the previous section under *vocabulary.*

Writing Skills

Many programs combine improvement of writing skill with the teaching of word-processing. Many of the programs also have provisions for evaluating the quantitative aspects of what is written by the student.

Software: Grammar and Writing. Available from Scholastic Inc., P.O. Box 7502, 2531 E. McCarty St., Jefferson City, MO 65102. The program consists of four discs, each representing one part of the program. Part 1 of the program provides instruction on parts of speech by challenging the student to use the various parts of speech correctly in context; part 2 provides practice in forming basic sentences; part 3 provides practice in the correct usage of verbs and pronouns; and part 4 focuses on creating and editing paragraphs.

Software: Success with Writing. Available from Scholastic Inc. This is described as a "complete writing composition course" by its creators. Students progress stage-by-stage from note taking and developing ideas to editing and revising. The program also contains models devised to check the writing structure and the reading level of the written product. The completed text can be transferred to word processors such as The Bank Street Writer III, or Apple Works.

Software: Composition Strategy: Your Creative Blockbuster. Available from Behavioral Engineering, 230 Mt. Herman Rd., Suite 207, Scotts Valley, CA 95066. This program interacts with the student by providing prompts that direct the student's thought processes as he or she is engaged in writing. After a sentence is typed, the program presents a key word such as "because," "before," or "whenever" and requires the student to continue the writing by incorporating the prompt provided.

Software: Skills Bank II, Writing Series. Available from Softwriters Development Corporation. This series contains 16 discs and provides lessons in organizing sentences and developing paragraphs. It contains quizzes and tests.

Readability Estimates

Even though originally intended for estimating the ease with which a passage in a text book can be read, readability formulas can be used for evaluating certain quantitative aspects of written work. The two basic criteria for assessing readability are semantic difficulty measured in terms of the quality of vocabulary used and syntactic complexity that is measured in terms of sentence length. Several readability formulas are available. The three frequently used formulas are by Dale and Chall

(1948), Fry (1977), and Raygor (1977). The Dale and Chall formula is based on traditional methods and uses the number of uncommon words and average sentence length in a sample writing. The Fry formula counts the number of syllables and sentences per 100 words. Three written passages are sampled and the mean scores are checked against the table provided. The Raygor readability estimate is based on the number of words with more than six letters from a sample of 100 words as well as the mean number of words in a sentence. Any one of these three formulas can be used to evaluate the written works of high school and college students.

As noted earlier, readability formulas provide a quantitative measure that cannot be used to evaluate the quality of the written material. Another problem in using readability formulas is that estimating the readability indices for a large number of students is a tedious and time-consuming task. The enormity of this problem, however, has been minimized to a large extent by the personal computer. Students in the academic skills class can be asked to use these programs and evaluate their own writing.

When selecting the program, caution should be exercised to see that the program is compatible with the word processor that is used. The following books and articles can be consulted for more detailed information regarding use of the computer for estimating readability levels of written essays.

Books and Articles: Blanchard, J. S., Mason, G. E., and Daniel, D. 1987. *Computer Applications in Reading* (3rd ed.). Newark, DE: International Reading Association.
Hague, S., and Mason, G. 1986. Using the computer's readability measure to teach students to revise their writing. *Journal of Reading* 1:14–17.
Kennedy, D. 1985. Determining readability with a microcomputer. *Curriculum Review* 25:40–42.
Strickland, D. S., Feeley, J. T., and Wepner, S. B. 1987. *Using Computers in the Teaching of Reading*. New York: Teachers College Press.
Standal, T. 1987. Computer-measured readability. *Computer in the Schools* 4:88–94.

Software: *School Utilities*, Vol. 2. Available from Minnesota Educational Computing Consortium, 3490 Lexington Ave. N., St. Paul, MN 55126. This program can provide six estimates of readability based on six formulas including the ones by Dale and Chall, Fry, and Raygor. *Readability Analysis.* Available from Cambridge Developmental Laboratories. In this program, the passage to be evaluated is typed in and the computer counts syllables, words, and sentences and calculates word and sentence length as well as word difficulty. It can provide three different estimates based on the Spache Primary Reading Formula, the Dale-Chall Readability Formula, and the Fry Reading Scale.

Success With Writing. Available from Scholastic Software. This program combines a word processor and a teaching guide for writing. Also included is a text analyzer module which estimates the level of student's writing.

Chapter 6

Counseling and Student Advocacy

INTRODUCTION

Students with reading disabilities who are successful enough in high school to gain admission into a post-secondary institution might be assumed to have a fair measure of self-confidence. But this is rarely the case. Most RD students, upon entering college, feel insecure and suffer greatly from fears of failure. Understandably, they also frequently suffer from fears common to freshmen who leave familial and familiar environments and venture into an unknown territory for the first time. For students with reading disabilities, these normal fears are often compounded by a belief that everyone at college is much smarter than they are, that college courses will be much harder than anything they have ever encountered, and that instructors might look down on them if they divulge the fact that they have reading problems. Further, students with reading disabilities might have been heavily dependent upon a parent or a particular teacher who encouraged, tutored, and supported them throughout their school years and they feel insecure and helpless without the presence of that significant person.

Thus, when a student with a known history of reading disability arrives at the first orientation or registration session, he or she may be already overwrought with anxiety and stress. Sometimes such a student will confide these concerns to the first available friendly person encountered; others will remain distant and uncommunicative, trying desperately to be "like every one else." Even though no two students are alike in their personality and requirements, all students with reading disabilities can profit from timely counseling. A student with a reading disability, however, differs from the college student who seeks counseling for purely psychological problems; the RD student may have emotional problems in addition to learning problems. Because of the peculiar nature of this combination of problems, an advisor who counsels students with reading disabilities is expected to deal successfully with personal problems as well as with learning problems. It is desirable, therefore, for an advisor to have expertise not only in the area of learning, reading, and reading disabilities but also in counseling skills. In combining these two roles an advisor is not only a counselor, but is also a *consultant*. An advisor is a consultant because she or he possesses expert knowledge that a student with RD seeks, and in doing so, the student expects the advisor to have answers to many questions. Miles (1988) succinctly describes this unique combination:

> Now in the area of counselling it seems to me that a distinction can usefully be drawn between what may be called "generalist" expertise and "specialist" expertise. In speaking of generalist expertise I have in mind the skills which are common to virtually all forms of counselling, for example the ability to show empathic understanding of human weaknesses, the willingness to be a good listener, and the recognition that the obtruding of one's personal views can sometimes be inappropriate. By "specialist" expertise I have in mind, for example, skills possessed by a doctor, a solicitor, or a stockbroker (p. 103).

Miles indicates that there are several instances where counseling calls for a combination of generalist and specialist expertise. An example is when a physician has to inform a patient and his family that the patient has a potentially fatal disease and then discuss the treatment options that are available.

Individuals with a combined expert knowledge in counseling and learning skills are, however, rare. Most advisors encountered in learning skills laboratories are likely to be experts in reading and learning who, nevertheless, may have no more than a passing acquaintance with the principles of counseling. With this possibility in mind, some fundamental principles of counseling are presented here.

BASIC PRINCIPLES OF COUNSELING STUDENTS WITH READING DISABILITIES

Even though there are numerous counseling methods and techniques, all of them can be placed in one of three models: (1) the medical model, (2) the behavioral model, and (3) the existential model. In the following sections, brief descriptions of these models are presented.

The Medical Model

The word *medical* should not be taken to mean that this approach to counseling advocates the use of medicine or drugs in treatment. Rather, this approach to counseling tries to identify the causal factors that have led to the presenting emotional and behavioral problems and attempts to eradicate the cause. The adjective *medical* is based on the rationale that a counselor, like a good physician who does not limit his or her treatment of physical illness to symptoms but actively looks for the cause with a view to eliminating it, also expends much effort in identifying the source of a psychological problem. Psychotherapy that adheres to the medical model deals with a problem at its origin because it is believed that in most instances, the psychological problem is not caused by current circumstances but by events of the past. Consequently, a counselor pays special attention to the developmental history of a client and attaches much importance to significant events and experiences of his or her past with an objective to link current problems with the past events. The life history of the student, therefore, is an important source of information used in this therapeutic process.

The psychotherapeutic method that is best represented by the medical model is psychoanalytic therapy. Sigmund Freud, the originator of psychoanalytic theory and therapy, believed that an individual's current behavior is, to a large extent, influenced by his or her past experience, particularly events that occurred during childhood. The client may not be aware of these past memories because much of it is stored in the subconscious (also referred to as the unconscious), particularly emotionally unpleasant memories. These subconscious memories, however, exert much influence on current behavior and thought. Because these memories are far removed from current behavior, the motives and the behavior they generate may not be congruous with each other and may often result in irrational behavior and thought patterns. For example, dislike developed toward a teacher in the elementary grades may be the motivational factor behind a student's reluctance to read textbooks while in college. The student may not be aware of this hidden motive until it is unearthed by a counselor and brought to his or her conscious attention. Once these submerged motives are brought to the conscious level, they can be dealt with in a rational manner. Even though Freud depended on clinical experience to develop the tenets of psychoanalytical theory, there have been sporadic attempts to subject the theory to scientific scrutiny. Some recent studies suggest that people can exert some control over their subconscious and that it can be used to carry out many intellectual tasks by developing and executing plans for reaching certain goals (Weis 1990). For example, the desire to become a hard-working student may be planted in the subconscious and can be expected to exert its influence on a student's study habits. A counselor, during therapy sessions, may not only make inferences regarding the already existing motives of a student, but also can introduce new ones and help a student achieve new goals.

The role of a counselor who tends to operate within the medical model would, therefore, include efforts to identify any potential unconscious motive that may be responsible for a reading-disabled student's disinterest in reading as well as efforts to make the student aware of this hidden motive. According to psychoanalytic view, once a client gains this insight, much of the problem can be resolved. In order to identify these putative causal factors of the past, psychoanalytically oriented therapists use different techniques, including free association, dream analysis, and interpretation of a student's current thoughts and feelings. However, several factors, such as forgetfulness, fallacious reasoning, and distortions of memory, may impede efforts to bring hidden motives to the surface.

An important set of forces that resist the recall of significant past events and hinder their accurate interpretation are the defense mechanisms employed by clients. For example, a college student who, as a child, thoroughly disliked reading may claim that he or she was fond of reading and had read many books during his or her elementary school years. Such a *denial* may not be the result of a conscious distortion of truth by a student but may be a defense constructed by his or her subconscious motives. If taken at face value, such a statement by a student can mislead the counselor. Deep probing of the student's history with the aid of questions such as "Can you name two of the books you read while in high school?" or "Who are your favorite authors?" can help the counselor to penetrate these defenses and reach the truth.

Freud and his followers have identified a number of defense mechanisms. In ordinary terms, defense mechanisms can be described as coping devices that are useful in preserving self-esteem. Defense mechanisms, therefore, serve the useful function of maintaining a feeling of self-worth in the face of events that threaten it. In addition to being known as coping devices, defense mechanisms are also referred to by descriptive terms such as "games people play" and "masks students wear." Even though defense mechanisms serve the useful purpose of maintaining one's self-esteem, in the long run excessive use of defense mechanisms will not lead to realistic solutions. For example, a student with a reading disability may not acknowledge that his or her poor performance on a test is due to a reading problem but may attribute the failure to factors such as excessive length of the test, the ambiguous nature of the questions, or the enormous amount of material to be read. This type of fallacious reasoning is referred to as *rationalization*. It is obvious that the chronic use of rationalization will not help a student to improve test performance. Other examples of defense mechanisms are *projection* ("It is not my fault; it is the professor who doesn't know what he is talking about"); *identification* ("Isn't it true that Leonardo da Vinci couldn't read either?"); *denial* ("I am not the best speller, but my reading is pretty good"). Smith (1989), in an article on the behaviors of learning disabled children who try to hide their problems, describes several "masks" these students wear. Included in this list of defense mechanisms are: *the mask of helplessness* (by constantly using statements such as "I don't know," "I don't understand," "I can't do it," the student gets everyone around to do his or her work); *the mask of invisibility* (the student tries to get through school by assuming a low profile, by not "making waves"); *the mask of the victim* (the student feels victimized and takes on a "poor me" attitude); *the mask of not caring* (the student assumes an "I don't care" attitude as though nothing is important); *the mask of contempt* (the student blames everybody and everything; he or she takes no pleasure in small successes and is angry at the world); and *the mask of frailty and illness* (the student constantly complains about health and other problems; nothing works and everything fails). According to Smith, by helping students understand the nature of their disability and the nature of the defense mechanism they are using, by helping them reach a comfort level and thereby gain self-confidence, these masks can be removed.

Since Freud's time, psychoanalytic theory and practice have undergone much change. Freud's followers who are responsible for having introduced such changes are frequently referred to as NeoFreudians. The NeoFreudians have rejected certain aspects of psychoanalytic theory as originally proposed by Freud and have elaborated on other aspects of it. They also have developed and emphasized their own key concepts within the framework of the psychoanalytic theory. For instance, Alfred Adler disagreed with Freud's view that neurosis is a product of childhood sexual conflicts and proposed that the major motivational force behind human behavior is an effort to overcome a feeling of inferiority and an attempt to strive for superiority. Avoiding inferiority and the striving for superiority are accomplished by adapting certain patterns of behavior that eventually become an individual's life-style. This is a useful concept to keep in mind while counseling students with reading disabilities since many of these students harbor a feeling of inferiority, possibly resulting from remarks made by some of their teachers, and even parents, that they were stupid, dumb, or lazy. In their attempt to conceal or overcome such a feeling, they adopt some maneuvering techniques that eventually become an established pattern of behavior, their life-style.

The Behavioral Model

Counseling approaches within the behavioral model concern themselves very little with the past history of students because counselors who are behaviorally oriented believe that we have little or no control over what has happened in the past. Rather, they are concerned with behavior as it occurs here and now. Behaviorally oriented counseling also disregards mental concepts that are advanced as putative explanations of human behavior. For this reason, behaviorally oriented counseling approaches make little use of concepts such as the subconscious, mental conflicts, and defense mechanisms. Behavior therapies, in their pure form, are based on principles of learning and, therefore, consider maladaptive behavior as learned. Such behavior can, therefore, also be unlearned. Consequently, therapeutic efforts undertaken to change or modify behavior make use of concepts such as conditioning, counterconditioning, reinforcement, and feedback. Behavioral counselors, generally speaking, set up specific counseling goals and focus on changing the subject's behavior by helping him or her to unlearn inappropriate behaviors and replace them with more desirable ones.

All behavioral therapies share two goals: eliminating undesirable behavior and installing desirable behavior in its place. Elimination of the undesirable behavior is accomplished by first identifying the reinforcing element that sustains such behavior and removing it. At the same time, a more desirable behavior is identified and appropriate reinforcers are introduced so that the substitute behavior can be learned quite readily. For example, skipping classes may be the undesirable behavior of a reading-disabled student and the reinforcer that sustains the behavior might be the "wild" time the student has with his or her buddies. The desirable behavior, therefore, is attending class regularly and this behavior can be reinforced by the instructor and the reading specialist who recognize and applaud the student's responsible behavior. The counselor, therefore, has to set up opportunities for consistent feedback to the reading-disabled student so as to facilitate the progress of the student in his or her studies.

Behavioral therapy of the purest kind does not deal directly with factors such as feelings and emotions but focuses instead on behavior. Therapists who subscribe to the behaviorist view are not interested in why a certain behavior occurs but rather are concerned with under what conditions a given behavior occurs. Recently, however, some theorists have recognized that man not only acts and behaves, but also thinks and feels. Certain "cognitive elements," therefore, have been incorporated into behavioral therapies. This "new and improved" version is sometimes referred to as cognitive-behavior therapy. Two counseling techniques that can be considered to have a cognitive behavioral flavor are *cognitive behavioral modification* (CBM) and *rational emotive therapy* (RET).

CBM is based, among other things, on the expectation that one's overt language can be used as a means to control and guide one's own behavior. For example, children who are impulsive are trained to say aloud before attempting to solve a problem:

> What is my problem? My problem is to find and circle the words on this list. What strategy shall I use? I will go slow and look carefully (Kirby and Grimley 1986, p. 79).

Cognitive behavioral modification techniques reportedly are successful in modifying the impulsive behavior of children diagnosed as having attentional deficit disorder (Kirby and Grimley 1986).

The essential features of rational emotive therapy are based on the belief that emotion and reason are closely interrelated; emotions affect thoughts and action. Conversely, action also affects thoughts and feelings (Ellis 1962; George and Cristiani 1990). Counseling based on the principles of the RET approach, therefore, focuses on both thought and behavior. The counseling process includes showing clients that some of their problem behaviors are due to illogical and self-defeating thinking and that such thinking can be changed into logical thinking and productive behavior. For example, reading-disabled students may say that they do not read much because they are not good readers. The therapist may counter this thought by saying that they are not good readers because they do not read much and not the other way around. The therapist may support his or her argument by citing the "Matthew effect." The therapist helps clients to change their inappropriate thoughts by questioning them and by challenging the validity of certain beliefs held by them. An additional goal of the therapist is to teach a client to question and challenge the validity of his or her own thoughts and actions. These are followed by reeducative plans that are often accomplished by requiring the client to complete homework assignments. Such homework can include specific activities that the client normally tries to avoid for fear of failure. For example, a therapist may question a client about why he or she usually avoids any contact with teachers or professors. After pointing out that the reason given by the student is an irrational avoidance behavior, the counselor may, as an assignment, require the student to approach two of his or her professors and have at least a one-minute conversation with each of them. RET can be used successfully by an advisor in counseling reading-disabled students because it has certain features that allow the counselor to play the role of an expert.

The Existential Model

Counseling approaches that can be placed in the existential model may or may not profess any allegiance to existential philosophy. However, they all share the belief that every human being is a worthy individual who is free to make his or her own decisions by choosing from among the several options available. Making a choice is not only a privilege of all human beings but is also their responsibility. Because decision-making is the client's responsibility, in the counseling situation a therapist may make the client aware of the many options available and let the client choose the one he or she thinks is best. A counselor does not make decisions for the client and does not assume a directing role. A counselor, however, actively listens to the statements made by the client and clarifies the client's thoughts regarding the many options available by reflecting on his or her statements and feelings.

The *person-centered counseling* (also referred to as *client-centered counseling*), which follows a non-directive approach developed and promoted by Carl Rogers (1951, 1980), can be accommodated within the existential model. According to Boy and Pine (1963),

The basic hypothesis of client-centered counseling is that effective counseling consists of a definitely created permissive relationship which allows the client an opportunity to gain enough understanding of himself to be able to take positive steps in the light of his new orientation (p. 13).

Person-centered counseling is based on the following principles.

1. The individual and not the problem is the focus of counseling.
2. Therapy should focus on the immediate situation and not the individual's past.
3. Therapy should place greater emphasis on emotion and feelings of clients than upon intellectual aspects.
4. A counselor believes that clients are basically responsible for themselves and for their decisions and actions.
5. Diagnosis is not considered essential for counseling.
6. A counselor accepts clients' rights to be different and accepts clients as they are.
7. Clients are made aware that a counselor does not have all the answers and that the clients will have to find solutions to their problems.

In its philosophical orientation, person-centered counseling differs in several respects from the more directive counseling procedures that can be placed in the medical and behavioral models. According to Boy and Pine (1963), assumptions that underlie directive counseling are:

1. Counseling is an intellectual process.
2. Because maladjusted behaviors leave a large portion of the mind of a majority of persons intact, it is possible to learn and relearn.
3. The counselor has superior information and experience and is, therefore, competent to give advice about how a problem can be solved.
4. Diagnosis is an integral part of counseling.

These assumptions are in stark contrast to the principles of person-centered counseling outlined above.

Is any one counseling approach belonging to one of the three models discussed above more suitable than the other for counseling the reading-disabled student? The answer is no. All the counseling approaches, regardless of their philosophical orientation, have certain features that are suitable for counseling the student with a reading disability; it is equally true that almost all these approaches have some features that are not well adapted for counseling the reading-disabled student. For this reason, a counselor should be flexible enough to adapt an eclectic approach by choosing the best features from each model and combining them into a method that is suitable for a particular student.

Students with reading disabilities also differ from each other in the type of reading deficit they have as well as the nature of their psychological problems. Some of the desirable features of the different counseling approaches along with the features that may render them unsuitable for counseling students with reading disabilities are shown in table 6.1.

Regardless of the philosophical orientation of a counselor and the

Table 6.1. Features of Different Counseling Approaches that are Suitable and not Suitable for Students with Reading Disabilities

Counseling method	Features that are suitable	Features that are not suitable
Medical model (Psycho-analysis)	Seeking cause of the problem; Past history of a student; Analysis of defense mechanisms; Analysis of life-style; Diagnosis.	Probing the subconscious; Study of unconscious motives; Dream analysis.
Behavioral model (Behavior/ Cognitive-behavior modifica-tion)	Use of reinforcers; Feedback; Extinction of undesirable behavior and teaching of desirable behavior; Peer support.	Cognitive processes cannot be easily modified; Student may become too dependent on counselor for support.
(Rational-Emotive therapy)	Cognitive self-instruction; Self-analysis of metacog-nitive skills; Replacement of illogical thinking with logical thinking; Homework assignments.	May make counselor assume responsibility for a student; Logical thinking in itself may not be able to improve reading skill.
Existential model (Person-centered therapy)	Helps student assume responsibility; Counselor remains as a non-threatening individual; Student becomes aware of the many options available.	Focuses on emotion rather than on intellect or behavior; Emotional problems can be the result of reading diffi-culty rather than its cause; Reading specialist may have definite answers to some of the reading problems but may not insist that a student follow his or her suggestions if a student wants to improve his or her reading skills. Diagnosis is discouraged.

theoretical biases he or she may have, there are certain principles that advisors of students with reading disabilities have to follow. Some of these principles are listed below.

1. During the initial meeting with a student, a counselor should strive to establish rapport rather quickly. Even though the ultimate goal of counseling a reading-disabled student is to improve his or her cognitive skills, a counselor has to strive to establish an affective relationship. Throughout his or her association with a student, a counselor has to be nonjudgmental about the student's weaknesses, habits, and life-style.

2. During the initial meeting, a counselor has to state in clear terms his or her role and the responsibility of the student. He or she also has to communicate to the student the approximate duration and frequency of counseling sessions.

3. A counselor should not indulge in moralizing and preaching but should provide a non-threatening, secure, and trusting environment for a student. A counselor has to be genuine, warm, and sincere.

4. A counselor has to obtain from a student a clear statement of his or her problems and his or her expectations from the learning skills program.

5. Throughout the counseling sessions, a counselor has to listen to a student with genuine interest and give him or her full attention.

6. A counselor has to present the diagnostic information to a student and describe fully the procedures involved and the rationale used in the interpretation of test results. A counselor has to describe the nature of different reading disabilities and support this exposition with the necessary scientific information. The procedure used in arriving at the diagnostic decisions has to be explained to a student. While doing so a counselor also has to present the weaknesses and the strengths of a student as revealed by the diagnostic tests. In presenting all this information, a counselor must be accurate, realistic, and forthright.

7. A student has to be given ample opportunities to ask questions about the diagnostic procedure and decisions and should be provided with a chance to express his or her own views about the entire diagnostic procedure, findings, and recommendations.

8. A counselor has to present to a student plans of actions available and explore each one. A student should have the freedom to choose any of them and reject those that he or she thinks will not be productive.

9. A counselor should have a plan for continually monitoring the progress of a student and communicate this plan to the student.

A student should be free to seek additional consultation from other specialists whenever he or she feels it is necessary.

10.   All the transactions that take place between a counselor and a student are private. Strict confidentiality must be maintained in these matters. Results of the diagnostic tests and other personal information are not to be shared with tutors, teachers, instructors, or institutions without a student's written permission.

11.   A student has to be informed in unequivocal terms about the seriousness of the program and the importance of his or her commitment to it. We find that some students have a tendency to treat the entire program lightly; these students tend not to show up for tutoring sessions, fail to keep appointments, and be tardy for counseling sessions. It is very important that a student understands from the very beginning that the program requires total commitment.

ILLUSTRATIVE CASE HISTORIES

Counseling: General Principles

As noted above, almost all students with reading disabilities are tense and anxious upon entering college. Invariably, these students also lack self-confidence.

Case 1

K.R., a freshman from a wealthy family in a large midwestern city, entered college after having had the benefit of the most advanced tutoring money can buy. He had been accustomed to having all reading materials taped, either from commercially prepared tapes available for the blind or by a tutor who rarely left his side. Upon entering college, K.R. approached the reading specialist at the orientation session in a state of near panic. "I was just told by the bookstore that the required texts are not available on tape. Then a student I met in the dorm told me not to even buy books before classes start because there might be changes. What am I going to do about my books?" Based on the diagnostic test results and an examination of K.R.'s history, the reading specialist determined that K.R. had specific reading disability but could indeed read; he just read very slowly. His comprehension was good, but he did not have confidence in his ability to comprehend the printed material. The reading specialist explained to him the nature and extent of his reading disability and told him that reader service was available and that some of the materials could be taped for him. Still, he would have to attempt to read some of the textbooks by himself because he could read. Convincing K.R. that he could do some reading by himself, however, was more difficult than helping him to improve his study skills and reading habits.

K.R. probably was using the defense mechanism of helplessness to avoid assuming responsibility. He also appears to have serious apprehensions about his comprehension skill which are not entirely logical and can be dispelled by showing him his own test performance. K.R. of course, has the option of trying to accomplish part of the reading by himself or to seek total help from outside. The counseling procedure, by examining his history, showing the defense mechanism he uses, pointing out his illogical thinking, and giving him a choice between being an independent reader or being dependent on others, makes use of all three approaches to counseling presented earlier.

Sometimes, RD students suffer from a lack of self-confidence as a result of some traumatic or unpleasant experience that had occurred earlier, as illustrated in the following case. A thorough analysis of the past history of a student, therefore, becomes essential for effective counseling.

Case 2

J.N. was a good-looking college freshman who had been recruited to play varsity volleyball. Identified by her high school as learning disabled, she was sent to the special tutoring services. Working regularly with a tutor, she achieved an excellent grade point average (GPA) by the end of the first semester in college. Still, J.N. had no confidence in herself. She would often refer to herself as "dumb" and "ugly." Such attitudes even manifested themselves in her personal, non-academic life, so that she allowed herself to remain in unhappy relationships, which often resulted in a state of depression. After a year, J.N. told the counselor that as a child she was very tall and heavy for her age and had worn glasses since age two. Further, while her mother quarreled with everyone at school, trying to find special help for her, J.N. had languished in classes for the mentally retarded in the first, second, and third grades. She had even ridden the special education bus with physically handicapped children during these three years, although she is obviously physically perfect. The self-image she conceived at that time had become fixed, and she still thought of herself as a tall, obese, and slow child. To this day, when someone comments on the beauty of her eyes—a fairly common occurrence—she becomes quite embarrassed.

The counselor decided that J.N.'s childhood history still has an important influence on her behavior. The counselor told her about the role of the subconscious and the defense mechanisms people use in adapting to poor self concept. It was suggested that she probably wears a "poor me" mask to avoid responsibility. Her good academic record and her athletic achievements were pointed out to her, and she was told that her emotions were not in line with rational thinking. The diagnostic procedure that led to her classification as SRD was explained to her, and her above-average performance in tests of listening comprehension was used as evidence of this conclusion. Her attention was drawn to the options available to her: that she could strive to be a normally achieving student or she could continue to feel inadequate and unhappy all the time.

In addition to problems of self-image and self-confidence, students with reading disabilities nearly always experience moments of

extreme frustration. Even in students who have been academically successful during the first and second years of college, these periods arise,
often near the end of the semester when the pressure of academic work
becomes almost unbearable for them, as seen in Case 3.

Case 3

M.R., having entered his junior year in college with a GPA of 3.0, was
progressing quite well. He saw his tutor twice each week and was able to
explain exactly what help he felt he needed. The counselor, on the basis of
her acquaintance with M.R., knew that he was a perfectionist, almost to
the degree of being compulsive. Even though he had satisfactory academic performance, by about midterm each semester, M.R. would fly into
the Center saying, in desperation, "I have to talk to you, I have to talk to
you." With the door closed, he would explain, "I don't know what's
wrong with me. I'm being mean to everyone, my roommate, my friends."
When his frustration level reached a certain point, he began taking it out
on the people around him. The counselor always listened, asking him
why he thought he was being mean, and M.R. would always respond that
there was so little time and that he knew he would not be able to get his
studying done on time. In order to deal with this problem, the counselor
listened while reflecting on M.R.'s problems and gave him a homework
assignment that required him to sort out the demands he was placing on
himself and arrange them in an order of priority. After M.R. compiled this
list, he was asked to meet these demands one at a time, according to priority. The counselor asked M.R. to report to her three times a week to
discuss how he was progressing. Once he realized that he did not have to
do everything immediately and once he had a mental picture of what had
to be done first, his frustrations subsided. M.R. also needed to realize that
no one is absolutely perfect and that we all make mistakes.

The perfectionist tendency of M.R. may have been his reaction to his
reading disability, a way to cope with the problem and compensate for
it. The problem experienced by M.R. is more emotional than educational. Counseling that combined an analysis of the nature of his compulsive behavior with a rational-emotive approach was found to be
very effective in his case.

Counseling: Self-Esteem and Motivation

A boost in self-esteem can be achieved only when suggestions made by
the counselor are backed by tangible evidence and sound reasoning. A
majority of students with reading disabilities are capable of better academic performance than they are achieving and they have to believe
that they can succeed if they apply the necessary effort. According to
Brophy (1987), success in increasing motivation and self-esteem of students depends on three factors: setting goals that are attainable, believing that they have the efficacy to succeed, and believing that they are in
control of factors that affect their performance.

Good performance in the classroom is the best evidence that a student is reaching the goals he or she has set. A counselor, therefore, has

to help students set up goals that can be reached in the near future rather than in the distant future, goals that are specific rather than general, and goals that are neither too easy nor too difficult to attain. For instance, the goal of getting a grade of B in the first test is closer than the goal of a grade of B in the course at the end of the semester; a goal of passing a course is more specific than the goal of majoring in certain field; planning to get a grade of C + can be more realistic and challenging than planning to get a C or an A.

Efficacy to succeed includes personal beliefs about one's capabilities to organize and implement actions necessary to attain desirable levels of performance (Bandura 1982). According to Schunk (1989), individuals acquire information to assess self-efficacy from their actual performances, vicarious experiences, positive feedback, and physiological indexes. Even though success tends to raise efficacy and failure tends to lower it, once a strong sense of efficacy is developed an occasional failure may not have much impact. It, therefore, becomes necessary that during the beginning semester, the academic program be so arranged that a student experiences success as often as possible. When students see fellow students succeeding, they too are likely to experience success vicariously. Positive feedback from credible sources such as teachers and instructors can have a positive impact on self-efficacy. Physiological indexes such as sweating and increased heart rate may be symptoms of anxiety that convey the information that one lacks the skills necessary to perform well. Efforts to reduce stress, therefore, can have a positive influence on a student's perception of self-efficacy.

Students with a high level of self-esteem feel that they have control over their success or failure. Such individuals are said to have an *internal locus of control;* individuals who believe that their success and failure are attributable to external factors such as luck and chance are said to have an *external locus of control.* Those who have the locus of control outside themselves also tend to use defense mechanisms excessively. Locus of control is a good concept that students with reading disabilities should be aware of. The life histories of some eminent men such as Woodrow Wilson and Hans Christian Anderson, who in spite of having experienced difficulties in learning to read were able to succeed, can be used to improve the self-efficacy levels of students with SRD. Available evidence suggests that these eminent men had specific reading disability (Aaron, Phillips, and Larsen 1988) and, therefore, these cases cannot be used in counseling students with NSRD or LAR.

Counseling: Peer Support

One of the devices that can be used successfully for improving self-confidence and self-image and for reducing stress and anxiety is a peer support group. Peer support groups are informally structured and vary in size and composition. Support groups, however, cannot be expected to materialize spontaneously and, for this reason, they have to be initiated and set in motion by a counselor. Students have to be informed that even though the composition and activities of the groups are informal in nature, they follow a well-structured time table. Senior students in the reading disability program can serve as leaders of these groups and as role models for younger students. The mere knowledge that one is not alone in struggling with reading problems often lifts the spirits of newly enrolled students. It is even more encouraging to identify with students who have made demonstrable progress and to know that students with reading problems can be successful in high school and college.

Groups can meet in different places such as the tutoring center, a local restaurant, the student union, or a recreational setting. These groups can operate both academic and social support programs. Ideally, these meetings should take place at least once a week. Because of students' other commitments, attendance will vary from one meeting to another. Nevertheless, students should commit themselves seriously to attending these meetings. A knowledge that a record of attendance is maintained and that the counselor is kept informed of the attendance and activities provides the impetus needed by some students who may be reluctant to attend. Even though these meetings occasionally can be social in nature—such as going out for pizza—most often they provide an opportunity to discuss problems and fears encountered by students and to share solutions tried and found successful. These meetings also provide a forum for sharing information regarding the nature of different academic majors, departments, courses, and instructors. Though these meetings may resemble gatherings of any group of college students, they are unique in that these people are gathered with the primary purpose of helping each other to survive and succeed in what many of them perceive to be an unsympathetic environment, and for sharing their knowledge about strategies for dealing with the challenges posed by an academic setting.

Many books that currently are available on learning disabilities claim that students with learning disabilities display abnormal social behaviors, such as withdrawal, excessive aggression, and even delinquency; however, these behaviors are rarely seen in college students with reading disabilities. When such behaviors are seen in high school students, there is no reason to consider these problems to be an essential component of the reading disability. Students with reading disabilities do experience anxiety and frustration; sometimes they want to give up. But many other college students experience similar feelings. When extreme behavioral and personality problems are seen in students with reading disabilities, they have to be dealt with as personality disorders and not as a form of reading disability.

Case 4
T.M. was the youngest of several brothers, all of whom attended ivy league schools. Because of his poor academic record, however, he was sent to a State school. His parents wanted very much for him to finish college but were not at all confident that he could succeed. T.M., however, was a very determined young man. He was quiet, though not shy, but the sort of person who would never stand out in a crowd. Relatively unnoticed, except by his tutor, he slipped in and out of the Center daily. He never made A's, but he never got F's, either. Until the annual hours were totaled after his first year in school, the director had not realized that he had spent approximately twenty-five hours per week in the Center with his tutor or using the facilities available there. In his junior year he told the counselor, "You know, it takes me all week to do what my roommate can do on a Saturday afternoon." T.M. never had a job, rarely had a date, never joined any social organization, and generally socialized only with his family on the weekends when he went home. Although it took him five years, he graduated with a degree in technology.

Although it seems that nearly all the students with reading disabilities report experiences of some sort of teasing from other students at some time or other, generally during the junior high years, such behaviors are seldom in evidence in high school or college. In fact, just the opposite is true. Other students frequently go out of their way to be helpful, once they know about the nature of reading disabilities. Knowledgeable professors and teachers promote conditions that facilitate interactions between students with reading disabilities and those without them. Under such circumstances, it is not unusual to hear statements such as, "Here, Jen, let me read to you first" or "You can make a photo copy of my notes; they could save you some time from rewriting your notes," etc. These gestures of helpfulness are frequently unsolicited.

In some instances parents of students with reading disabilities can be a problem rather than a help. This is not the norm, however. Most RD students who have been successful enough to reach post-secondary education levels have parents who have actively sought special testing and tutoring services for their children and have encouraged and helped them throughout their tenure in public school. Because problems of reading disabilities tend to run in families, frequently one of the student's parents or a close relative has also struggled with similar problems and, therefore, empathizes quite readily with their son, daughter, or nephew. In rare cases, however, there are parents who cannot face the thought that their child might have a reading problem. Because such parents lack an understanding of reading disabilities, they tend to equate reading disabilities with mental retardation and become hostile when told that their son or daughter has a reading disability. On the other hand, there are parents who, because they never entertained the thought that their child might have a problem, attribute RD to personality characteristics. "He is just lazy; he never would really try" is what these parents often say. Under such circumstances, a counselor has to shoulder the additional responsibility of explaining to the parents the nature of reading disabilities, ways of dealing with them, and the prognosis. Such an "expository session" is most effective when done in the joint presence of the parents and the student. More often than not, after such an information giving session, parents are relieved to know that there is a reason for the difficulties experienced by their child.

> *Case 5*
> J.T., a freshman with a pleasant smile and an engaging personality, was given the screening tests during the first week of school because of his low SAT scores. The pattern of his scores—mediocre comprehension, average vocabulary, low decoding, extremely low reading rate, and above average listening comprehension—indicated that he had SRD. When asked by the reading specialist if he had ever been tested for or diagnosed as learning disabled, he answered negatively, saying that his father, who teaches in the English department of a midwestern college, did not believe in reading disabilities and that it was his rule that if J.T. brought home any bad grades, he could not watch TV for a week. "I have three brothers," he said, "and I was the one who never got to watch TV." Then he asked, "May I tell my father what you've told me?" The reading specialist said that she would be pleased for him to discuss it with his father. The next day the reading specialist received a call from the father, who said: "I never thought he was really dumb, you know, but I was always so frustrated trying to get him to study. I just thought that anybody who tried could do well at school and that J.T. simply did not try."

Reading-disabled students with unsupportive parents or families need someone to lean on and frequently the supportive role then evolves upon the counselor or the mentor tutor. This can be an additional responsibility that every reading disability specialist faces.

The qualities that will help most students with reading disabilities are diligence and endurance, and all counselors and tutors need to emphasize this fact over and over. The ability to focus on the task at hand, the maturity to withstand the temptation to "go out with the guys," and the vision to keep an eye on the final goal are qualities that will enable students with reading disabilities to succeed in the academic world.

Counseling: Stress Management

Students with reading disabilities often experience anxiety, tension, and stress. Once in a while a student with RD appears to be supremely confident and presents a picture of an extremely competent person. This can very well be a mask the student wears. Stress management has become a specialty discipline that combines contributions from the psychological, medical, and physiological fields. If the stress experienced by a student appears to exceed normal limits, he or she may be referred to a clinic where special stress management techniques are available.

Students with reading disabilities also may be informed of the benevolent effects of physical exercise and its effectiveness in reducing stress. Students who experience frustration and anxiety should be encouraged to engage in some form of physical activity regularly. Many students take up jogging or running, since these are activities that are popular. Others may wish to make use of facilities such as weight rooms, tennis courts, or swimming pools available on most campuses. When these activities are not possible, a student may engage in brisk walking or even climbing stairs in the dorms. It is not uncommon for students with reading disabilities to complain that they have little time for activities that have no direct bearing on their academic work. These students need to be thoroughly briefed on the positive value of regular exercise and to be convinced of the positive impact exercise can have on feeling well. Because physical activities help to alleviate stress and thereby bring about a state of relaxation, they should be given importance in the counseling program.

ACADEMIC ADVISING

One of the most significant services a reading disability program can provide for students is enlightened academic advice about majors, course selection, course load, and selection of instructors. To advise well, counselors must be knowledgeable about the abilities of each student as well as have complete information about the available courses and instructors. Commonly, students with reading disabilities experience reading, spelling, and writing difficulties, although these vary in degree. It is imperative that a counselor take into account a student's talents and academic strengths as well as his or her interests while recommending courses of study. Students also need to be able to evaluate their own skills in an unbiased manner in order to develop realistic plans of study. For instance, someone with serious problems in math will not be able to handle physics, and this fact, by itself, will eliminate several potential majors. A student with nonspecific reading disability is unlikely to succeed in courses in classics or literary criticism, for these courses involve tremendous amounts of reading. For this reason, a literature major would be unsuitable for these students. Majors such as industrial technology, which provide plenty of hands-on experience, would be more suitable for such students with NSRD. Many students with specific reading disability also find math courses to be difficult, but often these difficulties are limited to the computational aspect of mathematical problem solving rather than the logic that is needed to solve these problems. For students with SRD, a mathematics or computer major cannot be ruled out entirely. Similarly, students with SRD, who invariably are poor spellers, may be able to write essays and stories that contain themes that are high in creativity and originality. These students can be expected to do well in literature courses but may encounter difficulties in composition courses that stress grammar and spelling. Some institutions have flexible liberal arts majors wherein students are able to select courses from a number of areas and so build an individualized curriculum. For many reading-disabled students, such a program would be ideal. At any rate, counselors need to be knowledgeable enough about the programs offered at their schools to be able to help these students select courses of study in which they have an opportunity to be successful.

A second important consideration for academic advising is course load: how many hours or classes should a student take? This, too, depends upon a student's level of skill as well as the types of classes he or she intends to take. Beginning freshmen should be given a minimal load with courses requiring excessive reading and writing carefully balanced. In other words, the advisor should advise the student to take per term no more than one or two courses that involve intensive reading or writing. These courses should then be balanced with other courses that involve less reading or lab-type activities or projects. Later in the student's academic career, when the student reaches the upper echelons of the major field, he or she may need to be advised to once again take a lighter load in order to maintain a respectable GPA. As noted earlier, a 12-hour load per semester is a reasonable responsibility that students with reading disabilities can be expected to handle. As a matter of precaution, they may start with a 15-hour load so that they can drop one of the courses should they find it difficult and still be able to satisfy the requirement for being a full-time student.

In choosing courses each term, a student is always constrained by, first, the courses that are offered and, second, by the requirements of the school or major department. However, some flexibility can be worked out even within those constraints. It is suggested that, in general, students with reading disabilities avoid foreign language classes because they are very time-consuming. Likewise, they should, during the initial semesters, avoid courses in areas such as philosophy and sociology, which tend to be primarily abstract.

Finally, the choice of instructors is another area in which the advisor can be helpful. Counselors need to be aware of which faculty members understand the nature of reading disabilities and the problems of students who have such disabilities and are willing to make available to these students options that would facilitate performance. Every educational institution has a few puritans who are inflexible in their demands; counselors ought to know who they are. Some instructors, for example, may not allow anyone to tape their lectures; some instructors do not allow students to have extra time when taking tests. It is easier to avoid such situations than to try to persuade these instructors and teachers to the counselor's way of thinking.

The academic success of a student is ultimately determined by the grade he or she receives in the courses, and this, in turn, is often determined by performance on the examinations given by the instructor. Information regarding the nature of examinations given by the instructor and his or her personal philosophy about testing in general are, therefore, important bits of information that should be taken into account while recommending instructors to a student. Some teachers follow what Canady and Hotchkiss (1989) call the "assign, test, grade, and teach" pattern. That is, these instructors require students to read the assignments first, they then test and grade them, and finally teach when they return the test. Students with reading disabilities are not likely to flourish under this type of teaching; for them, a reverse pattern of instruction is more suitable. Indeed courses that follow the "assign, test, grade, and teach" pattern can have disastrous consequences for the student with a reading disability.

Canady and Hotchkiss (1989) also note that some teachers fail to match testing with their teaching. That is, there is a mismatch between what is taught in the class and the material on which the test is based, the latter most often drawn from the textbook. Students with reading disabilities are likely to find these tests very difficult. These authors also caution against instructors who love to "ambush" the students by giving too many "pop quizzes" and surprise them when they least expect it. The policy followed by the instructor in the final grade assignment is also important. Some instructors grade the entire class on a "curve." This policy leads to comparing the individual student's performance to that of others in the class. It means that the instructor has already determined what percent of students in the class will get A's, B's, and so on. It also means that no matter how hard students try, a certain number of them are bound to fail. A grading policy that is better suited to students with reading disabilities is the criterion-based assessment wherein the standard to be achieved is preset and all the students who reach this criterion are assigned that grade. Some teachers average the scores obtained by the students on all the tests, whereas others would be willing to drop the lowest score in determining the grade for the course. The latter policy is more advantageous to the RD student than the former. Instructors also differ in their policy regarding discussing the test when it is returned. It is safe to steer away from instructors who are unwilling to discuss the test and will not tolerate any attempt by students to contest the validity of the questions in the test.

STUDENT ADVOCACY

Staff members of programs for the reading disabled, and especially the directors of such programs, have another educational responsibility besides the one they bear toward their students: they are responsible for informing the larger academic community about the nature of reading disabilities. Because the scientific study of reading problems is in its infancy and because only recently has reading disability been recognized as a legitimate handicap, many faculty members do not have an accurate knowledge of these conditions. Many teachers, unfortunately, equate it with mental retardation and consider it a façade that is used for concealing more serious intellectual deficiencies. Because students with reading disabilities look like normal students, many teachers cannot believe that these students have a genuine disability. These same teachers may be quite considerate of students who are blind, in wheelchairs, or who show visible signs of their handicaps, but to them, students with reading disabilities are simply lazy or dull.

Case 6
R.Y., because he had extended time allowed for the ACT and thus was able to make a respectable score on the verbal portion of the test that determines placement in freshman composition classes, was assigned to a regular freshman English class. However, after one look at his first in-class writing, his instructor called the learning skills center suggesting that R.Y. drop the class. The counselor explained that R.Y. had SRD and that his reading disability often manifested itself in erratic spelling. R.Y.'s words were recognizable, but he would regularly spell the same word in two different ways even in the same sentence. The counselor explained the disability and asked the instructor if he would allow R.Y. to remain in the class and just grade him on everything except spelling. The instructor was reluctant to do so. "How can I possibly pass someone who spells "necessary" as *nessesary* and "Germany" as *Jermany*?" he asked. However, with persistancy and gentle diplomacy on the part of the counselor, hard work on the part of the student, and much proofreading on the part of the tutor, R.Y. was able to pass the course with a C grade.

Keeping the faculty informed of the nature of reading disabilities can be done both formally through organized, campus-wide faculty development programs and informally in any regularly occurring encounters with the faculty. Many departments, particularly the English department, hold informal weekly seminars for the faculty and students. These seminars can provide an opportunity to disseminate information about the nature of reading disabilities. The student newspaper is yet another vehicle for informing both students and faculty about reading disabilities.

Formal faculty development programs for the understanding of reading disabilities may be presented in several different formats and settings. The scholarly approach should take precedent, with seminars or colloquia scheduled during a two semester period on various aspects of research in reading disabilities. These can feature local specialists as well as scholars from institutions nationwide. It might even be possible for an institution to publish the proceedings of such gatherings for distribution to its faculty. Additionally, presentations can be made to various departments, academic and administrative, on the campus. These can be conducted by resident scholars in the field and by the staff of the reading disability support program.

The organization and orchestration of these multilevel, multipurpose programs and presentations would be time-consuming and perhaps somewhat expensive (i.e., bringing in nationally known scholars) but eminently profitable for consciousness raising about the needs and characteristics of students with reading disabilities.

Within the structure of such programs, several strategies for teaching reading-disabled students need to be presented and discussed, both by the program staff and by the university faculty and administration. These strategies include the use of readers, tape recorders in classrooms, and untimed exams. Standard procedures need to be developed for use throughout the university for the inclusion of these alternate teaching and test-taking strategies. If the university were to advocate the students' right to such services, the pockets of faculty resistance and suspicion would be likely to disappear sooner or later. Unfortunately, in too many instances, education has become an "us versus them" scenario wherein faculty and students become adversaries. Such attitudes, then, frequently make faculty resistant to alternate strategies, especially with regard to testing. Education needs to become an "us and them" scenario wherein all parties in the intellectual community work together for the advancement of knowledge and for the common good. If it were to become university policy that students with reading disability be provided with these services, a great battle for the rights of students with reading disabilities will have been won.

Finally, information can be presented by panels of RD students themselves so that faculty and staff members will have an opportunity to listen to the students tell about their own learning and school problems and experiences. Only when such dialogue takes place will real understanding of the nature of reading disabilities occur. These student presentations can be held for both academic and administrative personnel as well as for audiences in the dorms. An excellent place in colleges to present such a panel is in teacher education classes. Prospective teachers are often amazed to see that students whose writing is barely readable are creative, witty, and intelligent. In such small group settings the RD students can communicate informally their own ideas and experiences to the prospective teachers and the audience can ask questions and respond to the presentations.

Case 7

DR., L.K., and J.N., three students with reading disabilities, agreed to visit a secondary education methods class for juniors who were to be student-teachers during the following semester. The instructor had announced previously that a panel of reading-disabled students would address the class that day. When the class members entered the room and saw the panel of speakers, several students from the audience were heard to whisper, "I know her; she was in my psychology class; I didn't know she had any problems; her grades were so good," etc. It was soon very clear to the instructor that the class members had expected persons totally different from those sitting before them. The instructor introduced each speaker and told the class how she met each one, what their majors were, etc. Then each speaker talked about his or her life in high school, how the learning disability was diagnosed, what kind of problems were encountered, how teachers had reacted, and the kind of feelings, fears, frustrations, and successes each had experienced. Class members soon began to ask questions, and everyone wanted to speak at once. One story about how an elementary teacher had ridiculed a student brought many class members close to tears. Afterwards, class members thanked the instructor for arranging the panel. Nearly all of them had taken the required class about dealing with special and gifted students in school, but all voiced the opinion that the two-hour panel discussion was more informative than any previous classes.

The final area of student advocacy is fund raising. Programs for students with reading disabilities must be funded to be visible; many students with reading disabilities do not avail themselves of the opportunities that exist on the campus because they are not aware of existing programs. Any university administration that applauds the idea of special provisions for students with reading disabilities is obligated to fund them. While this topic is discussed further in the final chapter of this book, it should be mentioned here that fund raising can be carried out in tandem with consciousness raising; that is, it can be discussed in all the types of presentations described above. Also, the director of the reading disability program can set up foundation accounts into which interested alumni can donate money for the program. At this juncture, some of the programs and presentations mentioned above may need to move beyond the university community into the wider business and educational communities. Alumni gatherings and meetings of social organizations such as the Rotary Club, the Lions Club, and the Kiwanis Club are ideal places to educate the wider public about reading disabilities and to solicit financial support.

READING-DISABLED STUDENT-ATHLETES

Athletes with reading disabilities present certain problems that are unique to this group of students. Because student-athletes must be full-time students to be eligible to participate in athletic events and because collegiate sports are extremely time consuming (20 to 30 hours per week during competitive seasons), the student-athlete with a reading disability is constantly under time pressure and is frequently overwhelmed by more work than students who are not in athletic programs. For this reason, counseling, advising, and tutoring (discussed above) and the proper scheduling of these services are very important for these students.

In addition to the problem of time management, student-athletes present some other unusual problems. Athletes, in general, reportedly often engage in superstitious and ritualistic behaviors. With the added stress and frustration growing out of their disability, such behaviors can assume neurotic proportions in the athlete with reading disability. The student may feel that he or she must wear certain clothes, colors, or numbers; eat certain foods at a certain time; see certain people before competition; or put on pieces of a uniform in a certain order. A lack of opportunity to perform any of these rituals in the exact way may send the student-athlete into a state of panic. These compulsive behaviors grow out of a desperate need to control events and can ultimately spread to nonathletic situations such as test taking. Students with these problems need special, professional counseling.

On the other hand, student-athletes with reading disabilities present a unique opportunity for student advocacy. Because they are often well-known and frequently in the public eye (Bruce Jenner is a good example) and also because they are often admired by their fellow students, open public discussion of their reading problems by the student-athletes themselves can create a wider awareness of reading disability than lectures or magazine articles. Such examples and testimony also help to enhance the self-confidence of fellow students with reading disabilities who are not athletes. Because some of these athletes are also good speakers, they can appear before faculty, administrative, and alumni groups and secure support for programs designed to help the reading disabled.

Chapter 7

A Model for an RD Program and its Administration

INTRODUCTION

Because the study of reading disabilities is a relatively recent phenomenon, many schools have yet to develop programs designed to provide academic and personal support that students with reading disabilities need in order to achieve success in academe. A few post-secondary institutions, such as Southern Illinois University, however, have had excellent supportive programs for years and a few, such as Indiana State University, have had research programs for some time. Only recently have many universities and colleges begun to develop such programs and to recruit students with reading disabilities actively. As the competition for students among post-secondary schools escalates and as more secondary schools identify and provide support for students with reading disabilities, the need for all post-secondary institutions to recognize the needs and abilities of these students will increase. In this chapter we provide some guidelines for schools that have yet to develop support programs for students with reading disabilities.

PHILOSOPHY

An academic support program for students with reading disabilities must begin with an appropriate philosophical perspective. It is important for persons who propose, plan, and administer such programs to maintain a success-oriented attitude. Any program designed to help students with reading disabilities must be structured so as to function on a positive and optimistic note. Students with reading disabilities should not be regarded as handicapped in the traditional sense; administrators and all employees of such programs, as well as the sponsoring institutions, should regard these programs in the same light as they would regard English as a Second Language (ESL) programs—as a way to help certain students cope with and succeed in the system. Everyone working within the program should have high expectations for the enrolled students at all times, for such attitudes on the part of administrators and tutors will be unconsciously assumed by the students themselves, helping them to accomplish what they believe they can.

RATIONALE

When the need for support programs for reading-disabled students arises, the burden of proof for the need of such programs falls generally upon those who propose the founding of them, whether these persons are faculty, counselors, or administrators. Thus, it is important for these persons to explain the fact that learning disabilities are officially recognized as handicaps under Public Law 94-142:

> Specific learning disability means a disorder in one or more of the basic psychological processes involved in understanding or in using language, spoken or written, which may manifest itself in an imperfect ability to listen, think, speak, read, write, spell, or to do mathematical calculations. The term includes such conditions as perceptual handicaps, brain injury, minimal brain dysfunction, dyslexia, and developmental aphasia. The term does not include children who have learning problems which are primarily the result of visual, hearing, or motor handicaps, of mental retardation, or of environmental, cultural, or economic disadvantage [Section 5(b) (4) of P.L. 94-142] (Wallace and McLoughlin 1988, pp. 5–6).

While this is the official, federal definition, the National Joint Committee on Learning Disabilities (NJCLD) has proposed its own definition:

> Learning disabilities is a generic term that refers to a heterogeneous group of disorders manifested by significant difficulties in the acquisition and use of listening, speaking, reading, writing, reasoning, or mathematical abilities. These disorders are intrinsic to the individual and presumed to be due to central nervous system dysfunction. Even though a learning disability may occur concomitantly with other handicapping conditions (e.g., sensory impairment, mental retardation, social and emotional disturbance) or environmental influences (e.g., cultural differences, insufficient/inappropriate instruction, psychogenic factors), it is not the direct result of those conditions or influences (Wallace and McLoughlin 1988, p. 7).

A second fact that must be made explicit in the rationale is that students with reading disabilities who manage to complete secondary schools in decent standing often have intellectual abilities that range from the average to the superior. While, as the NJCLD definition above points out, undoubtedly there are people who are less intellectually able who are also reading disabled, these are not the ones who finish high school with a C average or lower. Often, these persons must struggle with the traditional school chores of reading and writing even though they may have special skills. The institution that does not make the effort to differentiate the reading disability subtypes, allocate the monies, or develop the necessary supportive program may be wasting valuable resources.

Doubtless, before the age of universal literacy, these types of reading disabilities did not exist, at least not as we recognize them. Strengths exhibited were skills respected, whether they were literary, artistic, political, rhetorical, or organizational. However, in our society of nearly universal schooling, the measure of learning and ability has changed. Success in school depends heavily on one skill—literacy. Research with reading disabilities shows that there are alternate means to desired academic ends. If blind students can be taught, so can those who have decoding problems with reading. The fact that reading-disabled students have no visible physical handicaps should not be a deterrent to the understanding of their academic problems and needs.

Other types of student support programs, such as tutorial and counseling programs, often are not prepared to handle these reading-disabled students. These other programs frequently have personnel who may not be adequately trained to work with reading-disabled persons. The personnel already may be overworked and understaffed and, thus, unable to handle additional students in need of special help and attention.

ADMINISTRATIVE AND PHYSICAL PLACEMENT

There are two types of placement to be considered when planning the development of an academic support program for reading-disabled students: administrative (under what lines of authority the new program is placed) and physical (where on the campus the offices are housed). The former is by far the most important consideration, since programs can wither and die if placed too far from the source of institutional authority. The site of the administrative offices varies from school to school, but generally the best place for a reading disabilities support program is either in an academic department or in an existing learning skills center.

Some institutions may wish to place the new program under the auspices of the office of student life, since in many cases services for handicapped students are located there. However, student life programs are devoted almost entirely to residential and social programs and to behavior control, with no academic focus. Even the services for handicapped persons within student life programs are usually concerned with the problems of access and mobility for persons whose physical handicaps preclude their movement on campus in a normal manner.

Administrative Placement

One appropriate administrative placement is within an academic department, very likely a department in the school of education, if the school has the potential to support such a program. The most obvious choice is within special education or educational psychology, but elementary or secondary departments would also serve. If located in an elementary education department, however, it is imperative that the program not degenerate into one that simply allows fledgling elementary educators to practice elementary teaching skills that are inappropriate for college students. Another possibility is that the program be located in a new department in the school of education but not within an existing department. The program then benefits from the resources and expertise of all persons within the school and provides an opportunity for research for all interested parties.

A second acceptable location is within an existing learning skills center on campus, since such centers usually offer tutorial and academic support programs for undergraduates. Here, the program can take advantage of experienced tutors and existing equipment and tutoring facilities. Many such centers also provide a selection of mini-courses in study and survival skills helpful to reading-disabled students.

Wherever the academic support program for reading-disabled students is located administratively, it should be placed so that there are not too many supervisory persons between the director and the vice-president of the institution. More than one chair or director and one dean is unacceptable. Often programs located far from the higher echelon of power within the institution starve from a lack of monetary and political sustenance and eventually wither away.

Physical Placement

Physical placement of the new support program may be less important than the administrative placement, but it must be given careful consideration. The facility should be centrally located on the campus, in an area that is easily accessible, well-lighted, and populated at night, and the safety of students must always be given primary consideration. The facility must also be large enough to accommodate twenty-five students at any one time.

An ideal layout consists of a large general study room with tables and chairs, reference materials, word processors, and some comfortable lounge chairs. Adjacent to or opening from this room are several smaller offices for the tutors and for individual tutoring. The director's office also opens onto this area. Sound-proof booths should be provided so that hired readers may tape text materials. While aesthetic considerations are necessarily last, it is nevertheless true that students will be more likely to enjoy working in a pleasant atmosphere.

PERSONNEL

The number of professional, full-time employees of an academic support program for students with reading disabilities will, of course, vary with the number of persons enrolled in such a program. According to Wallace and McLoughlin (1988), the estimates of the prevalance of learning disabled persons in the general population run anywhere from 3% to 15%. During school year 1983–84 almost two million children, or nearly 5% of the nation's public school enrollment, were categorized as learning disabled. A post-secondary institution might find that approximately 2% of its student population is reading disabled, although the figure can vary from institution to institution depending upon their admission standards.

The professional staff should include at least three positions: a director, a tutor coordinator, and a counselor–advisor. There should be a sufficient number of professional staff members to provide services to all the students who are identified as reading disabled. We propose that every center have a tutor coordinator and one counselor–advisor for every fifty reading-disabled students. Additionally, several graduate assistants will be assigned to the principal staff members to help in coordinating their areas of responsibility. Finally, there needs to be at least one full-time secretary and a group of trained part-time tutors, readers, and proofreaders. If the program is quite large, several more professional staff members will be needed.

Director

The director should be a person with a doctorate in an appropriate field, such as reading, psychology of reading, learning styles, etc., and should have experience in working closely with students with reading disabilities. This person should also exhibit excellent skills in speaking and writing and in dealing successfully with administrative work in personnel and budgets. The first duty of the director is to hire capable persons for the other staff positions, with the aid of a university search committee. The director also develops a set of logical, objective guidelines for the evaluation of work done by each staff member and initiates an annual review of each position so that adequate personnel records will be kept, insuring quality in and fairness toward the entire staff.

Supervision of staff may be more art than science and may depend more on innate personality than on training. However, a director who meets formally with the staff every week at a scheduled time and informally with anyone who needs to visit will make great strides toward establishing an atmosphere in which people can work together successfully. Further, a director who builds rapport with staff members so that they feel free to share their ideas, complaints, innovations, concerns, and actual disagreements will find the program much enriched. Although control is necessary and sometimes criticism must be voiced, it can be done constructively. All persons involved need to know that they are needed and appreciated for their contributions to the program. Praise is, in fact, almost as good as money as a motivator.

A second responsibility of the director is to develop the testing component of the program (see Chapter 3). The director budgets for and orders adequate testing materials. These are often expensive when ordered for large groups, although some testing materials may be used over and over. The staff should be trained to participate in the testing process as supervisors and scorers, so the director should schedule at least one staff workshop each year on testing procedures. Finally, the director schedules test dates, both for groups of students during the campus orientation periods and for individuals when they initially enroll in the program or when they are referred by faculty members. It is always helpful to obtain high school testing records of a student as well as the high school Individualized Education Program (IEP) if such items are available, since such data may save the student from repetitive testing. An IEP record will be extremely helpful in designing a program for a student, for it will explain just what help the student has been receiving and perhaps indicate what strategies have been successful. All testing records must be kept confidential, but all entering students are asked to sign a waiver so that their scores and records may be shared with their tutors and may be used anonymously for research.

In addition to planning group testing for orientation, the director schedules entry interviews with students and their parents. These may be group sessions held during orientation or they may be held individually with either the director or the counselor–advisor. Incoming students need to understand just what the program has to offer and what their obligations are once they enter the program. If the program is to cost more for these students, parents need to know just what they are paying for. This interview sets the ground rules for everyone involved, for it is important that students and their parents realize that the program is not a panacea for the problems and frustrations faced by reading-disabled students.

At the other end of the process, a director schedules exit interviews with all students who are graduating or leaving school for any other reason. Similarly, these sessions may be group meetings for graduates at the end of the school year or they may be individual sessions held with the director or the counselor–advisor. Scheduling these interviews may be somewhat more difficult to accomplish, since a successful student may have progressed to the point where he or she no longer depends upon the program to the extent of weekly or even monthly visits. The ultimate goal of any student-support service is to make itself unnecessary, and the exit interview provides an excellent opportunity for the evaluation of a program by the persons for whom it is most important. It also may often be a source of valuable suggestions or recruiting material, for the testimony of a successful graduate certainly carries great weight. It is generally wise to provide some evaluation instrument for use by exiting students so that they may offer their comments anonymously, providing a more objective source of data for program evaluation.

In addition to being responsible for program organization, budget management, personnel supervision, testing, and student interviews, the director gathers, coordinates, packages, and distributes the statistics about the program. This is necessary for continued political and financial survival, for continued recruitment, and for program evaluation. Records are kept on the grades and class attendance of each student and on the student's attendance for tutoring, counseling, readers, proofreaders, or other program offerings. Further, percentages and averages are kept so that the successes and failures over time can be evaluated. A program must demonstrate worthwhile results to be viable, and only statistics for each period of operation will show those results. Charts can be developed for each term showing the number of students involved; the percentage having above a B average, above a C average, on probation, dismissed, etc.; the attendance records, recorded in percentages, for program activities and classes; the entry, exit, and graduation rates; the majors of students, and so forth. Administrators, faculty, students, parents, and the general public all are interested in records like these.

While many of the materials developed for and within a program for the reading disabled are communal staff projects, the ultimate responsibility for the cost, usefulness, appearance, and general value of such materials rests with the program director. These materials include all office forms and form letters; all tutoring materials, such as study guides, sample tests, text outlines, taped materials, computer programs, and workbooks; all release, entry, exit, and evaluation forms; all program brochures and handbooks. Brochures and handbooks are valuable materials both for publicizing and explaining a program. A brochure, suitable for mailing and of high quality, both in design and content, is an important asset in recruiting students and promoting the program. It can be mailed by the admissions office in response to inquiries and can be circulated to secondary schools either on a local or national level, depending upon the recruiting focus of the institution.

A handbook for enrolled students is an excellent vehicle for presenting necessary institutional and program information and rules and regulations. Handbooks may range from the simple to the complex, but should contain descriptions of program services, locations, hours of operation, rules and regulations, lists of student responsibilities, and copies of all forms that students must sign to participate. Handbooks may include guidelines for study, lists of various counseling or community services, or suggestions for handling university red tape. What is included will ultimately depend upon the type of institution, the type of program, the types of students enrolled, and the skill of the staff in discovering and presenting just what their students need.

Perhaps the bulk of the director's time is spent in meeting and consulting with other administrators, with faculty members, and with parents and other concerned persons. A large part of the director's responsibility is in the area of public relations and promotion. Meeting regularly with other administrators is necessary to run any program smoothly. Contacts with persons in the offices of admissions, the registrar, student life, financial aid, and the immediate supervisor must occur frequently, and relations with all of these groups must be nurtured. Meetings with faculty, while more sporadic, are also extremely important, for the faculty must understand, appreciate, and support the program for it to exist at all. Further, faculty provide valuable academic support for students with reading disabilities, since their cooperation is necessary for the use of alternate methods of study and testing. Therefore, their cooperation must be encouraged and appreciated by the program staff. On the other hand, the director must often spend time diplomatically educating the faculty about reading disabilities. Some professors have never heard of reading disabilities and are likely to regard persons so designated as lazy or slow. Thus, the educational responsibilities of the director go in two directions: toward the instructors as well as toward the students.

Another responsibility of the program director is the academic advising of students enrolled in the program. If the program is too large, he or she may share this responsibility with the counselor–advisor. This will vary depending upon the system of academic advising within any particular institution. In some schools students must see academic advisors each term for specific signatures without which students may not register for classes. Other schools have academic advisors available for those who wish to consult with them but will allow students to register as they wish, feeling that it is the students' responsibility to read the catalogue and decide which courses to take. Although there are probably several variations of these two themes, schools seem either to have very free or very controlled registration.

Students with reading disabilities need to consult with the director or counselor–advisor before enrolling in classes. They need to know which courses are required for their individual course of study, they need to know how they stand vis-a-vis the requirements for graduation, and they need to be careful not to enroll inadvertently in courses for which the reading or writing loads will be inappropriate for them. Remembering that it takes longer for students with reading disabilities to do a task than it takes those without disabilities, advisors must try to help students select courses that they will have time to complete. Students whose problems lie in a particular area need to be urged to take courses in which they will be able to achieve.

If an institution uses a controlled system of registration, a program director must work closely with the advisors in each academic area in order to develop the best program for each student. If registration is less controlled, all students enrolled in the program must be encouraged to work closely with the program director or counselor–advisor in order to develop programs in which they can be the most successful.

Closely related to academic advising is the director's role vis-a-vis students with reading disabilities and the financial aid office. Many students receive financial aid of some kind, and the rules for receiving federal financial aid require that a student be enrolled in and earn a minimum of twelve credit hours per term. However, federal rules for the handicapped now allow students with reading disabilities to enroll in fewer than twelve hours and still qualify for aid. Thus, the director must be sure that all necessary data about the status of these students are current with the financial aid office in order to prevent the cancellation of a student's aid.

Some students with reading disabilities may qualify for aid from the office of Vocational Rehabilitation through each State Department of Human Services, a government service for the disabled. This agency will sometimes pay for tutors or notetakers, may provide equipment of various kinds, or in some instances, will pay tuition for disabled persons to attend college. Reading-disabled students may qualify for these funds, so the director should refer students to the appropriate persons in this agency. Additionally, some reading-disabled students may be able to use recordings for the blind, and the director coordinates the ordering of these materials.

Finally, a director participates in the academic community by serving on university committees, teaching occasionally in his or her academic area, belonging to professional organizations, being professionally active, and by publishing. All of these activities are necessary to maintain not only respectability within the academic community but also to continue to stay abreast of the current research and thought in one's own field. A stagnant staff will offer only a stagnant program, one unable to provide the most up-to-date services to their students.

Tutor Coordinator

The second professional staff member necessary in any academic support program for students with reading disabilities is the tutor coordinator. The minimum degree requirement for this position should be a master's degree in an appropriate area, such as reading, special education, or English, for example. The responsibilities of this person include hiring, training, and supervising tutors; keeping careful statistics about the hours spent in tutoring, the students tutored, the courses in which they have been tutored, and success rates of the students in their courses and, if necessary, helping with academic advising.

Although the program director helps with the hiring of tutors and readers, the main responsibility for recruiting persons well-qualified for these positions rests with the tutor coordinator. Generally, contacts should be made with all department heads, with the graduate advisors, and with the work-study directors within the financial aid office. Recommendations then can be followed with phone calls, interviews, and, for interested and capable parties, official transcripts. Posted or published notifications of job openings may also be helpful. While it is often best to employ graduate students, there are also juniors and seniors who will be excellent tutors. Each person employed in a tutoring position should have a cumulative grade point average of at least 3.0 or a B average and the recommendation of the department head or senior professor in the major area. Being an excellent student, however, is not enough to qualify one for a tutoring position. Tutors must be patient, positive, intuitive, empathetic persons who can analyze students' problems and design learning situations without succumbing to the temptation to do a student's work for him or her. It can be quite difficult to watch a student struggle through an assignment, agonizing over every detail, when the tutor can do it in a fraction of the time. Thus, hiring tutors is a major responsibility and a time-consuming task for the tutor coordinator.

Training tutors is also important. New tutors may have great academic ability but little knowledge about the job for which they have been employed. There are three levels of tutor training that fall to the tutor coordinator: the development of day-long workshops to be given at the beginning of each term, the creation of a packet of materials on techniques for tutoring, the collection of books and articles on the subject, and the day-to-day observation and feedback that any person new to a job needs in order to master it.

A day-long, tutor-training workshop gives the tutor coordinator an opportunity not only to tell new tutors about techniques and procedures but also to demonstrate them. In this format, experienced tutors can assume teaching roles and be extremely valuable resources for initiating new employees into the program. Videotaped tutoring sessions (with the written permission of all persons taped, of course) can be shown and discussed; role playing can be demonstrated; and office procedures and paperwork can be thoroughly explained. This gives employees a chance to become acquainted before everyone becomes too busy.

A packet of tutor training materials may include, besides office forms and written statements of office and payroll procedures, a statement on the nature of reading disabilities, a bibliography on the subject, a statement on building rapport, a discussion of working in a multi-cultural context, an explanation of the various types of reading instruction for improving comprehension (see Chapter 5), a discussion of study skill techniques, a list of techniques for encouraging students and for keeping them on task while visiting the center, and steps for tutors to take when they feel that they cannot cope with a tutoring situation.

The day-to-day observation of tutors at work is done informally, but the tutor coordinator sets up regular group and individual meetings with the tutoring staff in order to provide guidance and continuing training. Such meetings will also provide the feedback necessary to keep any tutoring program viable.

Statistics gathering and record keeping are important responsibilities of the tutor coordinator. As mentioned earlier, programs must prove their worth if they are to continue to exist, and this requires accurate statitistics. The record of the number of hours spent in tutoring, both total and for each student; the number of students tutored and the areas of tutoring for each; the number and types of courses for which students sought tutoring; the instructors of the courses for which students sought help; and the grades and success rates for all students receiving tutoring are invaluable items for analyzing not only the success of the program but also for designing instruction to benefit students.

One significant, daily aspect of the job of the tutor coordinator is to schedule all tutoring appointments. This requires meeting with students who need or wish to receive tutoring in a particular skill or subject and with students who wish to tutor. It also requires a thorough knowledge of the skills and personalities of the tutors involved, in order to match students and tutors successfully. The tutor coordinator must have up-to-date tutor schedules at all times and be able to estimate how much tutoring a student will require based on the student's request, the student's testing records, and the student's previous performance. Thus, the tutor coordinator spends a large amount of time meeting with students to schedule or evaluate their tutoring.

Finally, the tutor coordinator must, during times of heavy advising, such as registration and orientation, help the director with the academic advising and testing of students.

COUNSELOR–ADVISOR

Like the position of tutor coordinator, that of counselor–advisor requires a minimum of a masters degree in an appropriate area, perhaps experience in reading or special education with some background in the theory and practice of counseling. The responsibilities of this person include counseling individual students; setting up and conducting workshops dealing with topics such as test anxiety, speaking in classes, and facing the fact that one has a reading disability without trying to hide it; participating in the academic advising and testing component of the program during registration and orientation; and maintaining adequate records of students' attendance in classes.

Because of the frustrations inherent in the situations of reading-disabled students, counseling needs to be a regular component of their support program, at least during their freshman year. All freshmen enrolled in the program should be scheduled to meet with the counselor–advisor regularly during the first semester on campus. Students beyond the freshman year who are in the program should plan to meet with the counselor at least once each semester. Of course, there will be a number of students whose problems are such that they need more individual attention and may need to see the counselor several times a week or even daily. Like the rest of the academic support program, the goal here is to make the student less dependent on the program as time progresses; however, experience has shown that great amounts of encouragement, understanding, love, and facial tissues will be required.

For the reading-disabled, academic work is never easy, and sometimes it becomes overwhelming. At these times, the students need to know where to go to find help, encouragement, and a friendly person who wants to listen to their problems. Often they only need to talk and do not really need any particular advice or help. For this reason, the counselor and all other staff members need to have an informal, open door atmosphere in their offices so that students feel comfortable walking in at anytime to discuss their feelings in a relaxed, accepting, non-threatening environment. Very often, the student with a reading disability is riddled with self-doubt about his or her own intellectual ability. A few words of encouragement will make a great deal of difference in the academic life of these students.

In order to provide this kind of counseling, the counselor should have a good background in the area of reading and be knowledgeable in the differential diagnosis of reading disabilities. It often happens that a student will form a close relationship with a staff member other than the counselor and feel more comfortable talking to that person, or a tutoring session may turn into a counseling session during the natural progression of a conversation about problems with a class. A student will be unlikely to settle down to reading a literature assignment, for instance, when depressed about some comment made by an insensitive teacher. In these cases all staff members must function as counselors, and so the counselor should also conduct workshops for the tutoring staff to teach them how to deal with these situations positively. Tutors also must be able to recognize when to call in a professional, for there are some cases when peer tutors should not be involved.

If an academic skills course, as described earlier in this book, is available on campus, reading-disabled students should be required to enroll in it. If one is not available, the program should develop its own, following the guidelines discussed in Chapter 4, and the counselor–advisor will develop and teach the course. If the program is large enough to require several sections of the course, the counselor will recruit and supervise graduate assistants who will teach course sections. When a program has its own skills course, it becomes the duty of the counselor–advisor also to schedule classes, reserve rooms, order books, and enroll students.

In addition to the academic skills course taken by all freshmen, occasional two hour workshops on such topics as stress management, surviving without a tutor, résumé preparation, and interviewing skills may be desirable. Sometimes a popular or required workshop may need to be offered several times. Some may be so well attended that they are offered every term.

Counseling workshops for the tutoring staff probably should be offered in conjunction with the tutor training workshop at the beginning of each term. They should be mandatory for new staff and for all tutors if there is evidence of such a need.

The class attendance monitoring done by the counselor–advisor will require contact with numerous faculty members. To reduce the time consumed by this task, it is helpful to develop a card which can be sent to the teachers of each student on which the instructor can indicate current attendance, grades, problems, and comments. These can be processed by the secretarial staff so that the counselor–advisor will have time for an analysis of and reaction to the information thus collected. Frequently, a sudden drop in class attendance is the first sign of a student's having given up or being overcome by depression because of the frustration caused by academic demands.

Access

The director has access to all grade reports, admission information, financial aid records, and student life records of enrolled students. When enrolling in the program, students are required to sign a contract with the program that includes permission for these types of information to be sent to the program director.

Budget

There are two basic rules for budgeting in academe: always ask for more than appears to be needed and always remember that the money will run out before the fiscal year ends. It is a given that a program will never receive everything it asks for, so in order to get what is needed, it is necessary to overestimate the request. Further, emergencies, student pay raises, and equipment failures are certain to occur at the worst possible times, so that even the best laid budgetary plans can go awry. This, then, necessitates flexibility as well as caution in budgeting.

The budget must allocate funds for salaries, equipment, furniture, and materials. Salaries will always be the largest expenditure on this list. The director's salary should be commensurate with the salaries received by other twelve month, middle-grade administrators in the institution, the tutor coordinator and counselor somewhat less, the tutors paid according to education levels, and readers, at least minimum wage. Equipment can be a large budgetary item, especially if the program is fortunate enough to have personal computers and a copy machine. Of course, machines like these require maintenance agreements that must be budgeted for. Furniture includes all tables, chairs, desks, chalkboards, file cabinets, bookcases, and cabinets and repairs on each. Materials include office and classroom supplies, dictionaries of various sorts, testing supplies, and software. Frequently, it is necessary for a program to purchase texts for commonly tutored courses so that the tutors will have time to read the materials and prepare study guides to accompany the lessons.

It is not really possible to present a typical budget because of the overwhelming number of potential variations and conditions that occur among different institutions. For example, at some schools, all student workers receive minimum wage for hourly work. At others, they are paid as much as $10 per hour for tutoring. Though those with advanced degrees should be paid more than undergraduate workers, this may not always be possible. In some cases, schools hire persons who are not students as part-time tutors, and these may be homemakers, retired persons, off-duty public school teachers, and so forth. Occasionally, a program is lucky enough to develop a volunteer tutoring staff from interested persons inside and outside of the academic community; this makes a budget go much further. Finally, the salaries of the professional staff will vary enormously from institution to institution; schools on both coasts, for instance, pay a great deal more than schools in the central areas of the country. Thus, to set up a hypothetical budget here would not be helpful. However, the ratio of students to tutors should not exceed ten to one, and a smaller one is desirable, for instance, six to one.

An academic support program at the post-secondary level for students with reading disabilities can be very rewarding, both for the individuals involved and for the parent institution. A successful, visible, highly respected program can attract the attention of prospective students, their parents, and their high school counselors and, thus, enhance the image of the school even as it enhances enrollment. Students with reading disabilities who choose to pursue a collegiate career may be gifted individuals whose presence will be an enormous asset to any campus. Any institution that chooses not to comply with federally mandated services for the handicapped in this context runs the risk of lawsuits and negative publicity, a risk that many schools cannot afford.

With the necessary academic and emotional support, students with reading disabilities can succeed in post-secondary educational programs. Many who have already done so have continued their success in the professional world beyond college. For the staff members of academic support programs, there is an immense reward in following the successes of their former students.

Appendix

Name _____ Grade _____

Instructions: Read these words aloud.

List 1

1. dog	14. fact	27. sing
2. cat	15. large	28. coming
3. pages	16. cells	29. songs
4. chance	17. city	30. became
5. larger	18. page	31. green
6. special	19. having	32. children
7. region	20. except	33. gone
8. decide	21. strong	34. cannot
9. girl	22. cold	35. begin
10. uncle	23. bring	36. game
11. changes	24. center	37. moving
12. discover	25. eggs	38. audible
13. edge	26. certain	

Mean number of words correct for grade 8 = 37.69

SD = 1.26

READING TEST

Name _____ Grade _____

Instructions: Read these words aloud.

List 2

1. king	16. ring	31. circle
2. church	17. engine	32. general
3. huge	18. process	33. village
4. chart	19. vegetable	34. giant
5. spring	20. gold	35. playing
6. charge	21. forces	36. gentle
7. record	22. danger	37. decimal
8. garden	23. capitol	38. glass
9. carry	24. hungry	39. pause
10. glad	25. cattle	40. thorough
11. include	26. fingers	41. applause
12. Germany	27. corn	42. necessity
13. necessary	28. bags	43. docile
14. strange	29. occur	
15. increase	30. begins	

Mean number correct for grade 8 = 41.37

SD = 1.21

READING TEST

Name _____ Grade _____

Instructions: Read these words aloud.

List 3

1. car	10. rat
2. mute	11. bite
3. sit	12. glade
4. came	13. care
5. hug	14. huge
6. rate	15. cut
7. mug	16. bit
8. cute	17. glad
9. site	

List 4

1. wait
2. cause
3. ghost
4. daughter
5. tough
6. laughter
7. build
8. caught
9. sign
10. guess

Mean number of words correct for grade 8 = 15.87

SD = 1.04

Mean number correct for grade 8 = 9.81

SD= 0.41

READING TEST, NON-WORDS

Name _____ Grade _____

Instructions: These are not real words. Try to read them aloud.

List 5

1. gare	13. gite	25. tite
2. duncle	14. fedge	26. cad
3. ract	15. git	27. dit
4. gar	16. bage	28. cilly
5. bace	17. ling	29. cept
6. recide	18. gog	30. colp
7. kaces	19. gend	31. kar
8. gade	20. cend	32. pare
9. skare	21. grone	33. sute
10. chape	22. chind	34. kare
11. skar	23. gen	35. par
12. kute	24. pice	36. sut

Mean number correct for grade 8 = 30
SD = 4.46

WRITTEN SPELLING TEST

Instructions: I am going to say a word and then I will read a sentence in which the word is embedded. Finally, I will say the word again. You have to write it down.

1. dog	The *dog* makes a good pet.	dog
2. cat	The *cat* is also a pet.	cat
3. pages	There are many *pages* in the book.	pages
4. chance	He has a *chance* of winning the game.	chance
5. larger	Jane's house is *larger* than Bill's.	larger
6. special	Christmas is a very *special* day.	special
7. region	They live in the northern *region* of the country.	region
8. decide	You must *decide* by tomorrow if you can come or not.	decide
9. girl	She is a pretty *girl*.	girl
10. uncle	You would like my *uncle*, but not my aunt.	uncle
11. changes	When Bill goes swimming he *changes* his clothes.	changes
12. discover	Did Columbus *discover* America?	discover

(continued)

WRITTEN SPELLING TEXT *(continued)*

13.	edge	They live on the *edge* of the town.	edge
14.	fact	That is an interesting *fact*.	fact
15.	large	That is a *large* house, not a small one.	large
16.	cells	There are many *cells* in our body; you have to use a microscope to see them.	cells
17.	city	We live in the *city*, not in a village.	city
18.	page	Please turn to the first *page* of your book.	page
19.	having	Jim was *having* a good time.	having
20.	except	I like all kinds of food *except* spinach.	except
21.	strong	Bill is very *strong*. He is not weak.	strong
22.	cold	It is *cold* outside, but hot inside.	cold
23.	bring	Will you *bring* me my plate?	bring
24.	center	He hit it in the *center*, not outside.	center
25.	eggs	I had *eggs* for breakfast.	eggs
26.	certain	Are you *certain* of that, or are you not sure?	certain
27.	sing	I like to *sing* but not dance.	sing
28.	coming	John is *coming* home tomorrow.	coming
29.	songs	He knows many *songs* and he sings them.	songs
30.	became	Jill *became* a school teacher.	became
31.	green	The grass is *green*.	green
32.	children	Parents have *children*.	children
33.	gone	He must have *gone* home.	gone
34.	cannot	I *cannot* answer that question.	cannot
35.	begin	We will *begin* a new lesson tomorrow.	begin
36.	game	Basketball is a fun *game*.	game
37.	moving	They are *moving* to their new house.	moving
38.	audible	If the speech is *audible* you can hear it.	audible

Mean number correct for grade 8 = 36.6

SD = 2.2

READING TEST

Name _____ Grade _____

Instructions: Here are some common words. Read them aloud *as fast as you can* taking care not to make mistakes.

Function Words

List 1		*List II*	
let	also	every	should
has	must	never	except
ago	even	could	behind
off	such	along	though
why	once	while	during
any	soon	might	almost
yet	ever	often	before
nor	upon	which	without
will	else	since	perhaps
much	thus	ahead	although

Mean time for grade 8 = 12.0	Mean time for grade 8 = 14.31
SD= 3.8	SD= 3.91

READING PASSAGES: GRADE LEVEL 10 A

Instructions: Read this passage aloud.

The Cherokee Indians say that Uktena was the most terrible animal that ever lived in America. Its den was in dark Nantahala Gorge in Western North Carolina. It was a snake as big as a tree trunk and a mile long. Its one eye, between two horns, was a precious gem. Whoever was seen by that eye died. Any Indian who was brave enough to kill Uktena and get that eye would be able to know the future. Many tried and died. At last a very brave Cherokee shot Uktena with an arrow while the snake was stretched along the top of Cliff mountain. Uktena slithered back and forth across Nantahala Gorge, tore up trees as it rolled down the mountain, and died at the bottom of the gorge. The brave Indian recovered the gem, and the story goes that it is kept by each succeeding chief of the Cherokees.

DECOMPOSED LIST OF WORDS: GRADE LEVEL 10 A

Instructions: Read these words aloud.

Indians	Nantahala	seen
trunk	Cherokee	America
rolled	ever	dark
succeeding	den	lived
precious	most	animal
Western	Uktena	big
two	while	mile
Carolina	arrow	tree
enough	each	snake
whoever	goes	horns
back	kept	brave
stretched	last	very
recovered	Gorge	shot
get	between	along
slithered	chief	story
eye	forth	terrible
kill	down	top
that	tore	cliff
say	brave	long
bottom	any	know
able	died	mountain
future	gem	across

READING PASSAGES: GRADE LEVEL 10 B

Instructions: Read this passage aloud.

The electric eel, a native fish of South America, defends itself from attacks of enemies by a natural electric battery. A discharge from this battery is powerful enough to stun even the largest animals. Where roads pass through ponds frequented by these peculiar fish, it has often been found necessary to change the line of the road for fear of them.

These fish are used for food by the native Indians, but they are dangerous to catch because of their ability to shock the fishermen. In order to overcome this difficulty, the Indians have devised a very ingenious method of disarming the fish. Horses are driven into the ponds and the eels expend their electrical charge on the horses. Then the fish are easily harpooned and caught. It is only after a long rest and some food that they are able to build up ability to shock their enemies again.

DECOMPOSED LIST OF WORDS: GRADE LEVEL 10 B

Instructions: Read these words aloud.

ponds	horses	catch
charge	fishermen	dangerous
harpooned	necessary	ability
able	found	shock
build	battery	caught
often	by	electrical
fish	eel	enemies
change	native	itself
line	where	from
fear	pass	electric
even	animals	natural
stun	because	disarming
powerful	order	method
frequented	overcome	driven
defend	rest	them
attacks	long	been
peculiar	easily	these
into	road	roads
expend	enough	south
again	largest	discharge
shock	used	America
difficulty	food	through
ingenious	Indians	devised

READING PASSAGES: GRADE LEVEL 11 A

Instructions: Read this passage aloud.

Long before the days of printing, minstrels wandered from castle to castle singing before kings and their retainers. Their songs were usually about the character and the brave deeds of a real hero. Often these minstrels, these "gleemen," used their imagination and added mythical deeds. No one at the time attempted to write down any of these tales, for few knew how to write. The stories were originally handed down by word of mouth, very much in the same way as were the legends of the American Indians. But about A.D. 700 the stories relating to the brave deeds of a hero, Beowolf, were collected by some Anglo-Saxon poet of the time. This poem has since been translated into modern English and today we can enjoy reading the first epic poem in English literature. Beowolf fought two dreadful fights to save a king and one to save his own people.

DECOMPOSED LIST OF WORDS: GRADE LEVEL 11 A

Instructions: Read these words aloud.

enjoy	originally	write
English	people	few
save	stories	knew
epic	printing	tales
Beowolf	days	time
A.D. 700	minstrels	attempted
legends	before	down
handed	songs	fights
word	long	much
mythical	singing	Indians
added	fought	mouth
retainers	kings	American
wandered	from	literature
castle	before	first
their	two	today
gleemen	these	reading
imagination	often	translated
hero	real	poet
deeds	character	modern
brave	about	poem
some	usually	Anglo-saxon
collected	own	
dreadful	one	

READING PASSAGES: GRADE LEVEL 11 B

Instructions: Read this passage aloud.

A great black and yellow V-2 rocket forty-six feet long stood in a New Mexico desert. Empty, it weighed five tons. For fuel it carried eight tons of alcohol and liquid oxygen. Everything was ready. Scientists and Generals withdrew to some distance and crouched behind earth mounds. Two red flares rose as a signal to fire the rocket. With a great roar and burst of flame the giant rocket rose slowly and then faster and faster. Behind it trailed sixty feet of yellow flame. Soon the flame looked like a yellow star. In a few seconds it was too high to be seen, but radar tracked it as it sped upward at 3,000 miles per hour. A few minutes after it was fired, the pilot of a watching plane saw it return at a speed of 2,400 miles per hour and plunge into earth forty miles from the starting point.

DECOMPOSED LIST OF WORDS: GRADE LEVEL 11 B

Instructions: Read these words aloud.

forty	flame	feet
burst	miles	tons
tracked	hours	alcohol
high	per	ready
radar	speed	liquid
star	minutes	withdrew
seconds	point	distance
pilot	plane	crouched
oxygen	saw	some
everything	fired	earth
scientists	watching	behind
generals	return	mounds
fire	great	signal
roar	yellow	3,000
flares	rocket	upward
rose	forty-six	sixty
five	black	flame
two	V-2	trailed
red	stood	faster
fuel	Mexico	2,400
eight	desert	speed
carried	new	earth
giant	empty	plunge
rose	weighed	starting
slowly	long	

READING PASSAGES: GRADE LEVEL 12 A

Instructions: Read this passage aloud.

When the Spaniards came to Columbia, South America, they were told of a tribe of Indians who possessed fabulous wealth. Many years before, the wife of an Indian chief had thrown herself into a lake to escape punishment and had become the goddess of the lake. Because they believed she had the power to make their tribe prosperous and victorious, whenever a new chief was chosen this tribe made a grand pilgrimage to Lake Guatavita to honor the goddess and take her presents. First in the procession came wailing men, who bore signs of mourning for the chief who had died; then came men decked with ornaments of gold and emeralds, with feathers in their hair; then braves in jaguar

(continued)

skins; then priests in black robes and tall caps. Finally came the nobles and chief priests, among them the new chief, who rode in a barrow covered with gold disks.

DECOMPOSED LIST OF WORDS: GRADE LEVEL 12 A

Instructions: Read these words aloud.

gold	came	before
rode	tall	years
barrow	robes	wealth
covered	caps	fabulous
honor	finally	Columbia
pilgrimage	nobles	came
decked	black	Spaniards
when	signs	told
south	priests	America
were	whenever	tribe
Indians	Guatavita	many
she	presents	possessed
power	procession	punishment
their	wailing	chief
prosperous	bore	become
chosen	jaguar	they
made	hair	because
grand	braves	goddess
feathers	victorious	believed
emeralds	escape	make
gold	into	men
ornaments	thrown	mourning
died	herself	skins
then	wife	first

READING PASSAGES: GRADE LEVEL 12 B

Instructions: Read this passage aloud.

Their airplane had been forced down at sea. They barely had time to inflate the yellow rubber dinghies and climb into them before the plane sank. Would a rescue plane find them? One did finally. To the surprise of the anxious watchers, they saw a boat hanging under it. The boat was aimed and dropped from the plane. Parachutes opened and let it down gently about a hundred yards from the dinghies. A sea anchor shot from the front. A long, light line shot from each side. *(continued)*

When the men pulled themselves into the boat by these lines, they found it equipped with two outboard motors, sails, compass, charts, waterproofed instructions for everything in four languages, dry clothes, food, cigarettes, knives, fishing tackle—everything but a welcome mat. All this was provided to make sure that they would keep afloat and alive until they could make harbor or be rescued.

DECOMPOSED LIST OF WORDS: GRADE LEVEL 12 B

Instructions: Read these words aloud.

their	each	rescue
tackle	anchor	sank
sure	charts	anxious
outboard	airplane	plane
two	forced	boat
everything	opened	watchers
mat	down	saw
provided	front	aimed
afloat	equipped	hanging
harbor	rubber	hundred
rescued	surprise	gently
four	finally	yards
dry	parachutes	light
languages	dropped	line
cigarettes	motors	long
knives	compass	pulled
food	sails	side
clothes	welcome	themselves
inflate	fishing	instructions
yellow	barely	everything
dinghies	time	waterproofed
climb	them	keep
under	find	alive
shot	would	sea

READING PASSAGES: GRADE LEVEL 13 A

Instructions: Read this passage aloud.

Space is said to be pervaded by ether, an invisible medium by which all waves of energy are thought to be transmitted. Of these ethereal vibrations, the most important for plants are the light waves, since all plants grow by the action of light, which a substance in their leaves converts

(continued)

into energy. Various species of plants, however, thrive best on different varieties of what we call light. For example, there is a marked difference between sunlight and moonlight, owing to the fact that the vibrations of light from the sun run in all directions, but the vibrations of moonlight are polarized and run in one direction only. Certain plants, such as the cucumber, thrive best in this polarized light. Since the discovery of this scientific fact, various experimental farms have been established where the light has been polarized in order to further the growth of certain species of plants.

DECOMPOSED LIST OF WORDS: GRADE LEVEL 13 A

Instructions: Read these words aloud.

directions	certain	most
owing	scientific	plants
moonlight	cucumber	grow
between	experimental	action
sunlight	certain	light
example	polarized	invisible
marked	difference	ether
varieties	however	pervaded
best	thrive	said
different	species	space
fact	various	medium
thrive	converts	which
discovery	substance	waves
farms	leaves	energy
established	vibrations	thought
further	ethereal	transmitted
growth	important	

READING PASSAGES: GRADE LEVEL 13 B

Instructions: Read this passage aloud.

That we are as yet ignorant of even the simplest relations between different odors is abundantly evident from the current uncertainties regarding their classification. Many thousands of different scents can be discriminated; just how many is not known. And with each passing day the organic chemist is adding new ones. It is quite possible, however, that only a few elementary odors are needed to account for the whole range of possible smells. The situation may be much as it is in

(continued)

the case of color, where three primaries are sufficient to synthesize the total gamut of visual hues. Were we as certain of the facts of odor mixture as we are the facts of color mixture, we should be able to approach with confidence such problems as those of odor specification and flavor analysis. As matters now stand, our information along these lines is at best characterized as sketchy.

DECOMPOSED LIST OF WORDS: GRADE LEVEL 13 B

Instructions: Read these words aloud.

sketchy	problems	abundantly
characterized	mixture	evident
elementary	specification	different
chemist	analysis	uncertainties
quite	flavor	current
possible	matter	regarding
such	sufficient	classification
confidence	color	thousands
three	case	scents
primaries	situation	organic
synthesize	whole	day
total	account	passing
gamut	range	discriminated
visual	odors	known
hues	needed	adding
certain	simplest	stand
facts	ignorant	new
odor	relations	lines
approach	between	best

References

Aaron, P. G. 1985. The paradoxical relationship between intelligence and reading disability. *Perceptual and Motor Skills* 61:1251–1261.

Aaron, P. G. 1987. Developmental dyslexia: Is it different from other forms of reading disability? *Annals of Dyslexia* 37:109–124.

Aaron, P. G. 1989a. *Dyslexia and Hyperlexia: Diagnosis and Management of Developmental Reading Disabilities.* Boston, MA: Kluwer Academic Publishers.

Aaron, P. G. 1989b. Orthographic systems and developmental dyslexia: A reformulation of the syndrome. In *Reading and Writing Disorders in Different Orthographic Systems,* eds. P. G. Aaron and R. M. Joshi. Boston, MA: Kluwer Academic Publishers.

Aaron, P. G. 1989c. Qualitative and quantitative differences among dyslexic, normal, and non-dyslexic poor readers. *Reading and Writing: An Interdisciplinary Journal* 1:291–308.

Aaron, P. G., and Clouse, R. 1982. Freud's psychohistory of Leonardo da Vinci: A matter of being right or left? *Journal of Interdisciplinary History* XIII(1):1–16.

Aaron, P. G., and Joshi, R. M. (Eds.) 1989. *Reading and Writing Disorders in Different Orthographic Systems.* Boston, MA: Kluwer Academic Publishers.

Aaron, P. G., and Phillips, S. 1986. A decade of research with dyslexic college students: A summary of findings. *Annals of Dyslexia* 36:44–66.

Aaron, P. G., and Simurdak, J. 1989. Differential diagnosis of reading disabilities without using IQ tests. Unpublished manuscript. Blumberg Center for Interdisciplinary Studies in Special Education. Indiana State University.

Aaron, P. G., and Simurdak, J. In press. The Matthew effect: Decline of verbal IQ in children with learning disability. *Perceptual and Motor Skills.*

Aaron, P. G., and Whitefield, J. 1990. Dysfluency—Fluency: Implications for a new cognitive style for reading consultation. *Journal of Reading, Writing, and Learning Disabilities, International* 6(4):395–411.

Aaron, P. G., Bommarito, T., and Baker, C. 1984. The three phases of developmental dyslexia. In *Dyslexia: A Global Issue,* eds. R. N. Malatesha and H. A. Whitaker. The Hague: Martinus Nijhoff Publishers.

Aaron, P. G., Franz, S., and Manges, A. 1990. Dissociation between pronunciation and comprehension in reading disabilities. *Reading and Writing, An Interdisciplinary Journal* 3:1–22.

Aaron, P. G., Olsen, J. A., and Baker, C. 1985. The dyslexic college student: Is he dysphasic too? *Cognitive Neuropsychology* 2(2):17–42.

Aaron, P. G., Phillips, S., and Larsen, S. 1988. Specific Reading Disability in historically famous persons. *Journal of Learning Disabilities* 12:523–38.

Aitchison, J. 1987. *Words in the Mind: An Introduction to the Mental Lexicon.* New York: Basil Blackwell, Inc.

Alegria, J., Pignot, E., and Morais, J. 1982. Phonetic analysis of speech and memory codes in beginning readers. *Memory and Cognition* 10:451–56.

Alley, G., and Deshler, D. 1979. *Teaching the Learning Disabled Adolescent: Strategies and Methods.* Denver, CO: Love Publishing Co.

Allington, R., and Fleming, J. T. 1978. The misreading of high-frequency words. *Journal of Special Education* 12:417–21.

Allington, R., and Strange, M. 1977. Effect of grapheme substitution in connected text upon reading behaviors. *Visible Language* 11:285–97.

Anderson, R. C., and Freebody, S. 1981. Vocabulary knowledge. In *Comprehension and Teaching,* ed. J. T. Guthrie. Newark, DE: International Reading Association.

Aquino, M. R. 1969. The validity of the Miller-Coleman readability scale. *Reading Research Quarterly* 4:342–57.

Baddeley, A. D. 1966a. Short-term memory for word sequences as a function of acoustic, semantic, and form similarity. *Quarterly Journal of Experimental Psychology* 18:362–65.

Baddeley, A. D. 1966b. The influence of acoustic and semantic similarity on long-term memory for word sequences. *Quarterly Journal of Experimental Psychology* 18:302–309.

Baddeley, A. D., and Hitch, G. 1974. Working memory. In *The Psychology of Learning and Motivation,* (Vol. 8), ed. G. H. Bower. New York: Academic Press.

Baker, C. 1984. Effects of comparison/contrast writing instruction on the reading comprehension of tenth-grade students. Unpublished doctoral dissertation, Indiana State University, Terre Haute, IN.

Baker, L., and Brown, A. 1984. Metacognitive skills and reading. In *Handbook of Reading Research,* ed. P. D. Pearson. New York: Longman.

Bandura, A. 1982. Self-efficacy mechanism in human agency. *American Psychologist* 37:122–47.

Benson, D. F. 1977. The third alexia. *Archives of Neurology* 34:327–31.

Bereiter, C., and Scarmalia, M. 1987. *The Psychology of Written Composition.* Hillsdale, NJ: Lawrence Erlbaum.

Berger, N. 1978. Why can't Johnny read? Perhaps he is not a good listener. *Journal of Learning Disabilities* 11:633–38.

Blanchard, J. S., Mason, G. E., and Daniel, D. 1987. *Computer Application in Reading,* (3rd edition). Newark, DE: International Reading Association.

Blank, M. 1985. A word is a word—or is it? In *Biobehavioral Measures of Dyslexia,* eds. D. G. Gray and J. F. Kavanagh. Parkton, MD: York Press.

Bos, C. S. 1988. Academic interventions for learning disabilities. In *Learning Disabilities: State of the Art and Practice,* ed. K. A. Kavale. Boston, MA: Little Brown.

Bower, G., and Hilgard, E. 1981. *Theories of Learning.* Englewood Cliffs, NJ: Prentice Hall.

Boy, A. V., and Pine, J. G. 1963. *Client Centered Counseling in Secondary School.* Boston, MA: Houghton Mifflin.

Bradley, L., and Bryant, P. E. 1983. Categorizing sounds and learning to read. *Nature* 301:419–21.

Bradley, L., and Bryant, P. E. 1985. *Rhyme and Reason in Reading and Spelling.* Ann Arbor, MI: University of Michigan Press.

Brophy, J. 1987. Synthesis of research on strategies for motivating students to learn. *Educational Leadership* 45(2):40–48.

Bruck, M. 1987. The adult outcome of children with learning disabilities. *Annals of Dyslexia* 37:252–63.

Byrne, B., and Ledez, J. 1983. Phonological awareness in reading disabled adults. *Australian Journal of Psychology* 35:185–97.

Calfee, R. C., Venezky, R. L., and Chapman, R. S. 1969. Pronunciation of synthetic words with predictable and unpredictable letter-sound correspondences. *Technical Report No. 11*. Research and Development Center, University of Wisconsin, Madison, WI.

Canady, R. L., and Hotchkiss, F. R. 1989. It's a good score, just a bad grade. *Phi Delta Kappan* 71:68–71.

Canney, G., and Winograd, P. 1979. Schemata for reading and reading comprehension performance. *Technical Report No. 120*. Center for the Study of Reading, University of Illinois, Champaign, IL.

Çapan, S. 1989. A linguistic study of reading and writing disorders in Turkish, an agglutinative language. In *Reading and Writing Disorders in Different Orthographic Systems*, eds. P. G. Aaron and R. M. Joshi. Boston, MA: Kluwer Academic Publishers.

Carroll, J. B. 1977. Developmental parameters in reading comprehension. In *Cognition, Curriculum, and Comprehension*, ed. J. T. Guthrie. Newark, DE: International Reading Association.

Carroll, J. B., Davies, P., and Richman, B. 1971. *Word Frequency Book*. New York: Houghton Mifflin.

Centra, J. 1986. Handicapped student performance on the SAT. *Journal of Learning Disabilities* 19:324–27.

Chafe, W. 1985. Linguistic differences produced by differences between speaking and writing. In *Literacy, Language, and Learning: The Nature and Consequences of Reading and Writing*, eds. D. R. Olson, N. Torrance, and A. Hildyard. New York: Cambridge University Press.

Chafe, W., and Danielewicz, J. 1987. Properties of spoken and written language. In *Comprehending Oral and Written Language*, eds. R. Horowitz and S. J. Samuels. New York: Academic Press.

Chall, J. 1979. The great debate ten years later with a modest proposal for reading stages. In *Theory and Practice in Early Reading*, eds. L. Resnick and P. Weaver. (Vol. 1). Hillsdale, NJ: Lawrence Erlbaum.

Cirilo, R. K., and Foss, D. J. 1980. Text structure and reading time for sentences. *Journal of Verbal Learning and Verbal Behavior* 19:96–109.

Conners, F., and Olson, R. In press. Reading comprehension in dyslexic and normal readers: A component skills analysis. In *Comprehension Processing in Reading*, eds. D. A. Balota, G. B. Flores de Arcais and K. Rayner. Hillsdale, NJ: Lawrence Erlbaum.

Conrad, R. 1964. Acoustic confusions in immediate memory. *British Journal of Psychology* 55:75–84.

Cordoni, B. 1982. Services for college dyslexics. In *Reading Disorders: Varieties and Treatments*, eds. R. N. Malatesha and P. G. Aaron. New York: Academic Press.

Cortina, J., Elder, J., and Gonnet, K. 1989. *Comprehending College Text-Books: Steps to Understanding and Remembering What You Read*. New York: McGraw Hill.

Cossu, G., Shankweiler, D., Liberman, I. Y., Tola, G. G., and Katz, L. 1988. Awareness of phonological segments and reading ability in Italian children. *Applied Psycholinguistics* 9:1–16.

Curtis, M. E. 1980. Development of components of reading skill. *Journal of Educational Psychology* 72:656–69.

Dale, E., and Chall, J. 1948. A formula for predicting readability. *Educational Research Bulletin* 27:11–20.

Danks, J. 1980. Comprehension in listening and reading: Same or different? In *Reading and Understanding*, eds. J. Danks and K. Pezdek. Newark, DE: International Reading Association.

DeFries, J. C. 1988. Colorado reading project: Longitudinal analysis. *Annals of Dyslexia* 38:120–30.

Déjerine, J. C. 1891. Sur un cas de cécité verable avec agraphie suivi d'autopsie. *Mémoires de Société de Biologie* 3:197–201.

Déjerine, J. C. 1892. Des differentes variétés de cécité verbale. *Mémoires de Société de Biologie* 4:1–40.

Deno, S. L. 1989. Curriculum-based measurement and special education services: A fundamental and direct relationship. In *Curriculum-Based Measurement: Assessing Special Children*, ed. M. R. Shinn. New York: The Guilford Press.

Deshler, D., and Graham, S. 1980. Tape-recording educational materials for secondary handicapped students. *Teaching Exceptional Children* 13:52–54.

Duker, S. 1965. Listening and reading. *Elementary School Journal* 65:321–24.

Durrell, D. D., and Hayes, M. 1969. *Durrell Listening-Reading Series: Manual for Listening and Reading Tests*, (Primary level). New York: Psychological Corporation.

Ehri, L. C., and Wilce, L. S. 1980. The influence of orthography on reader's conceptualization of the phonemic structure of words. *Applied Psycholinguistics* 1:371–85.

Ellis, A. 1962. *Reason and Emotion in Psychotherapy.* New York: Lyle Stuart.

Ellis, N. C., and Hennelly, R. A. 1980. A bilingual word-length effect: Implications for intelligence-testing and the relative ease of calculations in Welsh and English. *British Journal of Psychology* 71:43–51.

Ellis, N. C., and Miles, T. R. 1978. Visual information processing as a determinant of reading speed. *Journal of Reading Research* 1(2):108–120.

Fisher, P. F., and Frankfurter, A. 1977. Normal and disabled readers can locate and identify letters. Where is the perceptual deficit? *Journal of Reading Behavior* 9:31–43.

Fitzpatrick, E. M. 1982. *College Study Skills Program*, Level III. Reston, VA: National Association of Secondary School Principals.

Fodor, J. 1983. *The Modularity of Mind.* Montgomery, VT: Bradford.

Forness, S. R. 1988. Academic interventions for learning disabilities. In *Learning Disabilities: State of the Art and Practice*, ed. K. A. Kavale. Boston, MA: Little Brown.

Fox, B., and Routh, D. K. 1980. Phonemic analysis and severe reading disability in children. *Journal of Psycholinguistic Research* 9:115–19.

Frederiksen, J. R. 1982. Componential models of reading and their interrelation. In *Advances in the Psychology of Human Intelligence*, ed. R. J. Sternberg. Hillsdale, NJ: Lawrence Erlbaum.

Freud, S. 1910. *Leonardo da Vinci and a Memory of His Childhood.* Reprinted in *The Freud Reader*, ed. P. Gay. 1989. New York: W. W. Norton.

Freud, S. 1911. *On dreams.* Reprinted in *The Freud Reader*, ed. P. Gay. 1989. New York: W. W. Norton.

Freud, S. 1925. *Three Essays on the Theory of Sexuality.* Reprinted in *The Freud Reader*, ed. P. Gay. 1989. New York: W. W. Norton.

Frith, U. 1980. Unexpected spelling problems. In *Cognitive Processes in Spelling*, ed. U. Frith. London: Academic Press.

Frith, U., and Snowling, M. 1983. Reading for meaning and reading for sound in autistic and dyslexic children. *British Journal of Developmental Psychology* 1:329–42.

Fry, E. 1977. Fry's readability graph: Clarification, validity, and extension to level 17. *Journal of Reading* 21(3):242–51.

Fry, E. 1986. *Vocabulary Drills: Advanced Level.* Providence, RI: Jamestown Publishers.

Fry, E., Fountoukidis, D., and Polk, J. 1985. *The New Reading Teacher's Book of Lists.* Englewood Cliffs, NJ: Prentice Hall.

Funnell, E. 1983. Phonological processes in reading: New evidence from acquired dyslexia. *British Journal of Psychology* 74:159–80.

Garner, R. 1987. *Metacognition and Reading Comprehension.* Norwood, NJ: Ablex Publishing Corporation.

Garner, R., and Kraus, C. 1982. Good and poor comprehender differences in knowing and regulating reading behaviors. *Educational Research Quarterly* 6:5–12.

George, R., and Cristiani, T. S. 1990. *Counseling: Theory and Practice,* (3rd Edition). Englewood Cliffs, NJ: Prentice Hall.

Geschwind, N., and Behan, P. 1982. Left handedness: Association with immune disease, migraine, and developmental learning disorder. *Science* 79:5097–5100.

Gough, P. B., Tunmer, W. 1986. Decoding, reading, and reading disability. *Remedial and Special Education* 7(1):6–10.

Hague, S., and Mason, G. 1986. Using the computer's readability measure to teach students to revise their writing. *Journal of Reading* 1:14–17.

Hammill, D. D. 1990. On defining learning disabilities: An emerging consensus. *Journal of Learning Disabilities* 23(2):74–84.

Hankamer, J. 1989. Morphological parsing and the lexicon. In *Lexical Representation and Process,* ed. W. Marslen-Wilson. Cambridge, MA: The MIT press.

Hanson, V. L. 1989. Phonology and reading: Evidence from profoundly deaf readers. In *Phonology and Reading Disability,* eds. D. Shankweiler and I. Y. Liberman. Ann Arbor, MI: University of Michigan Press.

Harris, J. A., and Sipay, E. R. 1980. *How to Increase Reading Ability,* (7th edition). New York: Longman.

Healy, J. 1982. The enigma of hyperlexia. *Reading Research Quarterly* 17:319–38.

Heimlich, J. E., and Pittelman, D. S. 1986. *Semantic Mapping: Classroom Applications.* Newark, DE: International Reading Association.

Hella, J. 1988. GRE test scores of LD and nonLD students. Unpublished doctoral dissertation, University of California.

Henry, M. 1989. Decoding instruction based on word structure and origin. In *Reading and Writing Disorders in Different Orthographic Systems,* eds. P. G. Aaron and R. M. Joshi. Boston, MA: Kluwer Academic Publishers.

Henry, M. 1990. *Words, Tutor I; Tutor II.* Los Gatos, CA: Lex Press.

Hill, G. 1984. Learning disabled college students: Assessment of academic aptitude. Unpublished doctoral dissertation, Texas Tech. University.

Hinshelwood, J. 1895. Word-blindness and visual memory. *The Lancet* 1:1506–1508.

Hinshelwood, J. 1917. *Congenital Word-Blindness.* London: Lewis.

Hulme, C., Thomson, N., Muir, C., and Lawrence, A. 1984. Speech rate and the development of short-term memory span. *Journal of Experimental Child Psychology* 38:241–53.

Hunt, E. 1986. The next word on verbal ability. In *Reaction Time and Intelligence,* ed. P. E. Vernon. New York: Ablex.

Hunt, E., Lunneborg, C., and Lewis, J. 1975. What does it mean to be high verbal? *Cognitive Psychology* 7:194–227.

Jackson, M. D., and McClelland, J. L. 1979. Processing determinants of reading speed. *Journal of Experimental Psychology, General* 108(2):151–81.

Johnson, D., and Blalock, J. 1987. *Adults with Learning Disabilities.* New York: Grune and Stratton.

Johnson, D. D., and Pearson, P. D. 1984. *Teaching Reading Vocabulary,* (2nd edition). New York: Holt, Rinehart, and Winston.

Joshi, R. M., and Aaron, P. G. 1990. Specific spelling disability: Fact or artifact? *Reading and Writing: An Interdisciplinary Journal.*

Juel, D. 1980. Comparison of word identification strategies with varying context, word type, and reader skill. *Reading Research Quarterly* 3:358–76.

Just, M. A., and Carpenter, P. A. 1987. *The Psychology of Reading and Language Comprehension.* Boston, MA: Allyn and Bacon.

Kagan, J., Rosman, B., Day, D., Albert, J., and Phillips, W. 1964. Information processing in the child: Significance of analytic and reflective attitudes. *Psychological Monographs,* Whole No. 578.

Karlsen, B., Madden, R., and Gardner, E. F. 1977. *Stanford Diagnostic Reading Test.* New York: Harcourt Brace Jovanovich.

Katz, W. R., and Tarver, S. G. 1989. Comparison of dyslexic and nondyslexic adults on decoding and phonemic awareness tasks. *Annals of Dyslexia* 39:196–205.

Katz, R. B., Shankweiler, D., and Liberman, I. Y. 1981. Memory for item order and phonetic recoding in the beginning reader. *Journal of Experimental Child Psychology* 32:474–84.

Kean, M. L. 1977. The linguistic interpretation of aphasic syndrome: Agrammatism in Broca's aphasia, an example. *Cognition* 5:9–46.

Kennedy, D. K. 1971. Training with the cloze procedure visually and auditorially to improve the reading and listening comprehension of third grade underachieving readers. Unpublished doctoral dissertation, Pennsylvania State University.

Kennedy, D. K. 1985. Determining readability with a microcomputer. *Curriculum Review* 25:40–42.

Kintsch, W. 1977. On comprehending stories. In *Cognitive Processes in Comprehension,* eds. M. A. Just and P. A. Carpenter. Hillsdale, NJ: Lawrence Erlbaum.

Kintsch, W. and Kozminsky, E. 1977. Summarizing stories after reading and listening. *Journal of Educational Psychology* 69:491–99.

Kirby, E., and Grimley, L. 1986. *Understanding and Treating Attention Deficit Disorder.* New York: Pergamon Press.

Kleiman, G. M. 1975. Speech recoding in reading. *Journal of Verbal Learning and Verbal Behavior* 14:323–39.

Ladd, E. M. 1970. More than scores from tests. *The Reading Teacher* 24(4):305–311.

Langmore, S., and Canter, G. 1983. Written spelling deficit of Broca's aphasics. *Brain and Language* 18:293–314.

Leong, C. K. 1988. A componential approach to understanding reading and its difficulties in preadolescent readers. *Annals of Dyslexia* 38:95–119.

Liberman, I. Y., Mann, V., Shankweiler, D., and Werfelman, M. 1982. Children's memory for recurring linguistic and nonlinguistic material in relation to reading ability. *Cortex* 18:367–75.

Liberman, I. Y., Rubin, H., Duques, S., and Carlisle, J. 1985. Linguistic abilities and spelling proficiency in kindergarten and adult poor readers. In *Bio-*

behavioral Measures of Dyslexia, eds. J. Kavanagh and D. G. Gray. Parkton, MD: York Press.

Lundberg, I., Frost, J., and Peterson, O. 1988. Effects of an extensive program for stimulating phonological awareness in preschool children. *Reading Research Quarterly* 23(3):263–84.

Lundberg, I., Olofsson, A., and Wall, S. 1980. Reading and spelling skills in first school years predicted from phonemic awareness skills in kindergarten. *Scandinavian Journal of Psychology* 21:159–73.

Lytton, W. W., and Brust, C. M. 1989. Direct dyslexia. *Brain* 112:583–94.

Mann, V. A. 1986. Why some children encounter learning problems: The contribution of difficulties with language processing and phonological sophistication in early reading disability. In *Psychological and Educational Perspectives on Learning Disabilities*, eds. J. K. Torgesen and B. L. Young. Orlando, FL: Academic Press.

Maria, K. 1990. *Reading Comprehension Instruction: Issues and Strategies*. Parkton, MD: York Press.

Mangrum, C., and Strichart, 1984. *College and the Learning Disabled Student*. New York: Grune and Stratton.

Marshall, J. C., and Newcombe, F. 1973. Patterns of paralexia. *Journal of Psycholinguistic Research* 2:179–99.

Marshall, N., and Glock, M. D. 1978. Comprehension of connected discourse: A study into the relationship between the structure of text and information recalled. *Reading Research Quarterly* 14(1):10–56.

Marslen-Wilson, W. 1989. Access and integration: Projecting sound onto meaning. In *Lexical Representation and Process*, ed. W. Marslen-Wilson. Cambridge, MA: The MIT press.

Marzano, R. J., and Marzano, J. S. 1988. *A Cluster Approach to Elementary Vocabulary Instruction*. Newark, DE: International Reading Association.

McClelland, J. L., and Rumelhart, D. E. 1981. An interactive activation model of context effects in letter perception: An account of basic findings. *Psychological Review* 88:375–407.

McWhorter, T. 1983. *College Reading and Study Skills*. Waltham, MA: Little Brown Co.

Messic, S. 1976. *Individuality in Learning*. San Francisco, CA: Jossey Bass.

Miles, T. R. 1988. Counselling in dyslexia. *Counselling Psychology Quarterly* 1(1):97–107.

Miles, T. R., and Gilroy, D. E. 1986. *Dyslexia at College*. London: Methuen.

Miller, G. R., and Coleman, E. B. 1967. A set of thirty-six passages calibrated for complexity. *Journal of Verbal Learning and Verbal Behavior* 6:851–54.

Mitchell, D. C. 1982. *The Process of Reading*. New York: John Wiley.

Morgan, W. P. 1896. A case of congenital word-blindness. *British Medical Journal* 2:1368.

Morton, J., and Patterson, K. 1980. A new attempt at an interpretation and an attempt at a new interpretation. In *Deep Dyslexia*, eds. M. Coltheart, K. Patterson, and J. C. Marshall. London: Routledge and Kegan Paul.

Myers, M., and Paris. 1978. Children's metacognitive knowledge about reading. *Journal of Educational Psychology* 70:680–90.

Nagy, W. E., and Anderson, R. C. 1984. How many words are there in the printed school English? *Reading Research Quarterly* 19:304–330.

Nicholson, R. 1981. The relationship between memory span and processing speed. In *Intelligence and Learning*, eds. M. Friedman, J. P. Das, and N. O'Connor. New York: Plenum.

O'Brien, L. 1985. S.O.S. *Stengthening of Skills*. Rockville, MD: Specific Diagnostics Inc.

Olson, R. K., Wise, B. W., Conners, F. A., Rack, J. P., and Fulker, D. 1989. Specific deficits in component reading and language skills: Genetic and environmental influences. *Journal of Learning Disabilities* 22:339–48.

Orton, S. 1925. Word-blindness in school children. *Archives of Neurological Psychiatry* 14:581–615.

Orton, S. 1937. *Reading, Writing, and Speech Problems in Children*. New York: W. W. Norton.

Palincsar, A. S. 1986. Metacognitive strategy instruction. *Exceptional Children* 53(2):118–24.

Palmer, J., McCleod, C. M., Hunt, E., and Davidson, J. 1985. Information processing correlates of reading. *Journal of Memory and Language* 24:59–88.

Paris, S. G., and Myers, M. 1981. Comprehension monitoring, memory, and study strategies of good and poor readers. *Journal of Reading Behavior* 13:5–22.

Patterson, K. E. 1982. The relation between reading and phonological coding: Further neuropsychological observations. In *Normality and Pathology in Cognitive Functions* ed. A. E. Ellis. New York: Academic Press.

Patterson, K. E., Marshall, J. C., and Coltheart, M. 1985. *Surface Dyslexia*. Hillsdale, NJ: Lawrence Erlbaum.

Pauk, W. 1983. *How to Study in College*, (3rd edition). Burlington, MA: Houghton Mifflin.

Pauk, W. 1986. *Six-Way Paragraphs: Advanced Level*. Providence, RI: Jamestown Publishers.

Pearson, D., 1984. A context for instructional research on reading comprehension. In *Promoting Reading Comprehension*, ed. J. Flood. Newark, DE: International Reading Association.

Perfetti, C. A. 1985. *Reading Ability*. New York: Oxford University Press.

Perfetti, C. A., Finger, E., and Hogaboam, T. W. 1978. Sources of vocalization latency differences between skilled and less skilled young readers. *Journal of Educational Psychology* 70(5):730–39.

Phillips, S., Taylor, B., and Aaron, P. G. 1985. Developmental dyslexia: Subtypes or substages? Paper presented at the Indiana Psychological Association, Indianapolis, IN.

Pichert, J., and Anderson, R. C. 1977. Taking different perspectives on a story. *Journal of Educational Psychology* 69:309–315.

Raygor, A. L. 1977. The Raygor readability estimate: A quick and easy way to determine difficulty. In *Reading: Theory, Research and Practice*, eds. P. D. Pearson, J. Hansen. Clemson, SC: National Reading Conference.

Rayner, K., and Pollastek, A. 1989. *The Psychology of Reading*. Englewood Cliffs, NJ: Prentice Hall.

Richardson, S. O. 1989. Response to CBS 60 minutes issues. Indiana Branch of the American Council of Learning Disabilities. Spring, 1989.

Riedlinger, K. J., and Shewan, C. M. 1984. Comparison of auditory language comprehension skills in learning-disabled and academically achieving adolescents. *Language, Speech, and Hearing Services in Schools* 15:127–36.

Rogers, C. R. 1951. *Client-Centered Therapy*. Boston, MA: Houghton Mifflin.

Rogers, C. R. 1980. *A Way of Being*. Boston, MA: Houghton Mifflin.

Rothschild, L. H. 1987. Scholastic aptitude test preparation for the adolescent dyslexic. *Annals of Dyslexia* 37:212–27.

Salvia, J., and Ysseldyke, J. E. 1985. *Assessment in Special and Remedial Education*, (3rd edition). Boston, MA: Houghton Mifflin.

Sanford, A. J., and Garrod, S. C. 1981. *Understanding Written Language: Explorations in Comprehension Beyond the Sentence.* New York: John Wiley.

Scarborough, H. S. 1984. Continuity between childhood dyslexia and adult reading. *British Journal of Psychology* 75:329–48.

Scheiber, B., and Talpers, J. 1987. *Unlocking Potential: College and Other Choices for Learning Disabled People.* Bethesda, MD: Adler and Adler.

Schunk, D. H. 1989. Self efficacy and cognitive achievement: Implications for students with learning problems. *Journal of Learning Disabilities* 22(17):14–22.

Scott, C. M. 1989. Problem writer: Nature, assessment, and intervention. In *Reading Disabilities,* eds. A. G. Kamhi and H. W. Catts. Boston, MA: Little Brown Co.

Seashore, R. H., and Eckerson, L. D. 1940. The measurement of individual differences in general English vocabularies. *Journal of Educational Psychology* 31:14–38.

Seidenberg, M. S., and Tannenhaus, M. K. 1979. Orthographic effects on rhyme monitoring. *Journal of Experimental Psychology: Human Learning and Memory* 5(6):546–54.

Shankweiler, D., and Liberman, I. Y. (Eds.) 1989. *Phonology and Reading Disability: Solving the Reading Puzzle.* Ann Arbor, MI: The University of Michigan Press.

Siegel, L. S. 1989. IQ is irrelevant to the definition of learning disabilities. *Journal of Learning Disabilities* 22(8):469–79.

Smith, M. K. 1941. Measurement of the size of general English vocabulary through the elementary grades and high school. *Genetic Psychology Monographs* 24:311–45.

Smith, S. L. 1989. The masks students wear. *Instructor* XCVIII(8):27–32.

Sotiriou, P. 1989. *Integrating College Study Skills: Reasoning in Reading, Listening, and Writing,* (2nd edition). Belmont, CA: Wadsworth.

Sperling, G. 1960. The information available in brief visual presentations. *Psychological Monographs* 74:Whole No. 498.

Standal, T. 1987. Computer measured readability. *Computer in the Schools* 4:88–94.

Standing, L., Bond, B., Smith, P., and Isley, C. 1980. Is the immediate memory span determined by subvocalization rate? *British Journal of Psychology* 71:522–39.

Stanovich, K. E. 1986. Matthew effects in reading: Some consequences of individual differences in the acquisition of literacy. *Reading Research Quarterly* 21(4):360–407.

Stanovich, K. E., Cunningham, A. E., and Cramer, B. 1984. Assessing phonological awareness in kindergarten children: Issues of task comparability. *Journal of Experimental Child Psychology* 38:175–90.

Stanovich, K. E., Cunningham, A. E. and Feeman, D. J. 1984. Intelligence, cognitive skills and early reading progress. *Reading Research Quarterly* 19(3):278–303.

Stanovich, K. E., and West, R. F. 1989. Exposure to print and orthographic processing. *Reading Research Quarterly* 24(4):402–429.

Sternberg, R. J. 1985. *Beyond IQ: A Triarchic Theory of Human Intelligence.* New York: Cambridge University Press.

Stevens, S. H. 1984. *Classroom Success for the Learning Disabled.* Winston-Salem, NC: John Blair.

Sticht, T. 1979. Applications of the audread model to reading evaluation and instruction. In *Theory and Practice of Early Reading,* eds. L. B. Resnick and P. Weaver. Hillsdale, NJ: Lawrence Erlbaum.

Strickland, D. S., Feeley, J. T., and Wepner, S. B. 1987. *Using Computers in the Teaching of Reading.* New York: Teachers College Press.

Tiedemann, J. 1989. Measures of cognitive styles: A critical review. *Educational Psychologist* 24(3):261–76.

Torgesen, J. K., and Licht, B. 1983. The learning disabled child as an inactive learner: Retrospect and prospects. In *Topics in Learning Disabilities,* eds. J. D. McKinney and L. Feagans. (1:3–31.) Rockville, MD: Aspen Press.

Turkel-Kesselman, K., and Peterson, F. 1981. *Study Smarts: How to Learn More in Less Time.* Chicago, IL: Contemporary Books Inc.

Van den Bos, K. P. 1989. Relationship between cognitive development, decoding skill, and reading comprehension in learning-disabled Dutch children. In *Reading and Writing Disorders in Different Orthographic Systems,* eds. P. G. Aaron and R. M. Joshi. Boston, MA: Kluwer Academic Publishers.

Vellutino, F. R. 1979. *Dyslexia: Theory and Research.* Cambridge, MA: The MIT Press.

Venezky, R. 1976. *Theoretical and Experimental Base for Teaching Reading.* The Hague: Mouton.

Venezky, R. 1980. From Webster to Rice to Roosevelt: The formative years for spelling instruction and spelling reform in the U.S.A. In *Cognitive Processes in Spelling,* ed. U. Frith. London: Academic Press.

Vogel, S. 1985. Learning disabled college students: Identification, assessment, and outcomes. In *Understanding Learning Disabilities,* eds. D. D. Duane, and C. K. Leong. New York: Plenum.

Wallace, G., and McLoughlin, J. A. 1988. *Learning Disabilities: Concepts and Characteristics.* Columbus, OH: Merrill.

Weis, J. 1990. Unconscious mental functioning. *Scientific American* 262(3):103–109.

Wijk, A. 1966. *Rules of Pronunciation for the English Language: An Account of the Relationship between English Spelling and Pronunciation.* London: Oxford University Press.

Wise, B., Olson, R., Anstett, M., Andrews, L., Terjak, M., Schneider, V., Kostuch, J., and Kriho, L. 1989. Implementing a long-term computerized remedial program with synthetic speech feedback: Hardware, software, and real-world issues. *Behavior Research Methods, Instruments, & Computers* 21(2):173–80.

Wong, B., and Wong, R. 1988. Cognitive interventions for learning disabilities. In *Learning Disabilities: State of the Art and Practice,* ed. K. Kavale. Boston, MA: Little Brown.

Wood, T. A., Buckhalt, J. A., and Tomlin, J. G. 1988. A comparison of listening and reading performance with children in three educational placements. *Journal of Learning Disabilities* 8:493–96.

Woodcock, R. W. 1987. *Woodcock Reading Mastery Tests–*(revised). Circle Pines, MI: American Guidance Service.

Yule, W., and Rutter, M. 1976. The epidemiology and social implications of specific reading retardation. In *The Neuropsychology of Learning Disorders: Theoretical Approaches,* eds. R. Knights and D. Bakker. Baltimore, MD: University Park Press.

Zigmond, N., and Thornton, H. S. 1988. Learning disabilities in adolescents and adults. In *Learning Disabilities: State of the Art and Practice,* ed. K. Kavale. Boston, MA: Little Brown.

Index

(Page numbers in italics indicate material in tables or figures.)